SO-ATU-220

VITAL CHRISTOLOGY ISSUES

*Examining Contemporary
and Classic Concerns*

ROY B. ZUCK
GENERAL EDITOR

kregel
RESOURCES

Grand Rapids, MI 49501

Vital Christology Issues: Examining Contemporary and Classic Concerns by Roy B. Zuck, general editor

Copyright © 1997 by Dallas Theological Seminary

Published by Kregel Resources, an imprint of Kregel Publications, P.O. Box 2607, Grand Rapids, MI 49501. Kregel Resources provides timely and relevant resources for Christian life and service. Your comments and suggestions are valued.

For more information about Kregel Publications, visit our web site at http://www.kregel.com.

Cover design: Sarah Slattery
Book design: Alan G. Hartman

Library of Congress Cataloging-in-Publication Data
Roy B. Zuck
Vital Christology issues: examining contemporary and classic concerns / Roy B. Zuck, gen. ed.
    p.   cm. (Vital Issues Series; v. 10)
1. Jesus Christ—Person and offices. I. Zuck, Roy B.
II. Bibliotheca sacra. III. Series.
BT202.V58   1997   232—dc21   97-7365
                                                        CIP

ISBN 0-8254-4096-3

Printed in the United States of America

1 2 3 / 03 02 01 00 99 98 97

Contents

Contributors

Lewis Sperry Chafer
Late Founder, President, and Professor of Systematic
Theology, Dallas Theological Seminary, Dallas, Texas

Charles L. Feinberg
Late Academic Dean Emeritus, Talbot Theological
Seminary, La Mirada, California

Daniel G. Finestone
Late Pastor, Warren Point Presbyterian Church, Warren
Point, New Jersey

Don B. Garlington
Professor of New Testament, Toronto Baptist Seminary,
Toronto, Ontario

S. Lewis Johnson Jr.
Professor Emeritus of New Testament Studies, Dallas
Theological Seminary, Dallas, Texas

Robert P. Lightner
Professor of Systematic Theology, Dallas Theological
Seminary, Dallas, Texas

R. Larry Overstreet
Professor of Pastoral Theology, Northwest Baptist
Seminary, Tacoma Washington

Edward Robinson
Late Founder and First Editor, *Bibliotheca Sacra;* and Late
Professor, Union Theological Seminary, New York

Robert L. Thomas
Professor of New Testament Language and Literature, The
Master's Seminary, Sun Valley, California

John F. Walvoord
> Chancellor, Minister-at-Large, and Professor of Systematic Theology, Emeritus, Dallas Theological Seminary, Dallas, Texas

John A. Witmer
> Libraries Archivist and Associate Professor Emeritus of Systematic Theology, Dallas Theological Seminary, Dallas, Texas

Preface

A Hindu principal once asked a Christian schoolgirl in India why she refused to sing the praises of Krishna, while the Hindu girls were quite happy to join in singing "All Hail the Power of Jesus' Name." The girl answered, "I can't sing to anyone but Jesus."

Her reply underscores the most foundational fact of the Christian faith: Jesus Christ is central, and He alone is to be worshiped! He is the object of every Christian's worship because He is God. And because He is God, He is the only answer to the human problem of sin. The awfulness of sin is answered by the awesomeness of the Savior.

As the only way to heaven, Jesus affirmed, "I am the way, and the truth, and the life" (John 14:6). For this reason Jesus Christ, as Charles Spurgeon wrote, "is the great central fact in the world's history." His uniqueness is seen in the biblical truth that He is fully God and perfectly human.

The incomparable Christ has existed eternally as God the Son. Coming to earth He took on human flesh, "being made in the likeness of men" and humbled Himself (Phil. 2:7–8). His brief ministry on earth included several pinnacle experiences: His baptism, temptation, transfiguration, triumphal entry, trial, agony in Gethsemane, death, and resurrection. Believers cherish the life of this One "who gave Himself for our sins" (Gal. 1:4) so that "He might bring us to God" (1 Peter 3:18).

This ascended, glorified, exalted Savior, who now "intercedes for us" (Rom. 8:34) at the right hand of God the Father, will come someday to take us to be with Him (John 14:3; 17:25).

The chapters in this volume, taken from *Bibliotheca Sacra,* Dallas Seminary's theological journal, discuss the significance of these and other marvelous truths about our Savior, the One whose name "is above every name" and to whom every knee will someday bow in submission (Phil. 2:9–10).

ROY B. ZUCK

About *Bibliotheca Sacra*

A flood is rampant—an engulfing deluge of literature far beyond any one person's ability to read it all. Presses continue to churn out thousands of journals and magazines like a roiling, raging river.

Among these numberless publications, one stands tall and singular—*Bibliotheca Sacra*—a strange name (meaning "Sacred Library") but a journal familiar to many pastors, teachers, and Bible students.

How is *Bibliotheca Sacra* unique in the world of publishing? By being the oldest continuously published journal in the Western Hemisphere—1993 marked its 150th anniversary—and by being published by one school for more than six decades—1994 marked its diamond anniversary of being released by Dallas Seminary.

Bib Sac, to use its shortened sobriquet, was founded in New York City in 1843 and was purchased by Dallas Theological Seminary in 1934, ten years after the school's founding. The quarterly's 153-year history boasts only nine editors. Through those years it has maintained a vibrant stance of biblical conservatism and a strong commitment to the Scriptures as God's infallible Word.

Each volume in the Kregel *Vital Issues Series* includes carefully selected articles from the 1930s to the present—articles of enduring quality, articles by leading evangelicals whose topics are as relevant today as when they were first produced. The chapters have been edited slightly to provide conformity of style. We trust these anthologies will enrich the spiritual lives and Christian ministries of many more readers.

ROY B. ZUCK, EDITOR
Bibliotheca Sacra

For *Bibliotheca Sacra* subscription information, call Dallas Seminary, 1-800-992-0998.

CHAPTER 1

The Preexistence of Christ

Lewis Sperry Chafer

As the true starting point for all worthy thinking regarding Christ, believers do well to fix in mind the essential fact that the second person is intrinsically equal in every respect to the other persons in the Godhead and that He remains what He ever has been. No approach to a biblical Christology is possible that does not ground itself on and proceed from the all-determining truth that the incarnate second person, though He was "a man of sorrows, and acquainted with grief" (Isa. 53:3), is the eternal God. The Socinian distinction between the words *deity* and *divinity* and their claim that Christ was not deity but was divinity only in the sense that He partook of divine elements must be rejected. He is divine in the sense that He is absolute deity; otherwise the language of the Bible is entirely misleading. A candid mind must acknowledge the array of evidence as to Christ's deity or else show equally valid reason for not doing so. The trifling attempt of Unitarians to dispose of the vast body of truth that asserts the deity of Christ is unworthy of consideration. No more vital question has ever been propounded than "What do you think about the Christ?" (Matt. 22:42), and similarly, "Who do people say that the Son of Man is?" (16:13). Many outwardly religious people have said in reply, John the Baptist, Elijah, Jeremiah, or one of the prophets. Others who stood nearer to Him have said, "Thou art the Christ, the Son of the living God" (16:14–16).

No ground is left for argument with the Jew, the Muslim, or the atheist who repudiates the whole doctrine of Christ's supernatural being. The Arians professed great adoration for Christ, even acknowledging His preexistence, but, believing Him to be a creation of God, they rejected the truth of His eternal preexistence. In more recent times the controversy has been with the Socinians and their successors, the Unitarians, all of whom have sought to retain the worthy name Christian while dishonoring the One

9

whose name they espouse. This immeasurable insult to Christ would be serious enough were it confined to those who bear the Unitarian name, but these heretical teachings are again, as they have done before, penetrating the whole Christian profession under the gloss of scholarship that, being motivated by unbelief and being as dark as the natural human heart, tends ever to promote its cherished liberalism.

The greatest scholars of the Christian era have bowed with full submission to the authority of the Scriptures and have hailed its message as perfect and final. Unitarianism and its other self, modernism, reflect the downward pull of that unbelief that characterizes the unregenerate. The same truth abides that has sustained saints in life and filled the martyr with glory in death.

The same proofs that demonstrate to the satisfaction of the Unitarian (of whatever name) that God the Father is deity demonstrate with equal force that the Lord Jesus Christ is deity.

The first step in the proof that the Lord Jesus Christ has had equal and rightful place in the Godhead is taken when one recognizes the biblical fact that Christ existed before He came into the world in human form. Of necessity, evidence bearing on such a stupendous theme as the preexistence of Christ will be drawn only from the Bible. No other source of information exists. The demonstration that Christ preexisted is not, however, a complete proof that He is very God. Such proof does refute the Socinian contention, namely, that He is only human, for no human has ever existed before his birth; but it does not refute the Arian hypothesis that Christ is a created being who existed as such before entering this human sphere. Other truths from Scripture give decisive evidence of the deity of Christ. His preexistence is implied in a number of secondary passages. There are various phrases in which this implication resides. He said of Himself that He was sent into the world (John 17:18); likewise it is written that He came in the flesh (1:14); He shared human flesh and blood (Heb. 2:14); He was found in fashion as a man (Phil. 2:8); He said, "I am from above" (John 8:23) and "I am not of the world" (17:14); and He said He descended from heaven (3:13). No utterances such as these could have any place in the experience of human beings. They clearly imply that He existed before His incarnation.

Several major passages of indisputable import affirm the preexistence of Jesus Christ, thus pointing to His deity.

John 1:15, 30

In these verses John the Baptist twice asserted of Christ that "He existed before me." A time relationship is indicated, and though John was older in age than Christ, he declared that Christ was before him. The Unitarian notion that John was stating that by divine appointment Christ is higher in rank and dignity than John is impossible and cannot be sustained by unprejudiced exegesis. Had John made reference only to matters of appointment and dignity he would have said, He *is* before me, and not, "He *was* before me" (KJV). In point of time Christ preceded John.

John 6:33, 38, 41, 50–51, 58

Six times in John 6 Jesus declared that He came down out of heaven. To this may be added Christ's words to Nicodemus, "And no one has ascended into heaven, but He who descended from heaven, even the Son of Man" (John. 3:13). Similarly this point is made emphatic by repetition as presented in John 3:31, "He who comes from above is above all, he who is of the earth is from the earth and speaks of the earth. He who comes from heaven is above all."

As a pure invention, which has not a vestige of support either biblical or traditional, the Socinians offered the hypothesis that sometime after His birth Christ was transported to heaven that He might receive the word of truth, which was committed to Him, and from thence He came down from heaven. Later promoters of this form of doctrine have assumed that these passages assert that Christ had been "admitted to an intimate knowledge of heavenly things." Were this the case, Christ would be in no way superior to Moses or any of the prophets. Christ affirmed in John 3:13 that He is the only Man who has been in heaven and was then on the earth. To the same end John 6:62 not only anticipates the literal ascension recorded in Acts 1:10, but states that, when He would ascend, He would return "where He was before." On this controversy an early writer, Dr. Nares, may be quoted with profit: "We have nothing but the positive contradictions of the Unitarian party, to prove to us that Christ did not come from heaven, though he says of himself, he did come from heaven; that though he declares he had seen the Father, he had not seen the Father; that though he assures us that he, in a most peculiar and singular manner came forth from God, he came from him no otherwise than like the prophets of old, and his own immediate forerunner."

John 8:58

Most emphatic, indeed, is the Savior's claim to preexistence as recorded in John 8:58: "Before Abraham was born, I am." The phrase "I am" sets forth the meaning of the ineffable name, Jehovah, and asserts no less than eternal existence. It is evident too that the Jews recognized by this statement that Christ declared Himself to be Jehovah. This is seen in their bitter resentment. How could He, being not yet fifty years old, have existed before Abraham? (8:57). In answer to this query Christ replied that He not only existed before Abraham, but that He had *always* existed prior to the time when He was speaking. This is the claim embodied in the application of the eternal "I am" to Himself. For the last degree of blasphemy, which the Jews believed this to be, they were by their law obligated to stone Him to death. This they proceeded to do, but Christ displayed the very supernatural power He had professed by disappearing from their midst (8:59).

The Unitarian theories that Christ was asserting that His existence at that time merely preceded the time when Abraham would become the father of many nations through the preaching of the Gospel to the Gentiles or that Christ merely preexisted in the foreknowledge of God are not worthy of consideration. Faustus Socinus interpreted this passage in this way: "Before Abraham becomes Abraham, that is, the father of many nations, I am it, namely, the Messiah, the Light of the world." This statement was later included in the Socinian confession of faith. This momentous event is better described by Whitaker after this manner.

> "Your Father Abraham," says our Saviour to the Jews, "rejoiced to see my day; and he saw it, and was glad." Our Saviour thus proposes himself to his countrymen, as their Messiah; that grand object of hope and desire to their fathers, and particularly to this first father of the faithful, Abraham. But his countrymen, not acknowledging his claim to the character of Messiah, and therefore not allowing his supernatural priority of existence to Abraham, chose to consider his words in a signification merely human. "Then said the Jews unto him, Thou art not fifty years old, and hast thou seen Abraham?" But what does our Saviour reply to this low and gross comment upon his intimation? Does he retract it, by warping his language to their poor perverseness, and so waiving his pretensions to the assumed dignity? No! To have so acted, would have been derogatory to *his* dignity, and injurious to their interests. He actually repeats his claim to the character. He actually enforces his pretensions to a supernatural priority of existence. He even heightens both. He mounts up far beyond Abraham. He ascends beyond all the orders of creation. And he places himself with God at the head of the universe. He thus arrogates to himself all that high

pitch of dignity, which the Jews expected their Messiah to assume. This he does too in the most energetic manner, that his simplicity of language, so natural to inherent greatness, would possibly admit. He also introduces what he says with much solemnity in the form and with more in the repetition. "Verily, verily, I say unto you," he cries, "BEFORE ABRAHAM WAS, I AM." He says not of himself, as he says of Abraham, "Before he was, I was." This indeed would have been sufficient, to declare what he *now* meant to assert, his full claim to the majesty of the Messiah. He therefore drops all forms of language, that could be accommodated to the mere creatures of God. He arrests one that was appropriate to the Godhead itself. "Before Abraham *was*," or still more properly, "Before Abraham was MADE," he says, "I AM." He thus gives himself the signature of *uncreated* and *continual* existence, in direct opposition to *contingent* and *created*. . . . He attaches to himself that very stamp of *eternity,* which God appropriates to his Godhead in the Old Testament; and from which an apostle afterward describes "Jesus Christ" expressly to be "the same yesterday, and to-day, and for ever." Nor did the Jews pretend to misunderstand him now. They could not. They heard him directly and decisively vindicating the noblest rights of their Messiah, and the highest honours of their God, to himself. They considered him as a mere pretender to *those.* They therefore looked upon him as a blasphemous arrogator of *these.* "Then took they up stones, to cast at him" as a blasphemer; as what indeed he was in his pretensions to be God, if he had not been in reality their Messiah and their God in one. But he instantly proved himself to their very senses, to be both; by exerting the energetic powers of his Godhead, upon them. For he "*hid* himself; and went out of the temple, *going through the midst of them; and so passed by*" (Scripture quotes KJV; emphasis Whitaker's).

John 1:1–4, 14

This familiar portion reads, "In the beginning was the Word, and the Word was with God, and the Word was God. He was in the beginning with God. All things came into being by Him, and apart from Him nothing came into being that has come into being. In Him was life, and the life was the light of men. . . . And the Word became flesh, and dwelt among us, and we beheld His glory, glory as of the only begotten from the Father, full of grace and truth."

No Scripture is more conclusive as to the preexistence of Christ than this. Like the preceding passage (John 8:58), the thought of eternal existence is expressed by the use of the present tense with the thought implied that it is an eternal present. He is, not was, in existence at a time of beginning that was before He had created all things by the word of His power. He was not only with God, but He was God. He, who ever is, never began to be. With fullest assurance the inspired text recounts that this Eternal One "became

flesh, and dwelt among us." To the order of these events, the truth
they disclose, and the majesty here described, Warfield has made
an illuminating comment.

> John here calls the person who became incarnate by a name peculiar to
> himself in the NT—the "Logos" or "Word." According to the predicates
> which he here applies to Him, he can mean by the "Word" nothing else but
> God Himself, "considered in His creative, operative, self-revealing, and
> communicating character," the sum total of what is Divine (C. F. Schmid).
> In three crisp sentences he declares at the outset His eternal subsistence,
> His eternal intercommunion with God, His eternal identity with God: "In
> the beginning the Word was; and the Word was with God; and the Word
> was God" (Jn 1:1 [Warfield's paraphrase]). "In the beginning," at that
> point of time when things first began to be (Gen 1:1), the Word already
> "was." He antedates the beginning of all things. And He not merely antedates
> them, but it is immediately added that he is Himself the creator of all that
> is: "All things were made by him, and apart from him was not made one
> thing that hath been made" (1:3). Thus He is taken out of the category of
> creatures altogether. Accordingly, what is said of Him is not that He was
> the first of existences to come into being—that "in the beginning He already
> had come into being"—but that "in the beginning, when things began to
> come into being, He already was" [Warfield's paraphrase]. It is express
> eternity of being that is asserted: "the imperfect tense of the original suggests
> in this relation, as far as human language can do so, the notion of absolute,
> supra-temporal existence" (Westcott). This, His eternal subsistence, was
> not, however, in isolation: "And the Word was with God." The language is
> pregnant. It is not merely coexistence with God that is asserted, as of two
> beings standing side by side, united in a local relation, or even in a common
> conception. What is suggested is an active relation of intercourse. The
> distinct personality of the Word is therefore not obscurely intimated. From
> all eternity the Word has been with God as a fellow: He who in the very
> beginning already "was," "was" also in communion with God. Though He
> was thus in some sense a second along with God, He was nevertheless not
> a separate being from God: "And the Word was"—still the eternal "was"—
> "God." In some sense distinguishable from God, He was in an equally true
> sense identical with God. There is but one eternal God; this eternal God,
> the Word is; in whatever sense we may distinguish Him from the God
> whom He is "with." He is yet not another than this God, but Himself is this
> God. The predicate "God" occupies the position of emphasis in this
> declaration, and is so placed in the sentence as to be thrown up in sharp
> contrast with the phrase "with God," as if to prevent inadequate inferences
> as to the nature of the Word being drawn even momentarily from that
> phrase. John would have us realize that what the Word was in eternity was
> not merely God's coeternal fellow, but the eternal God's self.[1]

John 17:5

In His prayer to God the Father, the Savior said, "And now,
glorify Thou Me together with Thyself, Father, with the glory

which I had with thee before the world was." This unqualified declaration that He had shared personally and rightfully in the glory that belonged only to deity before the world was is another proclamation of the truth that Christ existed before His incarnation. Also being a part of His prayer to the Father, it is not subject to those restrictions required when people are addressed. He was speaking to the Father about things that belong to the eternal relationship within the Godhead. The Unitarian gloss proposes that Christ shared in the glory only in the sense that He was anticipated in the eternal counsels of God. If that were true, consistency would require that His petition to be restored to that glory was no more than a request to be returned to that nonexistent anticipation, with no expectation that He would ever attain to an actual glory.

Philippians 2:6

Here it is written, "who, although He existed in the form of God, did not regard equality with God a thing to be grasped." This decisive passage is adduced here because of its clear affirmation that Christ, before the Incarnation, existed in the form of God. Of the important foundation on which this passage is based, namely, the essential deity and preexistence of Christ, Warfield has written at length, a part of which is here quoted.

> The statement is thrown into historical form; it tells the story of Christ's life on earth. But it presents His life on earth as a life in all its elements alien to His intrinsic nature, and assumed only in the performance of an unselfish purpose. On earth He lived as a man, and subjected Himself to the common lot of men. But He was not by nature a man, nor was He in His own nature subject to the fortunes of human life. By nature He was God; and He would have naturally lived as became God—"on an equality with God." He became man by a voluntary act, "taking no account of Himself," and, having become man, He voluntarily lived out His human life under the conditions which the fulfilment of His unselfish purpose imposed on Him.
>
> . . . The terms in which these great affirmations are made deserve the most careful attention. The language in which Our Lord's intrinsic Deity is expressed, for example, is probably as strong as any that could be devised. Paul does not say simply, "He was God." He says, "He was in the form of God," employing a turn of speech which throws emphasis upon Our Lord's possession of the specific quality of God. "Form" is a term which expresses the sum of those characterizing qualities which make a thing the precise thing that it is. Thus, the "form" of a sword (in this case mostly matters of external configuration) is all that makes a given piece of metal specifically a sword, rather than, say, a spade. And

"the form of God" is the sum of the characteristics which make the being we call "God," specifically God, rather than some other being—an angel, say, or a man. When Our Lord is said to be in "the form of God," therefore, He is declared, in the most express manner possible, to be all that God is, to possess the whole fulness of attributes which make God God. Paul chooses this manner of expressing himself here instinctively, because, in adducing Our Lord as our example of self-abnegation, his mind is naturally resting, not on the bare fact that He is God, but on the richness and fulness of His being as God. He was all this, yet He did not look on His own things but on those of others.

It should be carefully observed also that in making this great affirmation concerning Our Lord, Paul does not throw it distinctively into the past, as if he were describing a mode of being formerly Our Lord's, indeed, but no longer His because of the action by which He became our example of unselfishness. Our Lord, he says, "being," "existing," "subsisting" "in the form of God"—as it is variously rendered. . . . Paul is not telling us here, then, what Our Lord was once, but rather what He already was, or, better, what in His intrinsic nature He is; he is not describing a past mode of existence of Our Lord, before the action he is adducing as an example took place—although the mode of existence he describes was Our Lord's mode of existence before this action—so much as painting in the background upon which the action adduced may be thrown up into prominence. He is telling us who and what He is who did these things for us, that we may appreciate how great the things He did for us are[2] (Scripture quotes KJV).

CHAPTER 2

Is the Angel of Yahweh the Lord Jesus Christ?

Daniel G. Finestone

In Old Testament times God revealed Himself to humans in varied forms. Sometimes He manifested Himself through elements of nature, such as fire or cloud. Other times He was seen in the form of a created being, such as a human or an angel. This study concerns the latter form of this self-revelation of God.

In the form of a man, God appeared to Abraham on the plains of Mamre, as He did also to Jacob at the Brook Jabbok. But perhaps the more frequent mode of theophany found in the Old Testament is in the appearances of the Angel of Yahweh or, the Angel of the Lord.

The Angel of Yahweh appeared twice to Hagar (Gen. 16; 21), and once to Abraham (Gen. 22), Balaam (Num. 22), Gideon (Judg. 6), Manoah and his wife (Judg. 13). He was present at the judgment on Israel after David's numbering of the people (2 Sam. 24), and he was the agent of destruction to Sennacherib's army (1 Chron. 21). In a vision, Zechariah saw Him as judging between Joshua the high priest of Israel and Satan their accuser (Zech. 3), and as the One who intervened on behalf of Israel's restoration after their seventy years of captivity (Zech. 1). The psalmist referred to Him as the deliverer of His people and the antagonist of their enemies (Pss. 34:7; 35:5–6). This close relationship to the covenant people of God is perhaps the reason He is sometimes called "the angel of the covenant."

Other designations of the Angel of Yahweh are "the angel of God" (Gen. 31:11), "My angel" (Ex. 23:23; 32:34), and "the angel of His presence" (Isa. 63:9), all doubtless referring to the same divine being.

The appearances of the Angel of Yahweh are always in connection with Israel's destiny. Other forms of theophanies have to do with crises in the history of the rebellion of people against

17

God's authority, as in the Garden of Eden and in Sodom and Gomorrah. These appearances of the Angel of Yahweh, however, are linked with the Lord's guidance of the chosen people in times of need and with their protection in times of distress. In this way the Angel was safeguarding the divine provision for the salvation God would bring through the person of His Son.

What relationship exists between the Angel of Yahweh of the Old Testament and the Lord Jesus Christ? Many devout scholars have replied that they are the same, the second person of the Trinity.

For this to be true, it must be established that the Angel of Yahweh is deity. Therefore one must determine whether the appearances of the Angel are distinguished from mere angelic manifestations. While the word *angel* means messenger, the context helps ascertain whether the angel referred to is a supernatural messenger or a human and whether the supernatural messenger is merely an angel, and thus a created being, or whether he is deity and thus the Creator.

Some scholars have carelessly classified all these appearances as merely manifestations of angelic beings, denying that any of these are appearances of deity in angelic form. The writers of Scripture, however, insist that all the appearances of the Angel of Yahweh are appearances of God Himself. They show that He is greater in dignity and power than any of the angelic host and that He is vitally related in the Godhead. The following five facts support the view that these are theophanies.

First, the Angel of Yahweh claimed deity. When revealing Himself to Moses at the burning bush, "the Angel of the LORD," (Ex. 3:2) said, "I am . . . the God of Abraham, the God of Isaac and the God of Jacob" (v. 6). Later, He proclaimed Himself to Moses as "I Am who I Am" (v. 14), clearly an assertion of deity.

Second, the Angel of Yahweh was addressed as deity. When He appeared to Hagar, she called the place of this miraculous manifestation, "Beer-lahai-roi" (Gen. 16:14), meaning "the well of the living one who sees me." She called the Angel who spoke to her, "Thou art a God who sees" (v. 13). Gideon, believing he had seen God, feared for his life when he had spoken with the Angel of the Lord. He exclaimed, "Alas O Lord GOD! For now I have seen the angel of the LORD face to face" (Judg. 6:22). He received divine assurance, however, that he would not die (v. 23).

Third, the Angel of Yahweh was paid divine honors. When in the presence of this Angel, Moses was commanded to remove his shoes, for the place where he stood was holy ground (Ex. 3:5). The Angel of the Lord received the sacrifice of Isaac, which Abraham had offered, by the words, "You have not withheld your son . . . from Me" (Gen. 22:11–12).

Fourth, the Angel of Yahweh was called God. In Moses' experience at the burning bush, the Angel of the Lord was in the bush (Ex. 3:2), and yet "God called to him from the midst of the bush" (v. 4), thus using "the Angel of Yahweh" and "God" interchangeably. Manoah, Samson's father, was curious about the identity of the Angel of the Lord (Judg. 13:17). When He departed, Manoah said, "We have seen God" (v. 22).

Fifth, the Angel of Yahweh promised to do what only deity can do. He promised Hagar He would make of Ishmael's descendants "a great nation" (Gen. 21:18; cf. 16:10); to Abraham He said, "I will greatly bless you, . . . I will greatly multiply your seed" (22:17); and to Moses He said, "I have come down to deliver them from the power of the Egyptians" (Ex. 3:8). These promises would have been meaningless if the Angel who spoke them was less than deity.

From this cumulative evidence it may be concluded that the Angel of Yahweh is one of the persons of the Trinity. In some passages this Angel is distinguished from God (Gen. 22:11, 15), but in others He is identified with God (e.g., 16:7, 13). All the mystery that surrounds the doctrine of the Trinity may also be found here.

With which person of the Trinity is He to be identified? Though Augustine identified Him with the entire Trinity, this is not a common view. Another view is that the Angel is a momentary descent of God into visibility. A third view is that the Angel is the Logos, a kind of temporary preincarnation of the second person of the Trinity.

Consensus throughout the centuries favors the third view for five reasons. First, Scripture is definite that God the Father has never made a temporary descent into visibility (John 1:18; 1 Tim. 6:16). Because Jesus Christ is the mediate revelation of God the Father (Matt. 11:27), every theophany in the Old Testament is in reality a Christophany.

Second, after the Incarnation the Angel of the Lord is never mentioned again, as though it were understood that the fuller identification was now recognized as the Lord Jesus Christ. This argument is based on the use and absence of the definite article that is invariably found in the Hebrew for "the Angel of the Lord" and yet is omitted from the Greek, implying that *an* Angel of the Lord in the New Testament is not the same person as *the* Angel of the Lord of the Old Testament.

Third, Zechariah associated the Angel of Yahweh with the Messiah and the house of David and with the Lord Himself: "In that day the LORD will defend the inhabitants of Jerusalem, and the one who is feeble among them in that day will be like David, and the house of David will be like God, like the angel of the LORD before them" (Zech. 12:8).

Fourth, Christ identified Himself with the Angel of Yahweh when He quoted to the Jews words similar to those He used in the theophany to Moses: "Before Abraham was born, I am" (John 8:58; cf. Ex. 3:14). The Jews evidently understood the significance of these words "I am," for they accused Him of blasphemy and sought to slay Him for it (John 8:59).

Fifth, some of the incidents of the Angel of Yahweh are characteristic also of the Lord Jesus Christ. In their compassion for women, the Angel was concerned for Hagar and Christ for Mary Magdalene. In their compassion for His people, the Angel said "I have surely seen the affliction of My people" (Ex. 3:7) and Christ said He had "compassion for them, because they were . . . like sheep without a shepherd" (Matt. 9:36). The Angel said to Moses, "I . . . will be with your mouth, and teach you what you are to say" (Ex. 4:12). And Christ told the disciples, "It shall be given you in that hour what you are to speak" (Matt. 10:19).

Since the Angel of the Lord was God the Son, the theophanies were actually Christophanies. Jesus Christ, as the Angel of the Lord, was the "messenger" (ἄγγελος) of God the Father. Then in the Incarnation He appeared "to put away sin by the sacrifice of Himself" (Heb. 9:26). And when He returns, His full glory will be revealed (Titus 2:13). How marvelous to think that some in Old Testament times saw the very One church-age believers will see at the Rapture!

CHAPTER 3

Did Jesus Claim to Be God?

John A. Witmer

Some time ago I was talking with a Jewish educational leader. Although he would disclaim being an expert, this man was quite knowledgeable in historical and contemporary Jewish thought. In the conversation I asked him to present his concept of Jesus. His reply in essence painted Jesus as a wandering rabbi who was seeking to correct the religious abuses of His times. This educator felt that Jews today would honor Jesus along with Hillel and others as one of their great teachers if Jesus' followers had not begun to worship Him as God. I challenged the Jewish educator on his view that the doctrine of the deity of Jesus Christ was a later development of the church and not the conscious claim of Jesus Himself. However, the rabbi, firmly convinced of his view, believed that Jesus did not claim to be the Messiah and had no consciousness of being the Messiah. I was just as firmly convinced that Jesus did claim to be God and that the faith of His followers in His deity was the result, at least in part, of this claim. The resulting conflict of views raises the subject of this chapter, "Did Jesus claim to be God?"

This Jewish leader had jokingly said that whenever three Jewish scholars discuss a subject, at least four views are expressed. On the subject of Jesus' claim to deity, however, Jewish scholars show surprising unanimity. Klausner, for example, asserts, "That Jesus never regarded himself as God is most obvious from his reply when hailed as 'Good master': 'Why callest thou me good? There is none good but one, God.' . . . Nor did he regard himself as Son of God in the later Trinitarian sense."[1] Elsewhere Klausner summarizes his view and supports the developmental idea as follows: "Jesus' own teaching is poles apart from the Trinitarian dogma; but it contained the germ which, fostered by gentilic Christians, developed into the doctrine of the Trinity."[2] Klausner did not agree completely with my friend, however, for he says,

"Jesus was convinced of his messiahship: of this there is no doubt."[3]

Liberals Deny Jesus Claimed to Be God

It is understandable that Jewish scholars, who reject the doctrine of the Trinity and its concomitant doctrine of the deity of Jesus, would advance the view expressed by Klausner and the teacher I met. But essentially the same position is embraced by a large segment of contemporary liberal Protestantism and avant-garde Catholicism. This is surprising, especially since many Protestants are vocal leaders in the World Council of Churches, which "is a fellowship of churches which accept our Lord Jesus Christ as God and Saviour."[4] Robinson, for example, asserts, "Jesus never claims to be God, personally," and, "It is, indeed, an open question whether Jesus ever claimed to be the Son of God, let alone God."[5] DeWolf insists that the New Testament "stops short of an absolute and unequivocal identification of Christ with God himself."[6] Perhaps the most extreme form of this position is stated by Ferré, who explains that "man's need to create gods made Jesus into a God . . . Jesus became the effective God of the Christian faith" and exhorts, "from Judaism and Islam Christianity should learn to repent of its central idolatry: its substitution, in effect, of Jesus for God, its making Jesus God."[7]

People like these state their positions with such emphasis and dogmatism and present the historic Christian doctrine with such condescension and even scorn that unwary readers accept their views. For example, Bauman writes, "Unfortunately, many modern Christians believe they solve the problem by stating flatly, 'Jesus is God.' . . . It must be pointed out that this statement is nowhere made by Jesus or by any writer in the New Testament."[8] Robinson more caustically declares, "The belief that we are at this point and in this person in touch with God has increasingly been left to the religious minority that can still accept the old mythology as physically or metaphysically true."[9]

This liberal view of Jesus' consciousness and claims has not swept the field of biblical scholarship. Nor is it opposed only by a few diehard, obscurantist fundamentalists. Many scholars even in the liberal theological camp recognize Jesus' consciousness of His deity and His unique filial relationship to God the Father. Connick reports,

> We have consulted a score of scholars concerning the question, "What did Jesus think of himself?" A bewildering variety of answers has emerged. . . . If we had space to examine the work of a second score of scholars, the diversity of thought would be increased. It ranged from one end of the theological spectrum to the other—from prophet to pre-existent Son of God.[10]

Connick's own conclusion is that "Jesus may well have used 'Son' as correlative to 'Father.' It expressed the fullness of his own personal consciousness of his intimate relationship to God."[11]

Other examples include C. J. Cadoux, who says that Jesus "sometimes spoke of God and himself as 'the Father' and 'the Son,' as if he were the Son of God in some absolute or unique sense" and, "Jesus knows himself to be in closest filial intimacy with God as His Father, so that . . . he occupies a special place of his own as 'the Son' over against 'the Father.'"[12] Methodist bishop Kern writes, "Jesus believed his sonship to God to be unique and essential and his appearance on earth to be a part of the cosmic purpose of an all-loving Father whose complete nature he shared."[13] And Taylor wrote, "It belongs to the self-consciousness of Jesus that He believed Himself to be the Son of God in a pre-eminent sense."[14] This demonstrates that biblical scholarship even in the liberal tradition amply supports the conservative position that Jesus claimed His deity and unique Sonship to God, a view classically presented by Geerhardus Vos in *The Self-Disclosure of Jesus.*[15]

The liberal denial of Jesus' conscious claim to deity, however, can be refuted by an examination of the biblical witness in the Gospels. Here, as in all other theological issues, the final question is, "What is written in the Law? How does it read to you?" (Luke 10:26; cf. Acts 17:11). The appeal to Scripture is not as simple as it sounds, however, because liberal theology embraces and builds on a totally different doctrine of the Bible than orthodox theology. Liberals reject verbal-plenary inspiration and the orthodox concept of the dual authorship of Scripture. Though they may hold to some view of divine inspiration, to liberals the Scriptures are basically human writings that developed over varying periods of time into their present form. As a result, the Scriptures reflect the religious beliefs of those who passed the stories on orally and of those who wrote them down, intermingled with the historical facts. Separating the facts from the faith—if possible at all—requires all the ingenuity of modern literary and historical criticism of the Bible. In relation to the Synoptic Gospels this involves the use of demythologizing.

For liberal theology the specific problem related to the question posed in this chapter is determining in the gospel accounts what Jesus actually said concerning Himself and what His followers put in His mouth. Bultmann, who says, "I am personally of the opinion that Jesus did not believe himself to be the Messiah,"[16] expresses the problem as follows:

> The common opinion is that this belief of the earliest Church rests upon the self-consciousness of Jesus, i.e., that he actually did consider himself to be the Messiah, or the Son of Man. But his opinion is burdened with serious difficulties. It does agree with the evangelists' point of view, but the question is whether they themselves have not superimposed upon the traditional material their own belief in the messiahship of Jesus. . . . Some advance the following reasoning as an argument from history: The Church's belief in the messiahship of Jesus is comprehensible only if Jesus was conscious of being the Messiah and actually represents himself as such—at least to the "disciples." But is this argument valid? For it is just as possible that belief in the messiahship of Jesus arose with and out of belief in his resurrection.[17]

Because of this problem Colwell wrote,

> The diversity of opinion as to what Jesus thought of himself is more strongly rooted in the inadequacy, the insufficiency of the evidence than in the particular presuppositions of the scholars. . . . There is not enough record of sayings of Jesus about Jesus to make it possible for the independent studies to arrive at the same conclusion.[18]

Similarly, Woolf writes, "It would be pushing our conclusions further than the premises warrant to say categorically that Jesus had no consciousness of a special and unique Sonship, but it is true to say that the historical material preserved in the two older sources is not aware of any such consciousness."[19]

If the faith of the early church was read back into the words and deeds of Jesus, as the liberals claim, then the authors of the Gospels did it, because insufficient time elapsed between the events themselves and the gospel records of the events for legend-filled accounts to develop. The time lapse between the public ministry of Jesus and the writing of the last of the Gospels is not more than seventy years at the most and probably around fifty years. Furthermore the legendary details could not have been woven into the Gospels after their original composition, for, as Dibelius writes, "The doubt as to whether our Gospels have been preserved in their original form turns out to be more and more unwarranted. . . . No book of antiquity has come down to us in such old, such numerous, and such relatively uniform texts as the Gospels and the Pauline Epistles."[20] Finally, the gospel writers must have put these claims into Jesus' mouth deliberately. Matthew and John were intimate associates of Jesus throughout most if not all of His public ministry. In addition, Mark is generally believed to have written his gospel under the supervision of Peter. Certainly these apostles knew that Jesus had said what they reported Him to say. The liberal explanation makes the gospel writers deceivers. Furthermore, this deception must have been a conspiracy of a large segment of the apostolic church, for a sizable group were disciples of Jesus throughout His public ministry (Acts 1:21–22), and yet no one accused the gospel writers of attributing to Jesus claims He did not make.

Obviously the gospel writers had a purpose in writing their accounts of Jesus' life and ministry. John plainly stated that "these [signs] have been written that you may believe that Jesus is the Christ, the Son of God" (John 20:31); but having such a purpose does not require the conclusion that John deliberately made Jesus say things He in fact did not say. All that having such a purpose implies is that John selectively recorded events and sayings that supported his purpose out of the mass of material available (cf. 21:25). In so doing, John and the other gospel writers were sustained and guided by the Holy Spirit (2 Peter 1:21). John referred to Jesus' promise to His disciples that "the Holy Spirit . . . will teach you all things, and bring to your remembrance all that I said to you" (John 14:26; cf. John 16:12–15).

Jesus' Claims to Deity

It is not the purpose of this study to settle the conflict between the orthodox and the liberal doctrines of the Bible. Nor is the purpose to refute demythologizing. The problem with the latter position is determining when one has reached the historical core, as the Bultmannians and post-Bultmannians seek to do. But it is necessary to present the case for the gospel writers as honest, sincere men of faith who were energized by the Holy Spirit and who accurately presented what Jesus did and said. As a result, the Gospels are considered as trustworthy documents that faithfully record the words of Jesus. Textual problems in the passages considered will be investigated.

Jesus' most emphatic claim to deity is the statement in His discussion with the Jews, "Before Abraham was born, I am" (John 8:58). The Jews brought the name of Abraham, their physical and spiritual ancestor, into the conversation (vv. 52–53). Jesus seized on it to lead on to His final claim in the verse already quoted, startling the Jews by saying, "Your father Abraham rejoiced to see My day, and he saw it and was glad" (v. 56). When the Jews responded with a question as to how a man as young as Jesus could have seen Abraham, "Jesus claims eternal existence with the absolute phrase used of God."[21] Jesus did not claim mere preexistence to Abraham, which would have been expressed by the imperfect tense of the verb used concerning Abraham, but eternal existence, the self-existence that belongs to God alone. Yahweh applied this same phrase to Himself as His name in His call to Moses at the burning bush (Ex. 3:14).

A second significant claim of Jesus to deity is His assertion in a later discussion with the Jews, "I and the Father are one" (John 10:30). The word translated "one" is in the neuter gender, not the masculine. There is obviously not a singleness of person between Jesus and the Father, but a "unity of essence."[22] Modern critics who deny the deity of Jesus object to this interpretation, a view almost unanimously accepted in the church until the advent of religious liberalism. They insist that it represents only a unity of purpose, pointing to Jesus' prayer for His disciples, "that they may be one, even as We are" (John 17:11; cf. vv. 21–23, as evidence). The argument is that the unity of believers is only a unity of purpose, and therefore the parallel unity of Jesus and God is the same. This view ignores the fact that Jesus described the unity between Himself and the Father as a personal interpenetration, "even as Thou, Father, art in Me, and I in Thee" (v. 21), which is far more than mere unity of purpose. This view also ignores the fact that believers in Jesus Christ are made members of the "body of Christ" (1 Cor. 12:12–13, 27) in a spiritual unity, are possessors of resurrection life, which is Christ Himself (Gal. 2:20; Col. 1:27; Col. 3:4), and are "partakers of the divine nature" (2 Peter 1:4). The strongest answer to liberals, however, and the strongest support of the orthodox interpretation of this statement is the reaction of the Jews to whom Jesus was speaking. It is the presumption of audacious intellectual pride to reject the understanding of the hearers of a statement for the interpretation of people removed from the events and the records by almost two millennia. Following

Jesus' statement, "the Jews took up stones again to stone Him" (John 10:31), and when Jesus asked why, they replied, "Because You, being a man, make Yourself out to be God" (v. 33). The Jews understood that Jesus was claiming deity by His statement, which to them was blasphemy.

A whole area of scriptural witness to Jesus' claim to deity is the way in which He spoke of Himself as the Son of God in a special and unique sense. That this identification of Himself as the Son of God was in effect a claim to deity is indicated in three passages of Scripture. The first is in the discourse just considered. In the light of the Old Testament designation of His people as gods (Ps. 82:6), Jesus wondered why the Jews accused Him of blasphemy because He said, "I am the Son of God" (John 10:36). In the immediate context Jesus had not called Himself the Son of God, but from this statement it is obvious that the use of that title by Jesus is the same as claiming unity with God, which the Jews understood as claiming deity. The liberals seize on this quotation from Psalm 82 to insist that Jesus was not claiming any special relationship to God for Himself, but the following context answers this misinterpretation.

A similar situation occurred when Jesus declared to the Jews, "My Father is working until now, and I Myself am working" (John 5:17). Before this, the anger of the Jews had been aroused by Jesus' healing on the Sabbath, which they considered breaking the Sabbath (5:1–16). But now, John explained, "the Jews were seeking all the more to kill Him" because He "was calling God His own Father, making Himself equal with God" (v. 18). This unique relationship to God as the Son, its manifestation in His ministry, and its purpose is explained in the following context (vv. 19–30).

The third situation where Jesus' acknowledgment of His position as the Son of God is taken as equivalent to a claim of deity is in His trial before the Jewish council. With slight variations of wording in the questions and the answers, the event is recorded in all three Synoptic Gospels (Matt. 26:63–66; Mark 14:61–64; Luke 22:66–71). Jesus was brought in the morning before the Sanhedrin and was asked by the high priest to answer under oath whether He is "the Christ, the Son of God" (Matt. 26:63). Mark wrote, "the Christ, the Son of the Blessed One" (14:61), and Luke divided the question into two (Luke 22:67, 70). In all three gospels Jesus in effect (the wording varies slightly) acknowledged this identity. Matthew and Mark added the statement, "Hereafter you shall see the Son of Man sitting at the right hand of Power, and coming on the clouds of heaven" (Matt. 26:64; Mark 14:62). Instead of accepting His statement under oath as truth and acknowledging Jesus as the Christ, the Son of God, the high priest and the council condemned Him by His own words as guilty of blasphemy.

All three of these passages point up a significant fact concerning Jesus' consciousness of and claims to His identity. This is the fact that the Jews who heard Him speak and did not accept Him and His message considered Him guilty of blasphemy, judging Him to be claiming to be God, and were aroused on several occasions to the point of attempting to stone Him in the Jewish manner of execution. Furthermore, it was under this judgment of blasphemy that the Jewish leaders finally sentenced Him to death. How could Jesus' followers jump to conclusions about His identity that Jesus Himself did not claim? Also it is difficult to conceive of His enemies drawing that conclusion without basis in His words. And it is even more difficult to conceive of Jesus being put to death because of a misunderstanding when a simple clarification would have saved His life.

Many liberals make the point that no evidence of such claims is found in what they call the older sources. These are Mark and a document they call Q, which is reflected in the material found in Matthew and Luke that does not occur in Mark. This argument is based on form criticism in particular and the whole liberal view toward the Bible in general. Furthermore, this conclusion simply does not accord with the facts. Bauman writes, "It must be maintained just as strongly, however, that Jesus knew himself to be the Son of God, partaking fully of the divine nature," and "This unique filial consciousness contributed a divine dimension to every word and act of his life. The author of John built his Gospel on this conviction, but it is just as obvious in the synoptics, where Jesus is *the* Son of God."[23] The clearest example of this consciousness and claim in the Synoptics is Matthew 11:25–30, especially the statement, "All things have been handed over to Me by My Father; and no one knows the Son, except the Father; nor does anyone know the Father except the Son, and anyone to whom the Son wills to reveal Him" (Matt. 11:27). Vos lists six occurrences in Matthew's gospel—several with parallel accounts in one or both of the other synoptics—when "Jesus represents Himself as the Son of God."[24]

When a person honestly and without liberal presuppositions faces the evidence of Scripture, he or she cannot fail to conclude that Jesus knew Himself to be the incarnate Son of God and claimed that identity. Some liberals admit the evidence but insist that Jesus was mistaken. Concerning this argument Kern writes,

> Either he was correct in his supposition, or he was deluded, or he was insincere. We reject the last possibility instantly. In the preface of his *Back to Methuselah* G. Bernard Shaw says: "Better by far to declare the throne of God empty than set a liar or a fool on it." That he could have been harboring a delusion seems difficult of belief. The ages would have punctured that self-deceit long ago. The answer seems unavoidable: Jesus must have been what he and his disciples thought he was: a unique revelation in humanity of the Absolute and All-Loving God.[25]

The believing heart responds to the evidence of Scripture concerning Jesus' conscious claims to deity with joyous assent. Like Thomas, Christians respond, "My Lord and my God!" (John 20:28).

CHAPTER 4

The Ministry of Christ in His Life on Earth

John F. Walvoord

T he four gospels provide the principal source of information concerning Christ in His life on earth. Though the narratives are selective, in keeping with the principle governing each gospel, and though only a fraction of the incidents that might be of interest are related, the picture provided in the inspired Scriptures is intriguing to all classes of scholars and is replete with theological significance.

Though the historical character of the Gospels makes them easy to understand, their theological interpretation is by no means uncomplicated. Few sections of Scripture require more careful analysis and precise interpretation. The reason does not lie in the complicated narrative but rather in the fact that the incidents recorded are more than just history. They constitute a revelation of God and His purposes.

The Major Spheres of the Earthly Life of Christ

One of the reasons the Gospels are difficult to interpret is that Christ lived in three major spheres, and His teaching as well as His life are related to them. The right understanding of this fact is essential to a correct interpretation not only of the Gospels but also of the entire New Testament.

THE SPHERE OF JEWISH LAW

The Law, inaugurated for Israel through Moses, was still in effect throughout the lifetime of Christ and in one sense it was not terminated until His death (Gal. 3:23–25; 4:5). In much of His teaching, Christ affirmed the Mosaic Law and declared it must be fulfilled (Matt. 5:7–19). In Jesus' life on earth He lived under the Law, His teaching constituted a major interpretation of it, and He kept it perfectly (2 Cor. 5:21). On numerous occasions Christ contradicted the customary teaching of the Law. He insisted, moreover, on its practical application to the spiritual issues of His day, in contrast with the common evasion and perversion of the Law by the scribes. As the Son of God, He also was free to interpret the Law authoritatively and in some cases He contrasted His own teaching with that of Moses.

Christ insisted that keeping the letter of the Mosaic Law was not sufficient. The Law could be properly fulfilled only by those who attained its highest form of interpretation, centering in the love of God and love of one's neighbor. In some cases Christ pointed out that the Mosaic Law represented divine condescension in that God accommodated Himself to the weakness of the people, as in the case of the teaching on divorce. Frequently, Christ appealed to the higher law of God of which the Mosaic Law was a particular expression.

THE SPHERE OF THE KINGDOM

Much of Jesus' teaching is directly related to the doctrine of the kingdom. The Gospels connect this line of truth specifically to the Old Testament revelation of the kingdom to be established on earth by the Messiah. The gospel of Matthew, in its opening portion, especially related Christ to David as the One who will fulfill the Davidic covenant. The gospel of Luke records the angelic messenger who promised Mary that her Son would reign on the throne of David and rule over the house of Israel forever.

In the opening section of Matthew the credentials of the King are presented and the predicted signs are recorded as fulfilled. In keeping with His relationship to the kingdom, Christ revealed in the Sermon on the Mount the spiritual principles that govern this kingdom, giving present application of these principles to the particular situation, as well as speaking prophetically of the spiritual qualities that are to enter into His millennial kingdom. In the Olivet Discourse, specific prophecies are given concerning the Great Tribulation, which will introduce His second coming and the establishment of His throne on the earth.

Though the New Testament doctrine of the kingdom necessarily is based on the Old, the tendency of scholars to limit the teaching of Christ to one phase of the kingdom or another is open to question. An examination of what Christ said about the kingdom should make plain that in some instances He spoke concerning the general government and authority of God over the universe. In other cases He dealt with the reign of God in the heart, a spiritual kingdom. In other cases He spoke specifically of the kingdom promises to David. It is therefore an error to limit His teaching to making all His kingdom messages apply to the millennial period alone. On the other hand it is equally erroneous to limit His teaching to a spiritual kingdom to be fulfilled in part before His second advent.

The kingdom teachings are found principally in the Old Testament, and the kingdom partakes to some extent of the legal character of that period. As presented in the teachings of Christ, however, the millennial kingdom is a distinct sphere of rule both in its content and in its application and is to be contrasted with the present age of the church or the past dispensation of Law.

THE SPHERE OF THE CHURCH

In addition to the teachings of Christ relating to the Mosaic Law and the millennial kingdom, prophecy is given of the church. The first mention of this is found in Matthew 16:18, following Israel's rejection of Christ as her King and the opposition to His message on the spiritual principles of the kingdom. Earlier, in Matthew 13, the entire interadvent age is revealed under the seven mysteries of the kingdom of heaven. Chronologically, the church coincides with much of the development of this period revealed in Matthew 13.

The chief revelation concerning the church, however, is found in the gospel of John in the Upper Room Discourse. Here, apparently for the first time, the essential principles are revealed that pertain to the purpose of God in the present interadvent age. The basic spiritual principles are given in John 13. In John 14 the fact that Christ will be in the Father's house during the present age and will send the Spirit to dwell in the believer is unfolded. In chapter 15 the vine and the branches speak of the organic union of the believer with Christ, of the new intimacy of being friends of Christ, and of the fact that believers are chosen and ordained to bring forth fruit. The opposition and persecution that will characterize the present age is revealed also in John 15, in contrast with the protection of the saints in the millennial kingdom. A major doctrine given in John 16 is the work of the Holy Spirit in relationship to the world and the believer. The great purposes of God as they will be fulfilled in the church are also implicit in the intercession of Christ recorded in John 17. The fact that believers will be perfectly united to God and that they will be in Christ and Christ will be in them forms the center of the revelation.

A study of the four gospels, therefore, demonstrates three major spheres of revelation. It is a hasty generalization, however, to characterize the Gospels as law or that they pertain to the church or to the kingdom. It is rather that Christ taught in all these spheres, and each utterance must be understood in its context and content.

The Office of Prophet

Without question Christ is the greatest of the prophets. His teachings contained in the four gospels demonstrate a great variety of subjects, a broader scope of prophecy, and a more comprehensive revelation than is found in any of the recorded prophets of Scripture. In almost every aspect of revelation Christ made a distinct contribution.

Unlike all other prophets, Christ revealed God the Father not only in His spoken ministry, but also in His life and person. As the Logos of John, Christ was eternally the source of knowledge, truth, wisdom, and light. When He became incarnate, He became a declaration in human flesh of what God is (John 1:4–18). In His life, death, and resurrection Christ was a revelation of God far beyond that of any prophet who preceded Him. Even after His resurrection Christ continued to exercise His prophetic office, teaching His disciples the things they needed to know to adjust themselves to the new age that they were entering. After His ascension, the Holy Spirit was sent to continue the prophetic work, revealing to the saints the truths that Christ would have them know (John 16:12–15).

The Office of Priest

Just as Christ fulfilled to the utmost the office of prophet, so also He qualifies as the High Priest and is the embodiment of all that is anticipated in the Old Testament priesthood. As a priest He fulfilled the primary definition of what constitutes a priest, "a man duly appointed to act for other men in things pertaining to God."[1] Not only in His person, but also in His work, Christ fulfilled the ministry of a priest, offering gifts, sacrifices, and intercession. He acted as a true Mediator between God and humankind. According to the Epistle to the Hebrews, Christ fulfilled the five necessary requirements of the priesthood:

1. He was qualified for the office (Heb. 1:3; 3:1–6).
2. He was appointed of God (5:1–10).
3. His priesthood was of a higher order than that of Aaron's; Christ's priesthood superseded Aaron's as Aaron's had superseded the patriarchal system (5:6, 10; 7:1–8:6).
4. All functions of the priesthood were performed by Christ (7:23–28; 9:11–28; 10:5–18).
5. His priesthood is eternal, indicating His superiority and finality (7:25).

The Office of King

One of the fundamental purposes of the Incarnation was the fulfillment of the earthly purposes of God in the Davidic covenant. The Old Testament had predicted the coming of a King who would fulfill the promises of God to David (2 Sam. 7:16; Pss. 2; 45; 72; 110; Isa. 9:6–7; Dan. 7:13–14; Mic. 5:2; Zech. 9:8). When Christ came, He fulfilled the requirements of the prophesied King, though the full revelation of His work as King was reserved for His second coming.

The record in the New Testament is both historical and prophetic (Luke 1:31–33; John 1:49; 18:37; 19:12; 1 Cor. 15:25; 1 Tim. 6:15; Rev. 1:5; 17:14; 19:16). The rejection of Christ as king by Israel (John 19:15) resulted in the postponement of the millennial kingdom, but it did not alter the certainty of complete fulfillment of His work as King nor the fact that in His person He is the King of Israel.

Taken together, the three offices of Christ as Prophet, Priest, and King are the key to the purpose of the Incarnation. His prophetic office is concerned with the revelation of the truth of God, the priestly office was related to His work as Savior and Mediator, and His kingly office has in view His right to reign over Israel and over the entire earth. In Christ the supreme dignity of these offices is reached.

CHAPTER 5

The Baptism of Christ

S. Lewis Johnson Jr.

T he Cross casts its shadow over the ministry of Christ from its opening stages to the eve of its close. This has been tellingly caught in the great painting of Holman Hunt, *The Shadow of Death*. The day is fast ebbing away, and the golden rays of the setting sun are slanting in through an open door. The weary toiler at the carpenter's bench, having just straightened Himself from His stooped and cramped position, stretches Himself for a moment. The sun, catching the outraised arms, throws on the wall behind Him the dark lines of a cross. It is Hunt's forceful way of stressing the fact that, even in the hidden years of obscurity, Jesus' decease at Jerusalem was inevitable.

The baptism of Jesus Christ, with its vision of the dove and the heavenly voice in the words traceable to the great Servant of Jehovah section of Isaiah, also points on to the baptism of His death (Mark 10:38; Luke 12:50). The accents are not so heavy as they shall become later, but they are definitely there. Ultimately the Cross shall so possess Him that it can be said "that He resolutely set His face to go to Jerusalem" (Luke 9:51; cf. v. 53), a text Sangster used for a sermon so movingly entitled, "His Destination is on His Face."

The narrative of Jesus' baptism, like that of His temptation, created acute difficulties for the early church. It seemed to say at first glance that Jesus underwent a "baptism of repentance for the remission of sins" (Mark 1:4). Were they not, then, His sins? How could He, the Son of God, occupy a position such as this? Furthermore, as Edersheim points out, "Nowhere in Rabbinic writings do we find any hint of a Baptism of the Messiah, nor of a descent upon Him of the Spirit in the form of a dove."[1] The embarrassment is itself the strongest evidence of the genuineness of the accounts. The church surely would not invent an incident that raised so many questions about its Lord. It is most likely that the complete account of the incident is to be traced to the Lord Himself.[2]

Jesus' Hidden Years

Jesus' baptism, the second major crisis in His life, is referred to in all four gospels. Intervening between the birth and the baptism are the so-called hidden years, years for which there is little information regarding the life of Christ. There are hints and suggestions in the records, but in the final analysis they yield only a whisper of His obedient existence.

HIS INFANCY (LUKE 2:21–39)

Luke related His circumcision, a rite that marked Him out as an heir of the blessings of the covenant made with Abraham (cf. Rom. 4:9–12), and His presentation to the Lord. There had begun, in the sphere of His flesh, life's progress from innocence to holiness (cf. Luke 1:35). Later it could be said of Him, "Although He was a Son, He learned obedience from the things which He suffered" (Heb. 5:8).

HIS CHILDHOOD (LUKE 2:40–51)

As Morgan wrote, "The whole story of the childhood of Jesus from infancy to His religious coming of age is contained in one verse."[3] The text reads, "And the Child continued to grow and become strong, increasing in wisdom; and the grace of God was upon Him" (Luke 2:40). The word "grow" is the broad term Luke used for His growth, while the remaining words of the verse spell out the details. The words "become strong" refer to the physical, while "increasing in wisdom" and "the grace of God was upon Him" refer to the mental and the spiritual. There was a beautiful harmony in His development, touching all the facets of His being.

In the following incident the curtain is drawn open for a short moment to permit a brief gaze into the silent years. A beautiful picture is seen of the youth of twelve trading probing queries and pellucid answers with the doctors. Since it was the time of the Passover Feast, the questions and answers may have revolved around this subject, one so uniquely fitted for the exposition of the significance of the coming Passover Lamb. Did He, as afterwards (Matt. 22:42–45), lead up with His questions to the deeper and fuller meaning of the festal rites? Was He even then attempting to prepare them and point them to the Lamb of God, who would take away the sin of the world? Was Calvary always in the air?

HIS YOUTH (LUKE 2:52)

In this verse Luke condensed the youth of God's Second Man in one brief statement, "And Jesus kept increasing in wisdom and stature, and in favor with God and men." The word "wisdom" includes His intellectual and moral growth, while "stature" refers to His physical development. That He could keep "increasing" in them attests to the complete humanity of the Lord's Messiah; He was perfect at each stage for that stage.[4] The result was favor with God and people. A favorite at Nazareth, with the perfect blend of holiness and love, He was the God-Man—a mystery indeed, but not a problem.

HIS LAND, HOME, AND KIN (LUKE 2:15)

Nazareth was the Lord's home until His manifestation to Israel. It has sometimes been thought that Jesus lived in "the sticks" of the day, a kind of backwater of history. That is far from the case. The apocryphal Book of Jubilees, 8:19, stated that Jerusalem was the navel of the earth, the center of the nations of the world. And Nazareth, too, was well within the sound of the reverberation of world events. At the crossroads of highways leading from the east to the west and from the north to the south, as well as being near Sepphoris, a Roman military colony and for many years Herod's capital, the little village of Nazareth was an interested spectator of the march of the empire. By way of the Roman coins, on which were borne the images of great men and significant events, together with innumerable coins of eastern currencies, the inhabitants of Nazareth were able to follow the events of the day. Jesus was interested in the coins (Mark 12:13–17), and there are many indications that He had a sharp eye for world politics (Mark 9:13; Luke 13:32; 22:25; John 10:1–21; 19:11). Amid the bustling family life of a large circle of kin within the tribe of Judah in the north and in the south, He was prepared for the future.

HIS OCCUPATION (MARK 6:3)

Mark wrote that those who listened to Jesus' teaching wondered, "Is this not the carpenter, the son of Mary, and brother of James, and Joses, and Judas, and Simon?" He learned His trade of carpentry from Joseph, becoming master of the tools and skills of his craft. As Morgan remarks, "He trod the path of a daily duty,"[5] learning thereby dependence on other wills. There were in Him no "fugitive islands of secret reservations," as someone has said. His life was as sensitive as a shadow, as selfless as a shadow, as obedient as a shadow.

HIS PHYSICAL APPEARANCE

The only portrait of Jesus' physical appearance found in the New Testament is that given to John in Revelation 1, and that one is symbolic in nature. A physical description is given of John the Baptist, but none is given of Jesus. A hint or two may be found in the fact that the rabbis had definite standards for the outward appearance of a proper Jew, especially a teacher. They could criticize very harshly if the standards were not met, but they did not scorn His physical presence. Evidently He measured up to their standards. One of them was the claim that the reflection of the divine presence could descend only on a man of tall and powerful stature. Jesus Christ must have met this standard, a fact supported by the ruggedness required for His frequent journeys by foot in the land.

The skin color of Palestinian Jews in antiquity was light brown, and their eyes were no doubt brown or blue. They were black-haired and wore their hair to the shoulders, and beards and mustaches were worn. Thus while Jesus may not have been able to make a professional football team today, He must have been "a man's man." One interesting fact is mentioned by John. Though Jesus was just over thirty years of age, the Jews said to Him, "You are not yet fifty years old, and have You seen Abraham?" (John 8:57). Apparently identifying with people in their cares and sorrows left its imprint on the Man of Sorrows.[6]

HIS SCRIPTURE KNOWLEDGE AND
UNDERSTANDING (JOHN 7:15)

Joseph undoubtedly taught Jesus the Torah from a very early age, as custom dictated. Jesus probably studied in the village schools also. He was able to speak Aramaic and Greek, the languages of ordinary conversation, and He could also read the Hebrew Bible (Luke 4:16–22). When He taught in Jerusalem the Jews marveled, saying, "How has this man become learned, having never been educated?" (John 7:15). The word γράμματα is found in Acts 26:24, where Festus blurts out, "Paul, you are out of your mind! Your great learning [γράμματα] is driving you mad." Festus had detected the knowledge and understanding of a man taught in the professional schools, but the Jews detected it in Him who never sat at the feet of the rabbis.[7] They seemed completely blinded to David's words, "The secret of the LORD is for those who fear Him, and He will make them know His covenant" (Ps. 25:14). And never man feared the Father as Jesus did.

The Account of the Baptism of Jesus in Matthew 3:13–17

THE RELUCTANCE OF JOHN (3:13–14)

Jesus had been born in Bethlehem of Judea about 5 B.C., in the reign of Emperor Augustus and, while the *Pax Romana* girdled the globe, He grew up, as noted, in Nazareth of Galilee. When Augustus died in A.D. 14, Jesus was about twenty years of age. A decade or so later the voice of prophecy rang out in the ministry of John after years of silence, and Jesus knew the beginning of His ministry had come. He therefore went down from Galilee to the Jordan "to begin a ministry in which he would proclaim a kingdom mightier than the Roman and tell of a world saved not by man who became God (like Augustus or Tiberius) but by God who became man."[8]

When Jesus arrived and submitted Himself for baptism, John strenuously attempted to hinder Him.[9] An inner conviction of the unique character of the One before him had come to John, perhaps from their relationship (Luke 1:36) or from the peculiar circumstances at Mary's visit to his mother (1:43–46) or from his own spiritual insight (Matt. 3:7). At any rate, the Baptist seemed to mean, "I have need of Your Spirit and fire baptism; why then should *I* administer water baptism to *You?*"

THE REPLY OF JESUS (3:15)

Jesus answered John the Baptist by saying, "It is fitting for us to fulfill all righteousness." With these first words of Jesus in Matthew, as Zahn says, the opposition of the Baptist was overcome.[10] The King must fulfill all the righteous requirements of the Law (5:20; 6:1). It was proper for Him as Son of Man to identify Himself with the nation in its preparation for the coming of the King (cf. Isa. 40:1–11).

THE REACTION OF HEAVEN (3:16–17)

Following the visible act of baptism the heavens were torn apart,[11] and then there was a vision and a voice. Important clues to the meaning of Jesus' baptism are found in the vision and the divine voice.

The vision of the Spirit, descending as a dove on Him, fulfills the words regarding the Servant of the Lord, "I have put My Spirit upon Him" (Isa. 42:1).[12] This is His anointing, as the Lord realized and the apostles preached. He could hardly make it plainer that this signified His inauguration into the office of Messiah than when He stood and read Isaiah 61:1, "The Spirit of the Lord GOD is upon me, because the LORD has anointed me," and then added, "Today this Scripture has been fulfilled in your hearing" (Luke 4:18, 21). The Spirit's coming was His anointing, and His anointing was His induction into the office of Messiah. Peter confirmed this when he said, "God anointed Him [Jesus of Nazareth] with the Holy Spirit and with power" (Acts 10:38). This, then, was the ordination of the Servant. Isaiah portrayed the Servant as a suffering Servant, and therefore it is fitting that the coming of the Spirit should be like the dove. The dove is the bird of sacrifice. Jesus then became the bearer of the Spirit so that He could carry out His ministry of death and ultimately baptize with the Spirit and with fire (Matt. 3:11).[13]

The voice from heaven, which confirmed the vision, was a kind of coronation formula for the Suffering Servant.[14] The words combined Psalm 2:7, the psalm of the messianic king, and Isaiah 42:1, a reference to the Suffering Servant. The words in effect informed Him that He was "born to suffer, born a king,"[15] and they became a preview of His destiny, a synthesis of ruling and of suffering of incomparable value. Some writers have claimed that at His baptism God the Father revealed to Jesus His messiahship. This is an intolerable view, because if this were so, it would imply that He was baptized like any other Israelite, namely, to confess His sins and give evidence of repentance. His messiahship was not revealed to Him there; His baptism simply confirmed His view of Himself. If this were not so, He could never have overruled John's objection as He did. But, having had His messianic dignity confirmed by the voice from heaven and the vision of the dove, He was the more able to affirm confidently, "The time is fulfilled, and the kingdom of God is at hand; repent and believe in the gospel" (Mark 1:15). Interestingly, the entire Trinity was involved in the scene, thus demonstrating how transcendently important was His baptism. Incidentally, the voice from heaven was the seal of approval on the hidden years. "He sets the seal of perfection upon the hidden years. We want to know more. We ask for no details; it is enough."[16] The King was now installed in the messianic office, but the anointing was not only for preaching; it was also for passion.

The Theological Significance of the Baptism

To most Christians the baptism of Jesus Christ is as much an enigma as it was to John the Baptist. This is reflected in the almost absurd statement that believers are "to follow the Lord in baptism," as if a believer's baptism is a carbon copy of His. However, it is doubtful if there is a single passage in the New Testament in which a biblical writer connects the baptism of Christ with Christian baptism.[17] But the baptism of Christ does have important theological significance.

CHRIST'S BAPTISM MARKED HIS IDENTIFICATION WITH ISRAEL (3:15)

John's baptism was founded on the redemptive work of the Lamb to come, and precisely for this reason it seems to be the exclusive responsibility of those who are the recipients of the work of redemption. How, then, can He who needed personally no redemption be baptized? The answer He gave John gives the clue. "To fulfill all righteousness" bears a close relationship to Paul's words that Christ was "born under the Law" (Gal. 4:4). It refers to the fulfilling of all the righteous requirements of the Law: Jesus must be circumcised though there was no necessity to put away the body of the flesh in His case (cf. Col. 1:11). He must be presented in the temple though He did not need deliverance from the house of bondage in Egypt (cf. Luke 2:22). The baptism signified not only the removal of sins; it also pointed to a positive preparation and dedication of heart to the coming King and His kingdom. He too belongs to this people, though He is their King, and must demonstrate His willingness to do the will of God. His baptism, then, was a phase of His humiliation under the Law, just as were His circumcision and His presentation in the temple.[18] He acknowledged John's authority at this stage in the unfolding of the program of divine revelation. He was baptized then as a representative person, knowing this was a divinely imposed duty for every Israelite.[19]

CHRIST'S BAPTISM SIGNALED HIS INAUGURATION INTO THE MESSIANIC OFFICE

This has already been discussed, but it should be emphasized here that this involved not only the work of redemption, but also the accompanying work of judgment (Matt. 3:11–12). This work is yet future.

CHRIST'S BAPTISM ILLUSTRATED THE GOAL OF HIS
   MINISTRY

When Jesus descended into the waters of the Jordan River and
then emerged from them, it may have been intended as a figure of
His death, for in Matthew 20:22 He described His death as a
"baptism." Thus John's baptism foreshadows His death, Calvary
was His baptism in death, the Great Commission is a charge to
preach with a view to uniting people with Him in His death, while
Paul in Romans 6 explained the subject in detail theologically.
John's baptism, then, mirrors the Cross.

CHAPTER 6

The Temptation of Christ

S. Lewis Johnson Jr.

Against the backdrop of the wilderness, with its "wild beasts" (Mark 1:13), two solitary figures wrestle for a gigantic prize, the kingdom of God and the souls of human beings. One is subject to the Spirit of God, the other is the infernal spirit, Lucifer himself. The one, the Last Adam, must retrace the history of Adam the first. Paradise lost must become paradise regained. Following Paul, Augustine said that the entire moral and spiritual history of the world revolved around two people, Adam and Christ. Satan's temptation of Christ is a decisive movement in that history.

The circumstances of the temptations of the first Adam and the Last Adam are in sharp contrast. For example, Adam was tempted in a garden, while Christ was tempted in the desert, that "great and terrible wilderness" (Deut. 8:15), as Moses described it. Adam the first was well prepared for the Tempter physically; he was strong and food was plentiful. But Adam the last, having fasted for forty days, was weak and hungry. Adam the first was the object of Satan's initial seductions in the history of humanity, but Christ was attacked after His opponent had had four thousand years of practice. The odds were all on the side of a fall.

Many questions arise as one meditates on the Lord's conflict in the desert. They are theological questions, and they cry out for discussion and solution. The principal question is, Is Jesus Christ impeccable? This is not to ask, Is He sinless? This is generally admitted. The holiness, however, of the God-Man is more than sinlessness. The question is, Was He unable to sin? Was He not only able to overcome temptation, but also unable to be overcome by it? This cannot be debated in detail; its discussion is beyond the limits and purpose of this chapter. The answer, however, must be that He was *non potest peccare* (not able to sin), not *potest non peccare* (able not to sin). Some things God cannot do, and Jesus was God (cf. Heb. 6:18; James 1:13).[1] There is something higher than the choice of the good; it is the happy necessity of good. This belongs to the divine nature of the Messiah.[2]

If one remembers that Jesus Christ is a divine person, one will have no difficulty here. He is not a human person raised to the power of deity by virtue of the Incarnation, because He existed before the Incarnation (Mic. 5:2; John 1:1). Instead He is a divine person who at a point in time took to Himself human nature as an additional nature. And His impeccability is guaranteed by the union of the divine and human natures in one theanthropic person. He is "as mighty to overcome Satan and sin, as his mightiest nature is."[3]

A further question naturally arises: Was, then, Jesus temptable? Again the answer is yes. The human nature of the God-Man was indeed temptable. However, divine nature could not desert the human nature, permitting it to sin, for then the guilt would attach itself to the entire person, but it could leave the human nature alone when no sin or guilt is involved. This it did in the Temptation. Therefore temptability depends on the constitutional susceptibility of human nature, and, since He was completely human apart from sin, He was temptable. An invincible army may actually be attacked. That Jesus was really attacked and that His testing centered in His human nature is evidenced by the statement that at the conclusion of the Temptation "angels came and began to minister to Him" (Matt. 4:11). Deity does not need nor can it use the help of its creatures.

Another question is this: Is the temptation account genuine? While acknowledging that the account may represent perhaps a real experience, Branscomb has said, "What we have are the reverent speculations of members of the early Christian community."[4] Branscomb's regard for the spiritual creativity of the early Christian community is excessively lavish. More likely, as Manson suggests, the story goes back to Jesus Himself and was transmitted by the apostles substantially as He told it to them. Manson asks, "Who in the Palestinian Christian community pictured in the first half of Acts could ever have invented the story?"[5] No, the account is not an invention; it is a bit of intimate autobiography told the apostles by its subject, Jesus. It has all the trustworthy trademarks of the Messiah Himself.

The occasion of the relating of the experience to the apostles is more difficult to determine. No doubt the occasion was relevant to the spiritual principles prominent in the temptation account. Since the messiahship of Jesus was so obviously the issue in the Temptation, then a later occasion in which this subject was in the foreground should be sought. Such a situation is found in Matthew 16, when, after Peter's confession of His messiahship, the Lord Jesus began His instruction concerning the necessity of His death and resurrection. Immediately Peter rebuked Jesus and received the stinging reply, "Get behind Me, Satan! You are a stumbling block to Me; for you are not setting your mind on God's interests, but man's" (Matt. 16:23). At this point, it would have been most fitting for Jesus to remind the apostles that Peter's attitude was strikingly similar to that of Satan as reflected in the Temptation, and to relate and expound the force of that wilderness experience.

The Personal Temptation (Matt. 4:1–4)

THE REQUEST (4:1–3)

The baptism by John the Baptist had marked the inauguration of the messianic ministry of Christ. By this the Lord's conviction was confirmed that He was "born to suffer, born a king."[6] The voice from heaven (Matt. 3:17), in words that beautifully combined Psalm 2:7 and Isaiah 42:1, had made it plain that He was the Son who should rule, the messianic King of Israel, and that He would attain His inheritance by carrying out the ministry of the Servant of Yahweh. This remarkable synthesis of exaltation and suffering was a preview of His destiny. The vision was the visible counterpart of the voice. The Spirit's coming identified Him as the King (cf. Isa. 42:1; 61:1), but the form of the dove, the symbol of suffering sacrifice, reminded Him of His work.

All three of the tests are variations of the one great temptation to remove His messianic vocation from the guidance of His Father and make it simply a political calling. "It may be put in this way, that what Jesus rejects in the Temptations are methods of 'bringing in' the kingdom of God: (a) the economic with all that apparatus so well known to us in these days of 'five-year' plans and the like; (b) the game of political intrigue backed by military force; (c) propaganda which would eventually create an artificial nimbus for the national leader."[7] And yet there are different emphases in the tests. The first has to do with the body, the second the soul, and the third pertains to the spirit. The first looks at Christ as the Son of God, the second as the Son of David (not out of harmony with the divine Sonship), and the third as the Son of Abraham.

The first test is directed toward the lust of the flesh, the second toward the pride of life, and the third toward the lust of the eyes (cf. 1 John 2:16).

In Matthew 4:1 the word τότε (then), one of Matthew's favorite particles, makes the connection with the preceding account of Jesus' baptism (cf. Mark 1:12, "immediately"; Luke 4:1, "and"). As Scroggie said, "After the testimony the test; and after the Dove, the devil."[8] Shortly after the baptism, Jesus was led by the Spirit into the wilderness for the temptation experience. Thoroughly weakened physically, He faced the archenemy of His vocation, Satan.

The opening question of the Tempter is related to the words that came from heaven at the baptism. It might be paraphrased this way: "If, for the sake of argument, as the voice at your baptism intimated, you are the Son of God, then demonstrate your messianic office by providing a kingdom of bread" (author's paraphrase; cf. v. 3).[9] The test was a shrewd thrust. Is it really true, Satan asked, that the God who said, "Thou art My Son" (Ps. 2:7), has also said, "You shall not eat" (Gen. 3:1)? A hungering Son of God! Could this be of God, especially when one remembers that one of the features of the kingdom the Messiah will bring is that of the messianic banquet (Luke 14:15; Luke 22:29–30)?

Satan, it will be noted, did not begin with a point-blank denial of the truth. That would be too obvious. As in much of contemporary theology, the unbelief is more subtle and deceptive. The Virgin Birth is not denied; it is simply considered an unnecessary doctrine. The deity of Christ is not rejected openly; it is explained away. Jesus is not the object of faith, but its founder and classic example. As Forsyth remarked of these apostates, "We must learn to believe not in Christ, but with Christ, we are told."[10] But if only one aspect of His teaching is considered, one can immediately see that this theology is bankrupt. Jesus affirmed, "Unless you repent, you will all likewise perish" (Luke 13:3, 5). Search His religious experience as deeply as one will, and there is no trace of repentance in it. The fact is that the church has always known, and rightly so, that Jesus is not only human, but more than human. He is "my Lord and my God," as Thomas affirmed (John 20:28). He does not ask only for devotion to His example, His actions, or His words; He demands devotion to Himself. Contemporary unbelief is simply an echo of the ancient serpent's skeptical query, "Has God said?" (cf. Gen. 3:1).

THE REPLY (4:4)

The reply of the Lord, a quotation from Deuteronomy (Deut. 8:3), alludes to the manna. He proved His sonship by a reply worthy of a son! Man lives by God, not by food alone.

The National Temptation (Matt. 4:5–7)

THE REQUEST (4:5–6)

That this request is slanted toward the national aspect of the messianic ministry is indicated by the mention of "the holy city" (i.e., Jerusalem; cf. 27:53), "the temple," and the quotation of the messianic Psalm 91. Satan urged the Lord to demonstrate His messiahship by a spectacular sign, a thing the Jews loved (1 Cor. 1:22). And Satan had learned something from the first test, namely, the importance of Scripture to the Lord Jesus. So this time he supported his request by the use of Scripture. But in so doing he made several mistakes.

First, he mistakenly tempted Jesus to presumption, or the forcing of God's hand. The promises of Scripture are always valid, but they are valid only at God's time. It is always wrong to put God to the test at one's own time.

Second, Satan made the mistake of opposing Scripture to Scripture. Psalm 91:11–12, Satan's citation, is probably a messianic passage and may refer properly to the Lord, but the text must not be used in such a way that it contradicts other valid passages. One must compare Scripture with Scripture, not oppose Scripture to Scripture. The latter is Satan's method here, for in the Lord's answer He cited Deuteronomy 6:16 and used it to contradict Satan's use of the Psalms passage. Scripture is to be explained by Scripture. The Devil put Scripture against Scripture, not beside Scripture. So the Lord did here—but against Satan's words!

Satan is knowledgeable in holy Scripture, knowing it far better apparently than many of the saints. His ministers also know Scripture. They pose as "servants of righteousness" (2 Cor. 11:15). As Morgan wrote, "Every false teacher who has divided the Church, has had an 'it is written' on which to hang his doctrine. If only against the isolated passage there had been the recognition of the fact that 'again it is written,' how much the Church would have been saved!"[11] Every Christian who has had to deal with representatives of false cults knows the truth of this. The heretical teachings of baptismal regeneration, soul sleep, universalism, and denial of eternal punishment, to name a few, are all supported by their adherents with the misuse of the Word of God. Acts 2:38 is wrenched from its context and made to bear the weight of entire denominations, without even a cursory consideration of its related passage in Acts 10:34–48. Oh, if they would simply remember, "it is written again" (KJV)!

THE REPLY (4:7)

The Lord's reply, again from Deuteronomy (Deut. 6:16), indicates that He does not pander to the Jews' love for a sign nor will He burgle the house of a person's soul. He will not realize His messiahship by force. He will not dazzle others into submission by carnal sensationalism.

The Universal Temptation (Matt. 4:8–11)

THE REQUEST (4:8–9)

The third test has universal aspects, relating to the Abrahamic promises of worldwide blessing, fulfilled ultimately in Israel's Messiah. Satan offered Him this worldwide blessing apart from the Cross. Some have said Satan had no right to offer the kingdoms to Jesus Christ. Billy Bray used to say in his quaint way that the Devil was wrong, adding: "The old rascal, to offer Christ the kingdoms of the world, why he never possessed so much as a 'tater skin.'" But, as Denney points out, "This saying, which in Luke is put into the lips of Satan, is not meant to be regarded as untrue. There would be no temptation in it if it was untrue."[12] The right apparently belonged to him by virtue of his victory over humanity, the rightful heir to creation, in Eden.

The ἐάν (if) of verse 9 introduces a third-class conditional clause, the more probable future one. If this condition is taken in its usual sense, it indicates that the Devil was quite optimistic, thinking success was likely in his effort to capture the Son of God.

THE REPLY (4:10–11)

If Satan thought he would be successful, he was sadly mistaken. Jesus would not assume that the end justifies the means. He will not use the world, nor its methods, to attain His destiny. He must not become the Messiah of the world nor of Satan but of God. As Horatious Bonar wrote, "The kingdom that I seek is Thine; so let the way that leads to it be Thine."

Some writers suggest Jesus was not conscious of a messianic ministry that touched the whole world, but this passage, as well as others (e.g., Mark 14:9), is a denial of that claim. Here in the beginning of His ministry it is evident that the stakes were high.

The reply, a third citation from Deuteronomy (Deut. 6:13), is the final thrust of the sword of the Spirit. The citadel is held, and the foe is vanquished. But did the Lord march from the battlefield as other conquerors? Thielecke answers this question in a striking way.

> By no means; how different is this victory from those of men! He rises to his feet, and immediately sets forth on his via dolorosa. He, too, goes forth into the world. Once again he will have to contend with the powers of evil which rise against him. He goes through this world, which is a theatre of war and a battlefield between God and Satan. By winning his first victory he has entered this world. Christ will fight for the souls of the men he meets, whether they be publicans or Pharisees, fools or wise men, rich youths or poor men, working-class men or lords of industry, the hungry and thirsty or well-fed and safe—he will fight for the souls of all these men alike, and he will die for all of them.
>
> Thus does the victor in this fight take his way hence (Matt. 26:46), going straight towards his cross, as though God had forsaken him (Mark 15:34).
>
> Is he not after all really the loser—a bankrupt king who has gambled away his crown—as he sets forth on his path from the desert to the cross? Has he not won a Pyrrhic victory? He travels the path beset with pain which leads to the cross, and not the way of glory and triumph which is also the way of God (for how can God's progress be other than triumphal?).
>
> Perhaps this contest in the desert was after all a drawn game. Perhaps in the long run the dread opponent will prove to have won the victory and regained his power over the world. Is there any man alive in the twentieth century who does not think that all the evidence points in this direction?
>
> But something more happens in the desert when the two go their ways: "The angels came and ministered unto him" (Matt. 4:11). He must after all have won the victory.[13]

One important practical lesson from Jesus' victory over Satan is the need for a knowledge and use of God's Word. Jesus defeated the Devil by the application of Scripture to his temptations. The threefold "it is written" (Matt. 4:4, 7, 10) highlights the victory and points the way to victory for the saints. And amazingly, His citations were from Deuteronomy, a book that is often overlooked in Bible study. How many texts from this section of Scripture have been hidden in the hearts of the saints? If victory depended on its use, would the prize be gained?

The Doctrinal Significance of Jesus' Temptation

It is important to observe that the Temptation marks Jesus Christ as One perfectly qualified to be the promised Davidic sovereign.

> In the Temptations the Messiah is being invited to take the centre of the stage in one role or another. It is significant that each time the response of Jesus puts God in the centre of the stage; and each time the implication is made perfectly clear: even the Messiah is only God's servant— indeed, just because he is Messiah he must be preeminently God's servant.[14]

This victory is one in a series that finds a thrilling consummation in this book in the exultant declaration, "All authority has been given to Me in heaven and on earth" (Matt. 28:18). And that, too, is a step in the process that shall be crowned with the climactic utterance of the voices in heaven at the sounding of the seventh trumpet of the Apocalypse, "The kingdom of the world has become the kingdom of our Lord, and of His Christ, and He will reign forever and ever" (Rev. 11:15).

Second, in experiencing victory in the Temptation Jesus Christ is seen as perfectly qualified to be the Savior. The Cross was anticipated in this conquest. In the Temptation there was, then, a pledge of the crucial victory of Golgotha, which Paul described in these words: "When He had disarmed the rulers and authorities, He made a public display of them, having triumphed over them through Him" (Col. 2:15).

Third, in the wilderness experience Jesus Christ is seen as perfectly qualified to be a sympathetic high priest. This is the principal use that the author of the Epistle to the Hebrews makes of the incident. He wrote, "For since He Himself was tempted in that which He has suffered, He is able to come to the aid of those who are tempted" (Heb. 2:18). And again, "For we do not have a high priest who cannot sympathize with our weaknesses, but one who has been tempted in all things as we are, yet without sin" (4:15). To those related to this High Priest there is no more appealing note on which to conclude a study of the Temptation than the exhortation that naturally follows: "Let us therefore draw near with confidence to the throne of grace, that we may receive mercy and may find grace to help in time of need" (4:16).

CHAPTER 7

Jesus, the Unique Son of God: Tested and Faithful

Don B. Garlington

The uniqueness of Jesus Christ is *the* characteristic feature of New Testament Christology. Claims such as those of Acts 4:12, that there is no other name whereby one may be saved, and of Colossians 1:18, that Christ alone is to have the preeminence in the universe, bear witness to the singularity of His person and work.

How can one account for the remarkable—indeed, the astonishing—devotion bestowed on Jesus of Nazareth? How is it that people inhabiting "the remotest part of the earth" (Acts 1:8), in syncretistic societies ancient and modern, have come to acknowledge Him as "the Savior of the world" (John 4:42)? There is only one way: people have accepted what the New Testament claims for Him. He is none other than God incarnate (John 1:1, 14), the Lord to whom every knee shall bow (Isa. 45:23; Phil. 2:10).

The thesis of this chapter is that Jesus' testing in the wilderness of Judea is one of the most significant indicators of His uniqueness. In fact it may not be stretching the point to say that the very purpose of the temptation narratives is to underscore His uniqueness. Though the temptations to which He was exposed are, at heart, the same as those that beset the people of God (Heb. 4:15), there is a personal and messianic aspect of His trial that places Him in a category of His own. While various individuals in the Old Testament and in postbiblical Judaism are set forth as examples of faith and perseverance, an awareness of which was very much alive in the first century (e.g., Sirach 44–50; 2 Macc. 7; T. Moses 9), He is portrayed in the Gospels and elsewhere as the One who gives meaning to all who went before Him.

The Connection of Jesus' Temptations with His Baptism

All the synoptics relate Jesus' testing in the wilderness with His baptism chronologically. However, in Mark 1:12 the links between the two are especially clear, because, in Mark's customary expression, "at once" (εὐθύς) after the baptism, the Spirit compelled Jesus to enter the wilderness.[1] The baptism and the temptations converge at two prominent junctures.

JESUS' RECEPTION OF THE SPIRIT

Jesus' baptism in the Holy Spirit on the banks of the Jordan River is a focal point of salvation history, at which a number of lines of thought converge. For Christians living in the milieu of first-century Judaism it was axiomatic that the Son of God had the Spirit of God, particularly in view of the fact that the Spirit was active at the time of the Exodus and Israel's wilderness wanderings (Isa. 63:14).[2] Lane noted that Jesus' expulsion into the desert was the necessary consequence of His baptism, inasmuch as the same Spirit who descended on Jesus at His baptism now led Him into the wilderness.[3] The connection of Jesus' anointing with the Spirit and His testing is highlighted by the way Matthew began his account with an infinitive of purpose, "to be tested" (πειρασθῆναι, Matt. 4:1), so that the testing of Jesus' obedience became the purpose of the Spirit's leading into the wilderness.

Assuming that Jesus received the Spirit in order to be tested, it is not surprising that all three synoptic gospel writers specified that His movements through the wilderness were Spirit-directed, as were those of Israel earlier (Isa. 63:14). Matthew stated that He was "led up by the Spirit" (Matt. 4:1), while Luke wrote that He was "full of the Holy Spirit" (Luke 4:1). Though these expressions are not as startling as Mark's "the Spirit expelled [ἐκβάλλει] Him into the wilderness" (Mark 1:12, author's translation), their impact is no less pronounced because "Jesus faces his opponent fully and manifestly equipped with divine power,"[4] as Isaiah 11:2 predicted. But the Spirit's leading was not confined to the climactic confrontation with Satan, because Jesus "was continually being guided" (ἤγετο) throughout the wilderness for the forty days (Luke 4:1). And afterward Jesus was able to begin His Galilean ministry in the power of the Spirit (v. 18).

THE VOICE FROM HEAVEN

Jesus the Son of God. The voice of God the Father declaring Jesus' sonship at His baptism is paradigmatic for everything that follows in the temptation narratives, because all the Adam/Israel/ messianic attributes of Jesus in the wilderness are undergirded by the concept of His sonship. When Satan challenged, "If you are the Son of God," he assumed that such is the case. Therefore the whole account is about the testing of the Son of God.

Jesus the Obedient One. While references to the voice of Yahweh are scattered throughout the Old Testament, Deuteronomy places special emphasis on His voice as speaking to His people. A key verse is 4:36: "Out of the heavens He let you hear His voice." Much of the book in fact is concerned with urging Israel to obey the voice of the Lord, thereby confirming Israel's status as His chosen people. The connection of Jesus with Israel is evident.[5] Just as Israel was summoned by the voice of God to be His people, so Jesus was called by the voice from heaven to undertake His mission as the ideal "Israel" of God. In this light, Jesus is set forth as the One who listened to the voice of God, thus compensating for Israel's failure to hear and obey. The voice announced that Jesus is the beloved Son, well pleasing to the Father, and the trial in the desert proved that such is the case. Therefore, "when Matthew and Luke recorded the voice from heaven, there was in the background to their thought the difference between the reaction of the Israelites to the voice of God and that of Jesus, the faithful servant, who was called, proved, and found obedient."[6]

The Place: The Wilderness

Each of the Synoptic Gospels sets the temptations in the wilderness, making that locale not merely the geographical site of the stories but also their ideological framework.[7] At least three points of relevance can be singled out.

THE WILDERNESS AND THE RED SEA

Jesus' baptism in the Jordan stands as a counterpart of Israel's crossing of the Red Sea at the onset of the Exodus. Thus Jesus transversed the Jordan and then, like Israel, spent a period of time in the wilderness. Jesus, another Moses, on whom the Spirit had been placed (Isa. 63:10–14), would lead the way. Davies and Allison suggest that this is intimated by Matthew's notice that Jesus was "led up" (ἀνήχθη, 4:1). "Just as God led Israel out of Egypt and through the waters and into the desert (Num. 20.5; 1 Βασ 12.6; Ps. 80.1 LXX; etc., all using ἀνάγειν), so does the Spirit of God lead Jesus into the desert after he is baptized."[8]

THE WILDERNESS AS THE PLACE OF GOD'S COMING DELIVERANCE

According to Hosea 2:14–23, the wilderness was the place of Israel's original sonship, where God had loved His people. Yet because they had forsaken Yahweh their Father, a "renewal" of the exodus into the desert was necessary for the restoration of Israel's status as the "son" of God. In this new exodus, God's power and help would be experienced again in a renewed trek into the wilderness.

JESUS' TESTING AS THE SON OF GOD

The phrase "Son of God" is loaded with significance in the Bible and in postbiblical Judaism.[9] This phrase features in three aspects of the temptation narratives.

Israel, the "son" of God. Gerhardsson addresses this concept.

> The theme "son of God" was deeply rooted in the traditional religious ideology of Israel. It was a favourite variant of the election and covenant themes and indeed in the late Jewish period these three were virtually inseparable; for many centuries Israel had been accustomed to thinking of itself as a chosen people, and as God's covenant people and as God's son.[10]

For Jesus, then, to undertake the role of Israel, God's "son," naturally led to the Son's experience in the desert.

Since Deuteronomy particularly focuses on the testing factor, it is natural that Jesus' replies to Satan are all from this book. In fact the passages quoted by Him function as an index to His self-perceived relationship to Israel.[11] Consequently in Deuteronomy and the gospel temptation records is to be found a pattern of sonship articulated in terms of the ideal Israel. Therefore Jesus' obedience must be affirmed in the wilderness, "the precise place where Israel's rebellion had brought death and alienation, in order that the new Israel of God may be constituted."[12]

Adam, the "son" of God. Jesus' wilderness experience has two links with Adam. (1) Matthew and Luke both connect Him with Adam in their baptismal accounts, by virtue of the new creation ideas surrounding that event.[13] (2) Luke inserted his genealogy of Jesus between the baptism and the temptations, thereby merging the phrase "Son of God" with Adam (3:38).[14]

Thus in His exposure to the assaults of Satan, Jesus was "Adam" as well as "Israel." Israel's sonship was modeled on Adam's,[15] since God is the Creator-Father in both instances. The wilderness forges a link between the two, for it represents reverse imagery, especially with Mark's mention of the "the wild beasts" (1:13). Opinion on the proper location of the animals is divided between the Paradise and wilderness settings. However, it may be that the Gospels glance at the beasts both in Adam's mandate to rule the earth (Gen. 1:26–28) and in their association with satanic powers (Ps. 22:11–21; Ezek. 34:5, 8, 25; Luke 10:19), thus suggesting the chaos that threatens to (re)impose itself on the ordered world (e.g., Job 5:22; Ezek. 5:17; 14:21; T. Ben. 5:2; T. Naph. 8:4; T. Iss. 7:7).

On the one hand the wilderness symbolizes chaos and judgment and is associated with demonic activity,[16] the antithesis of the beauty and blessing of Eden. In the Old Testament, blessing is associated with Eden-like land, that is, inhabited and cultivated land, whereas the wilderness is the place of the curse.[17] Therefore like Adam, Jesus was tested, but under the worst of conditions, not the best conditions. As symbolized by the wilderness, He labored under all the disadvantages brought on the creation by the First Adam. Mark's notice that the Spirit "expelled" ($\acute{\epsilon}\kappa\beta\acute{\alpha}\lambda\lambda\epsilon\iota$) Jesus into the desert may well be an allusion to Genesis 3:23–24, which records Adam's expulsion from the garden back to the dust from which he had been taken.

Yet on the other hand, Mark's reference to the beasts cannot be limited to Israel in the wilderness, because paradise and wilderness in biblical theology are contiguous: what Adam was unable to do in the garden, namely, to have dominion over the beasts of the field, Christ did in the wilderness. He, in a sense, turned the wilderness back into a paradise.[18] Guelich maintains that Jesus was living peacefully with the animals, a relationship found only at Creation (Gen. 1:28; 2:19–20) and expected in the millennium (Isa. 11:6–9; 65:17–25; Hos. 2:18). "Thus Jesus' peaceful coexistence 'with the wild animals' boldly declares the presence of the age of salvation when God's deliverance would come in the wilderness and harmony would be established within creation according to the promise, especially of Isaiah (11.6–9; 65.17–25)."[19] Guelich further remarks that both Adam and Christ were tempted while living at peace with the animals (Gen. 1:28; 2:19–20; Mark 1:13; cf. Apoc. Moses 10:2–4), but while Satan's victory over the first Adam led to enmity and fear within creation (e.g., Ps. 91:11–13; Apoc. Moses 10:1–11:4; Adam and Eve 37–38; cf. T. Naph. 8), these are removed by the triumph of the other Adam, who reconciles the creation to itself.[20]

Of relevance also is Daniel's Son of Man (Dan. 7), an Adam-like figure who defeats the beastlike kingdoms hostile to the kingdom of God.[21] In addition Psalm 91, which features in the second temptation, promises the one who trusts in God, "You will tread upon the lion and cobra, the young lion and the serpent you will trample down" (Ps. 91:13; cf. Job 5:23). Interpreted messianically, the psalm takes up the promise of Genesis 3:15 and paves the way for Jesus Christ, who defeated the Devil initially in the desert and climactically at the Cross, and ultimately will do so at His second coming (Rom. 16:20).

The Son of David, the Son of God. The identification of Jesus as David's son, the heir of the nations, will emerge from the ensuing exposition. Suffice it to say here that the declaration of the heavenly voice at His baptism, "Thou art My beloved Son" (Mark 1:11; Luke 3:22), is a reflection of Psalm 2:7. In the Psalms especially, the Israelite (Davidic) king was viewed as the "son" of God[22] (an indication of the intersection of Jesus' Davidic sonship and his Adamic sonship). As will be seen, Satan's challenge to Jesus to bow before him in order to possess the kingdoms of the world was a direct assault on His right as the Davidic son to command the obedience of the nations (Gen. 49:10; Num. 24:17–24; Ps. 2:8).

The Time: Forty Days and Forty Nights

In Scripture and Jewish tradition the figure of forty years is frequently associated with hardship, affliction, or punishment.[23] Also it is commonly recognized that the number forty has several links with the wilderness. One link is Israel's forty years of wilderness wanderings. Especially significant is Deuteronomy 8:2: "And you shall remember all the way which the LORD your God has led you in the wilderness these forty years, that He might humble you, testing you, to know what was in your heart, whether you would keep His commandments or not."[24] Also see Deuteronomy 13:3; Judges 2:22; 3:1, 4; and 2 Chronicles 32:31. A second association is Moses on Mount Sinai (Ex. 24:18; 34:28; Deut. 9:9–18). A third link is Elijah's forty-day trip through the wilderness to Mount Horeb (1 Kings 19:8, 15). In the case of Moses and Elijah particularly, "the forty days concentrate into one focal period the essence of their ministry; the innermost quality of their mission is revealed in them in a figurative symbol."[25] The common ground between the two is the Law: Moses was the lawgiver, and Elijah called Israel back to the Law away from idols.

The Conflict Between Jesus and Satan

THE FUNDAMENTAL PERSPECTIVE: THE TESTING OF
GOD'S SON

The Gospels portray Jesus' experience in the wilderness as a "testing" or "temptation," alternate ways of rendering the verb πειράζω. In fact Jesus' experience was both a testing and a temptation. The term has to do with "testing" when God stands in the forefront and with "temptation" when an evil force such as the Devil is more prominent. So the combination of the Spirit's leading of Jesus and the Devil's enticements gives the verb a double connotation here.[26] However, as Davies and Allison point out, Deuteronomy 8:2 is exemplary: "As God once tested Israel in the wilderness (Ex. 20:20), so now does the Spirit lead Jesus into the desert in order that he might face the ordeal with Satan: the confrontation is initiated by God."[27] By means of Satan's "temptations" God was "testing" His Son.

The several temptation narratives can thus be reduced to Jesus' identification with Israel, whose role of sonship is now concentrated in Him who is the beloved Son. Hence "the heart of the temptation is to be found in an attempt to induce Jesus to be unfaithful to a pattern of Sonship conceived in terms of the relationship between ideal Israel and the divine Father."[28]

Yet even the covenant with Israel is not fully comprehensible apart from the prior testing of Adam in Paradise. Though Deuteronomy 6–8 forms the basis of the dialogues between Jesus and Satan, the testing motif began in Eden and is repeated several times before Israel's formation as a nation, most conspicuously in the case of Abraham. In the beginning, God's partner in the creation covenant was charged with the mandate to subdue the earth and was promised, at least by implication, a reward at the end of his task (the "Sabbath rest" of Gen. 2:1–3; Heb. 4:9). However, Adam repudiated his formation as God's image and chose the way of self-determination. Rather than inherit "all the kingdoms of the earth" by obedience to God, he sought to become like God by compliance with the Tempter (Gen. 3:5). The Devil wanted Jesus to repeat Adam's error; the temptations were Satan's effort to induce Jesus to renounce His vocation as the *obedient* Son.

An important qualification is in order, however. Matthew in particular represented Jesus as more than Israel and Adam, God's

Son, image, and covenant partner; He is the divine person, God, who is to be worshiped in His own right and approached with reverence. One indication of this is that in relating Satan's demand that Jesus "fall down and worship" him (Matt. 4:9), Matthew drew on the same combination of terms he had already predicated of the Magi, who "fell down and worshiped Him" (2:11).[29] Matthew also used the verb "approach" (προσελθών, 4:3; NASB, "came").[30] The tempter approached Jesus for the purpose of enticing Him.[31] Significantly the combination of "tempt" (πειράζω) and "approach" (προσέρχομαι) occurs in other places in Matthew (and Mark) to describe the antagonism of the Pharisees and Sadducees. Throughout His public ministry they continued what Satan initiated in the wilderness (Matt. 16:1; 19:3; 22:18, 35; Mark 10:2).[32] Matthew, like the other Evangelists, pictured the Jewish leaders as the instruments of the Devil in his ongoing attack on Jesus. Like their ancestors (Ps. 78:18), they in satanic fashion put to the test the Lord their God.

THE ORDER OF THE TEMPTATIONS

Matthew and Luke differ in their order of the second and third temptations. It is normally assumed that Luke reversed Matthew's order to make Jerusalem the place of the climactic test, in accord with the temple theme of Luke and Acts.[33] Donaldson, however, has shown that Matthew's sequence is not necessarily original. In fact he suggests that a natural progression in a Palestinian setting would be desert-mountain-temple. Moreover, the temple, the focal point of Jewish religious life, ranks above the other settings. Thus Luke's most dramatic temptation has in view divine aid for the Son of God in the capital city.[34]

Nevertheless Matthew's order has a significance of its own. Several scholars contend that his arrangement reproduces in inverse order Jesus' quotations of Deuteronomy 8:3; 6:16, 13, so that the first gospel is seen to follow the sequence of events in Exodus: the provision of manna in the wilderness (Ex. 16), the testing at Massah (Ex. 17), and the worship of the golden calf (Ex. 32).[35] Furthermore, Gerhardsson, followed by Gundry, surmises that all three lead back to Deuteronomy 6:5, according to which the Israelite was to love Yahweh with all his heart, soul, and might.[36] If indeed Deuteronomy 6:5 is the bedrock of Jesus' replies to Satan, then the issue before Him was none other than the total consecration of Himself to the God of Israel and His refusal to settle for anything less than Yahweh the Creator and covenant Lord as the One to worship.

Moreover, in Matthew an upward spatial progression is evident: Jesus was first "led up" from the Jordan into the wilderness (4:1), then placed on the pinnacle of the temple (4:1), and finally taken to "a very high mountain" (v. 8). This progression corresponds to the dramatic tension that reaches a climax in the third temptation.[37] Donaldson has further demonstrated that Matthew is as theologically motivated as Luke in his arrangement of the temptations, inasmuch as the former presents a correspondence between the final temptation and the closing scene of the gospel, for which the mountain setting is one of the main links.[38]

THE CONNECTION OF THE THREE PLACES OF TESTING

Donaldson shows that each of the settings—wilderness, temple, and mountain—was a place where eschatological events were expected to occur.[39]

As to the wilderness, a consistent feature of the Prophets is the anticipation that Israel will be led once more through the desert on a new exodus. That the final act of divine deliverance would come from the desert was firmly entrenched in first-century Judaism.[40] For one thing there was the very existence of the Qumran community, which retreated into the desert to be tested like the original Exodus generation, "during the dominion of Belial" (1QS 1:18).[41] There they awaited the war of the sons of light against the sons of darkness at the advent of the Messiahs of Aaron and Israel (CD B 11), whose way was being prepared by the sect, in fulfillment of Isaiah 40:3–5. Also various anti-Roman revolutionary movements originated in the wilderness. Apart from the statements in Matthew 24:26 and Acts 21:38, Josephus, in his account of the siege of Jerusalem, related that when the temple had gone up in flames, the surviving insurgents asked permission to retreat into the desert,[42] the motivation being that in the wilderness the final messianic deliverance must surely take place, thereby turning the debacle into victory. Josephus said the wilderness is the place where the messianic (in his view, false) prophets repaired to rally their forces against Rome.[43] In some measure at least, this hope was founded on passages such as Deuteronomy 32:7–14 (esp. v. 10).

The temple and the mountain, especially when the latter is interpreted as Mount Zion, occupy a position of particular prominence in the Old Testament and in Jewish eschatological expectation.[44] One extrabiblical indicator is that the messianic figures at the time of the Jewish revolt (in the Josephus passages cited above) promised "signs of deliverance" to be performed at the temple.

FIRST TEMPTATION: STONES INTO BREAD

Jesus went without food for forty days and nights (Matt. 4:2). As stated earlier, the forty days are reminiscent of Israel's forty years in the wilderness and also of Moses' forty days of fasting before his reception of the Law (Ex. 34:28; Deut. 9:9–18).[45] At the end of the forty days, when Jesus' hunger was at its most intense and when He was most vulnerable, "the tempter came" and said, "If You are the Son of God" (Matt. 4:3).

The clause, "If You are the Son of God," assumes that such is the case: Jesus' sonship is the presupposition of the temptations, as established at the baptismal scene, where God the Father said He is the Son. Satan did not tempt Jesus to doubt His divine sonship but to presume on it in self-serving ways that would lead Him disobediently from the path of the Cross.[46] While the third temptation is the most blatant instance, all three of Satan's efforts were designed to seduce Jesus to use His sonship in a way inconsistent with His God-ordained mission—indeed inconsistent with the very nature of His sonship itself. Carson points out that the same taunt, "If You are the Son of God," was hurled at Jesus on the cross (Matt. 27:40), when for Him to have left the cross would have annulled the purpose of His coming.[47]

Jesus' sonship again displays a twofold association. One is Adam, the first "son of God" (Luke 3:38) to be tested by Yahweh, with Satan as the instigator of his temptation. Possibly the recurring notices that Satan "said" to Jesus allude to Genesis 3:1, 4. As the Tempter insinuated to Eve (and Adam) that God had not spoken truly, so he intimated the same to Jesus and proposed that His sonship can and ought to be asserted defiantly—in Adamic fashion—by turning stones into loaves. The other association is Israel, who was admonished in Deuteronomy 8:5, "Know in your heart that the LORD your God was disciplining you just as a man disciplines his son." Jesus, in other words, reprised the role of the covenant people (cf. Isa. 42:6; 50:1–11), whose grumbling about food occasioned their infidelity.

Satan's appeal to food resembled his tactic in the garden, but it was intensified by the fact that Jesus was solicited when, humanly speaking, He was most vulnerable and might have most plausibly used His power in an act of self-assertion. Adam, though not really hungry, made the fruit of the tree a vehicle for declaring his independence of his Maker. In this same vein the Devil tempted Jesus to express His sonship by behaving like the First Adam in an assertion of autonomy, using food as the warrant of His rebellion. He should take the initiative in providing for His needs rather than wait on the Father to do so.

Similarly Israel's rebellion in the wilderness was related to the demand for food (Ps. 78:17–20). Israel's dissatisfaction with the manna was tantamount to the rejection of the Lord Himself (Num. 11:20). The people thought the Lord's hand was shortened, so that His word of promise could not come to pass (v. 23). Psalm 78 confirms that the children of Israel "did not believe in God, and did not trust in His salvation" (v. 22); in spite of all He did for them, they did not trust Him (cf. Ps. 106:13–14).

The impact of Satan's temptation is that Jesus, like Adam first and Israel later, had a justifiable grievance against God and therefore ought to voice His complaint by "murmuring" (Ex. 16; Num. 11) and ought to provide for Himself the basic necessity of life, namely, bread. Satan, in other words, sought to make Jesus groundlessly anxious about His physical needs and thus to provoke Him to demand the food He craved (cf. Ps. 78:18). In short, the Devil's aim was to persuade Jesus to repeat the apostasy of Adam and Israel. Satan wanted to break Jesus' perfect trust in His Father's good care and thereby to alter the course of salvation history.[48]

Jesus rejoined with the words of Deuteronomy 8:3, "Man does not live by bread alone, but man lives by everything that proceeds out of the mouth of the LORD." The context of 8:1–10 must be taken into account, particularly verse 2, which includes the three elements underlying the temptation narratives as a whole: the number forty, the wilderness, and testing. In addition, verse 3 mentions hunger and verse 5 refers to Israel's sonship. In His own person, then, Jesus recapitulated Israel. He remembered all the way Yahweh had led (v. 2) and that He had provided all His people's needs as indisputable proof of His care (v. 4). Jesus was thus content to live by "every word that proceeds out of the mouth of God," that is, by God's interpretation of reality, as opposed to that of Satan (Matt. 4:4).

SECOND TEMPTATION: GOD'S PROTECTION OF HIS SON

According to Matthew's order, in the movement from the first temptation to the second, Jesus was taken from the wilderness to Jerusalem. The significance of this temptation centers around at least two factors.

First, Luke recorded the proposed leap from the temple as the climactic episode of his narrative: Jesus was made to face death in Jerusalem.[49] At the same time, Satan pointed out an alternative; angels would save Him. So Satan would have Jesus resort to divine intervention to deliver Him from death altogether.[50] However, as is clear in the book of Luke, Jerusalem was the place of His death (9:51; 13:32–33). Jesus was to undergo death in the capital city as one of the prophets (13:33), in fulfillment of God's plan (24:26, 46; cf. Matt. 26:54). Satan wanted Jesus to deny the relationship of faith in which He trusted God the Father to deliver Him from the pangs of death (Ps. 16:8–11; Acts 2:24–36).[51]

Second, the temple was the symbol of God's presence with Israel and the most conspicuous emblem that this nation is His people. The temple was the organizing center of Jewish life and "a theological symbol of tremendous emotive power."[52] Moreover, the geographical complex of Jerusalem and the temple has a significance of its own.[53] The holy city was located in the highlands of Israel, with Mount Zion and the temple as the most imposing location in the land.[54] Jerusalem was considered the "center of the nations, with lands around her," the "center of the world," whose inhabitants "dwell at the center of the earth" (Ezek. 5:5; 38:12; Jub. 8:12, 19; 1 Enoch 26:1; Sib. Oracles 5:250). Thus when Jesus stood on the pinnacle of the temple, He was, theologically speaking, at the center of the world.[55] From that vantage point the Messiah most naturally could claim the nations as His own and rule them with a rod of iron (Gen. 49:10; Num. 24:17–24; Ps. 2:9), beginning with the overthrow of the Romans (cf. Song 17:22–25, 30–32).[56] Satan's intention was that Jesus should make an impressive entrance onto the stage of Israelite history, enabling Him to rally around Himself those "zealous for the law" (1 Macc. 2:27).

The Devil quoted a portion of verses 11–12 of Psalm 91, the whole of which celebrates God's fatherly care of those who trust in Him. Whether the subtlety of the quotation lies in the omission of the words "in all your ways" (v. 11), the psalm does promise divine protection in all one's ways. Nevertheless the psalmist took it for granted that all these ways are in accord with the divine will and purpose.[57] When this is understood, Satan's proposal that Jesus throw Himself from the temple bears no resemblance to the intention of the psalm; in fact, it was a misapplication and therefore a distortion of the Scriptures.

Ultimately Psalm 91 is messianic, a fact Satan was no doubt aware of. So his intention was that Jesus the Davidic son should force His Father to vindicate Him in a way other than through the resurrection following the Cross.[58] A fascinating point of irony appears in Satan's use of the psalm, because immediately following the portion quoted by him there is the assurance, "You will tread on the lion and cobra, the young lion and the serpent you will trample down" (v. 13). At the Cross Christ bruised the head of the serpent (Gen. 3:15; Rom. 16:20).

Jesus' reply, "you shall not put the Lord your God to the test" (Matt. 4:7; see Deut. 6:16), was not intended to call into question Psalm 91 but rather the Devil's application of it. One should trust in God, but there are occasions when the appeal to such trust is nothing less than putting God Himself to the test; such "manipulative bribery"[59] turns justifiable reliance on the Lord's protection into blindness and presumption. The quotation comes from Moses' warning for the Israelites not to repeat their sin at Massah, when they demanded water from the rock (Ex. 17:1–7; cf. Num. 20:2–9). If it was wrong for Israel the "son of God" to demand miraculous confirmation of the Father's care, so it would be for Jesus the Son to demand the same. Jesus therefore would not repeat the example of the fathers by testing God.[60] As ever, Jesus must finally submit to the Cross. The death scene at the temple corresponds to that in Jerusalem at the climax of the Passion Week; not only was Jesus determined not to tempt God, but also He was ready to lose His life in obedience to the Father.

THIRD TEMPTATION: THE KINGDOMS OF THE WORLD

In keeping with his mountain motif, Matthew noted that Satan took Jesus to "a very high mountain" (Matt. 4:8), while Luke is silent about this. Matthew thus continued to pursue his Jesus-Moses/Jesus-Adam/Jesus-Son of God agenda.

As to Moses, Deuteronomy 3:27 and 34:1–4 describe the panoramic view of the Promised Land shown him on Mount Nebo, from which he could see the earth in every direction. The language parallels between Matthew and Deuteronomy are especially evident from the Septuagint[61] (to which may be added,

quite strikingly, the noncanonical 2 Bar. 76:3–4 and 1 Enoch 26;
87:3–4). As Yahweh showed all the land of Canaan (and the
earth) to Moses, so the Devil showed and promised the entire
world to Jesus, if He would worship him. The "showing" in
question was not simply visual perception, because, in its biblical
setting, seeing is possessing.[62]

With regard to Adam, Genesis 2:10–14 and Ezekiel 28:13–16
suggest the idea that the Garden of Eden was located on a mountain
(cf. 1 Enoch 24; 87:3; Jub. 4:26).[63] From the mountain of Paradise
Adam was able, so to speak, to gaze on the kingdoms of the world
and to see the domain destined to be his under God.[64] For Jesus,
however, the mountain was that of the wilderness, the mountain
of testing and temptation. From this mountain Satan sought to
have Jesus renounce God's lordship over the creation in favor of
Satan himself, the "ruler of this world" (John 12:31; 14:30; 16:11;
2 Cor. 4:4; Eph. 2:2),[65] who has been granted the prerogative to
bestow "all this domain," that is, world leadership and the
accompanying wealth of the nations, on whomever he desires
(Luke 4:6; cf. 1 John 5:19; T. Job 8:1–3; 16:2).

Certainly the most prominent association with the mountain
was that of "the Son of God." Several scholars have proposed that
the mountain is specifically Mount Zion, as confirmed by Psalm
2:6–8.[66] They point out that the ultimate source of Satan's
acknowledgment, "if You are the Son of God," is Psalm 2:7, as
echoed by the heavenly voice at the baptism and also by the fact
that the verse's declaration, "Thou art My Son," is followed
immediately by the promise of world sovereignty to the scion of
David. In fact Satan's promise, "all these things will I give You"
(Matt. 4:9), corresponds directly to the king's pledge of the same,
"Ask of Me, and I will surely give the nations as Thine inheritance"
(Ps. 2:8). The site of the temptation is "the place of the
enthronement of the Son—and thus, because of the messianic
interpretation of Ps 2, against a background of eschatological
Zion, the place where the world-throne would be established."[67]

The placement of Jesus on the mountain of temptation, where
He refused to acknowledge the Devil's "authority," is deliberately
juxtaposed to the mountain (Matt. 28:16) of the Great Commission,
on which He later affirmed that all "authority" in heaven and on
earth had been granted to Him (28:18). The irony of the situation is
intensified by the fact that even before this commission Jesus is
represented as One who taught with inherent "authority" (7:28–29).

Therefore He repudiated Satan's "authority" in view of the lasting dominion to be His as a result of willing obedience to God (which in principle He already possessed).

Jesus' rebuff of Satan is embodied in the words of Deuteronomy 6:13, which states that only Yahweh is to be worshiped. He is to be loved with all one's heart, soul, and might (v. 5)—a reflection on Israel's failure to love Him wholeheartedly as illustrated in the golden calf incident (Ex. 32). Jesus thus relived the solicitation to idolatry, to which the nation characteristically succumbed, while remaining the faithful Son. For Israel the desert was a place of apostasy, but for Jesus it was a place of fidelity to God. He is to have glory (Matt. 16:27; 17:1–8; 19:28; 24:30; 25:31; Mark 14:62), and that was to come through and as a result of the Cross (John 12:28; 13:31–32; 17:1–26). The Gethsemane narratives (cf. John 12:27–33; 14:30–31; Heb. 5:7) demonstrate that the glory of Jesus cannot be divorced from the *via dolorosa.*

As noted earlier, in relating Satan's demand that Jesus fall down and worship him (Matt. 4:9), Matthew alluded to Jesus as the recipient of the adoration of the Magi. The irony of the third temptation, therefore, is that the One who Himself ought to be worshiped is told to worship the being who wrongfully received the service of Adam in Eden.

The Aftermath

In Matthew, the temptations ended abruptly with Jesus' rebuke, "Begone, Satan!" (Matt. 4:10). The precise choice of words forms a verbal link with Matthew 16:21–23. In both places, Jesus chose the path of duty. "The end ordained by the Father is to be achieved by the manner ordained by the Father, namely, the cross. And any opposition to this is satanic. To reject the way of the cross is to be on the side of the Devil."[68] In Jesus' resistance of the Devil's way to universal rule His words "Begone, Satan" have a climactic effect. Thus vanquished, the Devil departed until "an opportune time" (Luke 4:13), that is, till Gethsemane.

Matthew recorded that angels came to minister to Jesus (Matt. 4:11). This too reflects an Old Testament background. The angel guided and helped Israel through the wilderness (Ex. 14:19; 23:20, 23; 32:34; 33:2), and an angel supplied Elijah with food in a wilderness (1 Kings 19:5–7). Presumably the angels gave Jesus food (possibly manna, the food of the wilderness; cf. Ps. 78:24–25). He thus received sustenance not by placing demands on God but by first submitting to His will. He was the embodiment of true humanity, the authentic image of God.

The Temptations and the Zealot Ideal

Each of the temptations reflects the zeal for Israel and the Law manifested by a large portion of first-century Judaism, whose most outspoken (consistent?) representatives were the various resistance groups against Roman rule in Palestine. In a nutshell, Jesus said no to the temptations, while zealotism said yes (*Zealot* and *zealotism* are here being used in a nontechnical [nonfactional] sense to designate the mentality of zeal for the Law that cut across most party barriers.[69] *Zealot* does not automatically mean "revolutionary"). Jesus is Messiah, but not the kind expected by many of His contemporaries.[70] Jesus of Nazareth could not have avoided facing the issues raised by Jewish nationalism. Therefore it is reasonable to infer—given both the place of the temptations, that is, the desert with all its messianic overtones, and the framework of the gospel narratives generally—that there was a politico-militaristic dimension to the choices placed before the Lord.[71]

From the time of the Maccabean revolt Israel's self-definition was shaped to no small degree by the kind of zeal for the Law exemplified by Mattathias, the "zealot" prototype par excellence (1 Macc. 2:23–28).[72] The ideal of Israel's sonship contemplated by much of first-century Judaism was indistinguishable from the fervor that finally led to the war of independence of A.D. 66–74. The irony of the situation, accordingly, is that a sizable portion of contemporary Israel viewed obedience as allegiance to a zealot-like deliverer who would uphold the Law and the kingship of Yahweh. Thus the implication of the Gospels is that Israel's supposed obedience is actually disobedience; only Jesus, the true Son of God, who declined to follow the zealot way, is obedient.

FIRST TEMPTATION

Turning stones into bread has to do not simply with providing for the necessities of life, but with the miraculous supply of manna in the wilderness, a phenomenon expected to be repeated in the new exodus.[73] This follows not only from the wilderness imagery of the temptation stories but also from the miracle of the loaves and fish, which provoked such excitement that the crowd wanted to make Jesus king (John 6:15).[74] However, He declined to use His power in the service of the kind of salvation event for which many of His contemporaries were longing.

SECOND TEMPTATION

The point of this aspect of the testing goes beyond the general idea that God protects and supports His own. More specifically, it reflects the zealot mentality of incurring risk for the sake of Israel with the hope that God would miraculously vindicate His warriors. In fact the whole zealot movement was motivated by the conviction that if God's people would fight, He would respond by bringing in the kingdom.[75] As France notes, Jesus was tempted to force God's hand, to see if His need would be met.[76] This is especially relevant if Davies and Allison are correct that it was precisely an attempt to force God's hand to which the zealots resorted during the war.[77] The case is strengthened if lying behind Luke's order of the temptations is an oblique reference to the geographical order in which the deliverance was anticipated to take place—from desert to mountain to temple[78]—and even more so if the rabbinic tradition that the Messiah would stand on the roof of the temple and proclaim salvation was extant in Jesus' day.[79]

In this light, not only did Jesus renounce the zealots' concept of Yahweh's safekeeping and vindication of His own, but also He later taught His disciples to wait for God to vindicate them in His own time.[80] He would not allow Satan to obscure the true nature of the kingdom, nor would He permit His church to employ violence in pursuing its sacred duty.[81]

THIRD TEMPTATION

Satan's most blatant demand was that Jesus worship him in exchange for the kingdoms of the world. Jesus' reply from Deuteronomy 6:13–15 parallels Exodus 34:11–17. In both, Israel is strictly enjoined not to go after the gods of the nations, for the Lord is a jealous God, who alone must be the object of His people's adoration. Most strikingly, the Exodus passage occurs in the course of Moses' second trip to the top of the mountain to meet God (34:2), where for forty days and nights he neither ate nor drank (v. 28). Thus the Old Testament context of this temptation is to be understood as the conversation between God and Moses on Mount Sinai. On the mountain, Moses was told of the pagan peoples who would be expelled from Canaan, with whom Israel was forbidden to make any covenant or to intermarry and, above all, whose gods were not to be honored. The nation was in no way to compromise its singleness of dedication to the one God (cf. Num. 23:9, uttered by Balaam from the top of the mountains).

Hence the third temptation focused on the integrity of the people of God,[82] concerned with their separation from and superiority to the nations. As is well known, the Messiah in second-temple Judaism was expected to subdue the nations on behalf of Israel, in keeping with Genesis 49:10, Numbers 24:17–24, and Psalm 2:8. Jesus, however, refused to exalt Israel by becoming a Psalms-of-Solomon sort of Messiah, seeking to preserve Israelite societal values intact.[83] His response to Satan from Deuteronomy 6:13 rather forcefully suggests that the (zealot) ideal of supremacy over the nations was nothing less than idolatry.

Conclusions

This exposition has sought to establish that the temptations of Jesus are among the most significant indicators of His uniqueness. Within the pages of the Old Testament and in the history of the Jewish race there are many notable instances of people and communities who were exposed to trial, testing, and temptation, often accompanied by great suffering. For this reason the synoptic temptation narratives are rich in such associations. In the foreground are Adam, Abraham, Israel, Moses, and Elijah (the latter two representing the Law and the prophets), while in the background are the Maccabean martyrs, the zealots, and possibly the Qumran community. Moreover, the temptations can be viewed as the transition into the entire gospel story of Jesus, who is said to be greater than all the possessors of the Spirit, holy people and places of Judaism, and the various contenders for messianic recognition. Yet none of them is ultimately of any avail, because all without exception are merely the forerunners (or competitors) of the Coming One, who alone is the zenith of salvation history and the consummation of God's plan for the ages. The question comes down to this: Who is the Son of God? And the answer of these authors is unambiguous: Jesus of Nazareth.

Particularly within their historical milieu, the Gospels stake a claim for the distinctiveness of Christ in two major areas. The first relates to Israel's perception of itself as God's new beginning after the fall of Adam. The Adam theology of Jewish literature is intended to advance a claim about Israel in the purposes of God. As such, it fulfills a specific purpose, namely, to mark out this nation as God's true humanity and the realization of His Creation designs. In brief, "Adam has become embodied . . . in Israel, the people of the Torah, and in her future hope."[84] This is why the temptation accounts are replete with allusions to Adam, with Jesus as his true successor and with the reminder that Israel in the wilderness was a failure. As the One begotten of the Holy Spirit (Matt. 1:20; Luke 1:34–35; 3:23), He entered the desert to defeat Satan and thus to rectify damage done by the first human being. Only He is the new Adam; only in His person and activity can the darkness of the chaos of sin be dispelled.

The second area of Jesus' distinctiveness has to do with the phenomenon of zealotism. In their determination to establish Yahweh's rule, the zealot types pursued relentlessly the course of national messianism. The several Evangelists, accordingly, portray the way of zealotism as nothing other than an entrapment in the "nets" (CD 4:13–18) that the Devil sought to cast about Jesus. Zeal for the Law, then, would not do, and the advocates of zeal were destined to lead Israel down the path of self-destruction. In the face of such messianism the Gospels advocated the messiahship of Jesus. In so doing, they associated two factors that would have appeared to first-century Judaism as an egregious self-contradiction. The one is the scandal of a crucified Messiah. While it is true that the zealots and zealotlike individuals were prepared to carry the cross for Israel, Jesus bore the cross in such a manner as to be an outcast from the covenant community.[85] The other is the way in which Matthew and Luke depicted Him as the Lord God who was approached by Satan, an assertion certainly calculated to confer on Jesus of Nazareth an unprecedented celebrity.

These conclusions are especially relevant in view of the growing trend of recent scholarship to dispute or at least downplay the uniqueness of Jesus. One tributary of this stream is the claim that the Christology of the New Testament, as distinct from that of later conciliar formulations, can be contained within Jewish parameters.[86] Another is the argument, valid in itself, that Christianity in its own way is as particularistic as the Judaism preceding it, inasmuch as salvation is available only in Christ.[87] For many scholars, however, the observation serves to denigrate Christianity's perception of itself as the definitive religion, especially when this item is placed on the table by those who detect, they think, an anti-Semitic bias in the New Testament.

Regarding the first point, the temptation stories portray Jesus

as the One who breaks the mold of Jewish precedents, because in
Him something genuinely new has been revealed (Matt. 12:6;
Luke 11:31). True, He was cast in the role of Adam, Moses,
Elijah, and Israel. But He cannot be limited by such personages,
because they are only the "shadows," while He is the "substance"
to whom they point (Col. 2:17). In one sense He is another Adam
and the image of God, yet He is the Lord God Himself, tempted by
Satan. It is of interest that Hebrews, which draws so heavily on the
imagery of the wilderness, presents the same interchange of ideas:
Jesus is God's image (χαρακτήρ) and is also the very outshining
(ἀπαύγασμα, 1:3) of God's own glory.

As to the second area, it is correct that Christianity is a new
particularism, not the particularism of race, culture, politics, or
language but of a person, the unique person of the Lord of heaven
who became human in order to be tempted, to die, and to then rise
again for the salvation of all who place their trust in Him.
Christianity finds its authentic self-definition in the proclamation
of a sole and exclusive Savior who is able to save to the uttermost
all those who come to God through Him.

CHAPTER 8

The Transfiguration of Christ

S. Lewis Johnson Jr.

The transfiguration of Jesus Christ is one of the most astonishing and perplexing of His earthly experiences. It is the one occasion in which the bright beams of His divine glory blazed through the sackcloth covering of His humanity. It is somewhat strange, then, that commentators and preachers have become as Peter who "did not know what to answer" (Mark 9:6).

It is also surprising to discover that standard systematic theologies say little if anything about the theological significance of the Transfiguration. During a series of meetings for the ministry of the Word in Pennsylvania, I had occasion to do some of my first study on this event. I asked permission of the pastor of the church in which the meetings were being held to use his fine library, in which were a number of the standard sets, such as those by Charles Hodge, William G. T. Shedd, A. H. Strong, and others. It was shocking to learn that the Transfiguration was almost completely neglected. Not a single one of the authors consulted discussed the theological significance of that event. Later I made mention of this experience in Pennsylvania to a group of earnest Christians in a home Bible class in Dallas. After the meeting one of the couples said that though they had been members of evangelical churches for years they had thought that the word *transfiguration* referred to the ascension of Christ! They added that they had never heard a sermon on the event, a sentiment I have heard expressed many times after I have preached on the subject.

Why has so little attention been given to the Transfiguration? Perhaps it has not been thought an event as vital as the other crises in Jesus' life on earth. True, the Transfiguration is surely not as vital as the death and resurrection of Christ. Nor does it have the same significance as the Incarnation. However, the Transfiguration is surely as important as Jesus' temptation and as important as His ascension.

71

Some have suggested that the Lord's transfiguration does not have "any direct bearing on human experience,"[1] that is, it has little relevance for believers. The practical significance of events such as the Temptation, with its signal lesson on the importance of the Word of God, and Jesus' agony on the cross, with its message of the imperative need for obedience to the will of God, is evident. But what is the practical meaning of the Transfiguration? How should it affect believers now? As will be seen, the Transfiguration has a deep practical relevance for believers.

The answer to the neglect of the Transfiguration is to be found in a third consideration. In the words of Clow,

> The story strains our faith and baffles our imagination. The shining of the face and the glistering of the garment present little difficulty. But the visitors from the world beyond, and the voice out of the cloud, provoke us to question whether the scene was a vision or a reality to mortal sense. Expositors love the easy way as much as others, and so they willingly turn aside from mystery to dwell upon the carpenter's shop, to enforce the parables by the seashore, and to expound the Sermon on the Mount.[2]

Probably, then, the mysterious nature of the Transfiguration helps explain the lack of attention given to it. This, however, does not excuse this lack. The New Testament writers themselves accord it an important place in their works. Each of the synoptics contains a fairly full account of the experience. While John did not mention it, Peter mentioned it in both of his letters (1 Peter 5:1; 2 Peter 1:15–21) and made it the basis of a significant exhortation in his last reference to it. This striking crisis in the Lord's life, therefore, is worthy of careful attention. The basis of this study is Matthew 17:1–8.

The Change in the Lord (Matt. 17:1–2)

In the quietness of Caesarea Philippi and in the shadow of snow-crested Mount Hermon, Peter's confession of Jesus' messiahship and sonship signaled the end of His ministry to the multitudes. The die was cast; the nation had not responded to its Redeemer's ministry. And so Jesus took three of His intimate followers, Peter, James, and John, to a spur of Hermon, about fourteen miles north of Caesarea.[3] Luke added that He went up to pray (Luke 9:28). The content of the prayer is not difficult to imagine. He had just announced to the disciples that He must go to Jerusalem and suffer many things from the hands of the Jewish authorities and be killed and on the third day rise from the dead.

The prayer was undoubtedly made in the light of His coming passion (cf. Matt. 16:21). The Transfiguration, then, seems to be the answer of the Father to the prayer of the Son—a prayer that would ultimately find its deepest expression on the cross, "My God, My God, why hast Thou forsaken Me?" (Matt. 27:46). The answer of the Father was not the removal of the Cross; that could not be prevented. It was rather a revelation of the glory of the kingdom to come, designed to encourage the Son as He moved toward His atoning sufferings.

The fact that Jesus was transfigured as He prayed is a fact of some practical importance. If His temptation account illustrates the importance of the Word of God in the believer's life, the Transfiguration illustrates the fact that communion with God produces transformation of life. This truth finds expression throughout the Word of God (Ex. 34:29–35; Ps. 34:5) and is given its doctrinal foundation by Paul in the memorable words of 2 Corinthians 3:18. "But we all, with unveiled face beholding as in a mirror the glory of the Lord, are being transformed into the same image from glory to glory, just as from the Lord, the Spirit."

The word used by Matthew to describe the Transfiguration is μεταμορφόω (transfigured). Derived from μορφή, meaning "form, shape, or appearance," the verb refers to an inward spiritual change. In philosophical language the μορφή often referred to the specific character or essential form of something, and this is its force in the compound verb the Evangelist used. It is impossible of course to describe adequately the change in the appearance and form of the Lord, but the transformation was not simply outward in character. In Luke's words, the fashion of His countenance became "different" (ἕτερον, Luke 9:29). Matthew, however, went beyond the face of Jesus, saying that "He was transfigured" (17:2). The transformation touched the inner being, the form, the nature—perhaps a kind of foregleam of the glory of His resurrection body.

But Matthew did not neglect to mention the transformation of Jesus' face, for he added, "and His face shone like the sun." This is the outward expression of the inward change. Just as the impurities of the body often appear as blemishes on one's countenance, so the glory of the transformation of the inner being has its counterpart in the shining face.

Matthew then mentioned the change in Jesus' garments, which "became as white as light." His soul, His face, and His clothes were all transfigured. Communion ennobles all, not only the inner and outer being, but the gestures, the gifts, the courtesies, the manners—all the habits of life. While the practical application is obvious, it is well to remember that the believer's transformation will not be completed until the conditions of 1 John 3:1–2 are met.

The Conversation with Moses and Elijah (Matt. 17:3)

Moses and Elijah were leading figures in the unfolding drama of the ages. Moses was the personification of the Law of God, while Elijah was perhaps the greatest of the prophets. The Law and the prophets testify of Him!

According to Luke 9:31, the subject of the conversation on the mount is His "departure" (ἔξοδος), which He was to accomplish in Jerusalem. The "exodus" there would be a greater one than that from Egypt, fraught with greater spiritual consequences. Then will come to pass that to which the deliverance from Egypt pointed.

The presence of Moses and Elijah indicates that there is indeed life beyond the grave, a topic that has been discussed through the ages. People have always sought to seize every hint and probability that nature might give to indicate that life survives the grave. But with only the dim light of nature and faced with the tragic human experience of death and decay, there is no apparent certainty. When, however, the light of divine revelation shines on the human predicament, there comes assurance and confidence. The simplest believer may climb far beyond the brilliant Socrates who, in the *Phaedo* with his cup of hemlock to come, has so appealingly and loftily argued for a life to come.

In addition, the incident may possibly tell much more than that there is life beyond the grave. It surely stresses the fact that the life beyond the grave is a conscious life. It may also point to the fact that the dead are conscious of the living. Consciousness of human events might seem to rob the dead of their happiness and bliss, until one realizes that God knows and sees and is still perfect in His peace. The reason is that He knows the end of the human events; He sees them in their final significance. Cannot something of the same be posited for those who are with the Lord?

The Counsel of Peter (Matt. 17:4)

Peter's suggestion that he make three tabernacles—one each for Jesus, Moses, and Elijah—was senseless and sinful. True, he seemed to sense value in the present situation so that he wished it could be prolonged. Mark 9:6, however, indicates that fear called forth the saying, and Luke 9:36 states that he did not know what he was saying. Besides being senseless, his words were sinful. In effect, they would have turned the Lord from His destined earthly goal, the Cross. But Jesus thought so little of the suggestion that He did not answer it. There is One, however, who did.

The Cloud and the Voice (Matt. 17:5–8)

God the Father interrupted Peter's senseless rambling. His words from the cloud united the Psalms (Ps. 2:7), the Prophets (Isa. 42:1), and the Law (Deut. 18:15) in an authoritative testimony to Jesus' sonship and messiahship. The voice is similar to the voice that shattered the heavens at Jesus' baptism (Matt. 3:17). That voice, however, was directed primarily to Jesus, confirming Him in His understanding of His office. This one was directed primarily to the disciples, confirming the testimony that Peter had just given by divine revelation (16:16 17).[4] In other words, the baptism confirmed the Son's messiahship to Him, while the Transfiguration confirmed the messiahship to the disciples. He is the King (Ps. 2:7) who shall do the work of the Suffering Servant (Isa. 42:1–53:12), and believers must listen to Him, not to fallible Peter, for He is the Prophet who is greater than Moses (Deut. 18:15–18). This event is significant for a number of reasons.

First, the Transfiguration *authenticates* the Son as Messiah by means of the voice from heaven. While rejected by human beings, He was accepted by the Father and was confirmed in His messianic office. The path to its ultimate glorious future passes by Golgotha's brow.

Second, the Transfiguration *anticipates* the kingdom that is to come on the earth. In fact, it is a kind of prelude to and pledge of the kingdom. A statement that precedes each of the accounts of the Transfiguration gives the clue to the theological significance of the incident. Matthew 16:28 reads, "Truly I say to you, there are some of those who are standing here who shall not taste[5] death until they see the Son of Man coming in His kingdom." Many interpretations put on these words might fill a book. Dodd, in reasoning that is extremely weak grammatically, has referred the statement to the coming of the kingdom in the earthly ministry of Jesus. The disciples would awake to the fact that the kingdom had come before they died.[6] Others have suggested Jesus was referring to the Resurrection, a view that fails to explain the force of the word τινες (some). McNeile refers the words to Pentecost as the beginning, but not the completion, of their fulfillment.[7] This too cannot explain the τινες.

Other views are that the destruction of Jerusalem in A.D. 70 is meant or that the life of God in the church was pictured.[8] Of remaining views one can say something similar to what H. A. A. Kennedy used to say when he wished to ridicule fancy theories constructed on insubstantial bases: "I need hardly remind you, gentlemen, that for these fantaSStic conclusions there is not a SSHred of evidence in the New Testament. The most charitable judgment that can be passed on this preposterous book is that its author is slowly drifting towards imbecility."[9]

There can hardly be any doubt that Jesus' statement in Matthew 16:28 refers to the Transfiguration for several reasons. (1) The careful notation of time in 17:1 indicates that the author regarded the following account as the fulfillment of Jesus' words. (2) The verb ἴδωσιν, "see" (16:28), is in harmony with the Transfiguration event.[10] (3) It handles nicely the word τινες (some), which is a feature of the account common to all the synoptics. As Plummer remarks, "No interpretation can be correct that does not explain εἰσίν τινες, which implies the exceptional privilege of some, as distinct from the common experience of all."[11] (4) Jesus' words in 16:28 agree with the apostolic commentary in 2 Peter 1:16–19, in which Peter plainly linked the kingdom with the Transfiguration as "the prophetic word made more sure." He claimed that he had made known "the power and coming of our Lord Jesus Christ" to his readers and that his presentation of it was not based on fables but on his personal experience on the Mount of Transfiguration (v. 16). Therefore, because the Old Testament promises of the kingdom were seen fulfilled in that vision, the word of prophecy was "made more sure." Peter also referred to the event in 1 Peter 5:1, in which he claimed to be a partaker already of the glory that is to be revealed at the manifestation of the Shepherd (1 Peter 5:4).[12] (5) With this view most of the church fathers agree. The Transfiguration, then, was a foretaste and foreshadowing of the messianic kingdom to come, and thus it was a convincing pledge of its consummation according to its Old Testament terms of description. It fell to Peter, James, and John—the "some" of the Lord's words—to have this inestimable privilege of sharing in the messianic glory before its time.

Third, the Transfiguration *illustrates* the inhabitants of the kingdom to come. On the mount were Jesus, the Messiah; and Peter, James, and John, the representatives of the theocratic nation. With Him were Moses, a saint who died, and Elijah, a saint who was raptured without dying, the two together representing the two types of believers in the church (1 Thess. 4:13–18). At the foot of the mountain there was the multitude, but the identity of the multitude is difficult to ascertain. If its character were Gentile, the illustration would be complete. The opposite may be more accurate, however. The future kingdom will be that of the Messiah, who will rule with His church and His nation over the nations of the earth.

Fourth, the Transfiguration *portrays* the personal resurrection of believers. The marvelous change that came over the Lord points to the change that will come over those who belong to Him. As Paul expressed it, when He comes He "will transform the body of our humble state into conformity with the body of His glory" (Phil. 3:21). His appearance "in glory" (Luke 9:31) anticipates the believers' appearance with Him "in glory" (Col. 3:4).

Fifth, the Transfiguration—and this is the use Peter made of the event—*confirms* Old Testament prophecy. What was formerly known by faith—the promises of the Scriptures concerning the messianic kingdom—were now known by sight through the Transfiguration. Therefore the apostle wrote, "And so we have the prophetic word made more sure," and then he added the appropriate exhortation that logically follows, "to which you do well to pay attention" (2 Peter 1:19).

Sixth, the Transfiguration *proclaims* the costliness of His sacrifice for sin. Though Jesus Christ was the only One who in His own merit gained and possessed the right to enter the presence of God, He nevertheless renounced any right He may have possessed in order to fulfill the Scriptures and die for humankind. With the examples of Moses, a man buried by God Himself, and Elijah, who entered heaven without dying, Jesus nevertheless left glory a second time for human salvation. He did not wish His crown without its jewels, and in a few days this same divine Lord was seen crying out in the agony of desolation, "My God, My God, why hast Thou forsaken Me?" (Matt. 27:46). Oh, the costliness of the offering for sin!

Seventh, as a converse of this truth, the Transfiguration also *demonstrates* the strength of Jesus' passion for souls. The perplexity of the Transfiguration has been resolved in a deeper understanding of its relationship to the kingdom of the Messiah, but the perplexity of the love of God's Son for sinful people has only increased. What an apt phrase is that of the Greek liturgy, "His unknown sufferings," for who can understand how much He cares? Believers stand amazed in the presence of Jesus the Nazarene and sing with a fervor produced by His loving-kindness,

> Were the whole realm of nature mine,
> That were a present far too small:
> Love so amazing, so divine,
> Demands my soul, my life, my all.
> —Isaac Watts

CHAPTER 9

The Triumphal Entry of Christ

S. Lewis Johnson Jr.

Not without design is the fact that the two most significant figures of history appeared in the same generation. One was *homo imperiosus,* imperial man, who destroyed Cato's romantic dream of the old republic and its freedom. Augustus, "The divine Caesar—and the Son of God," as a later Gallic inscription had it, shattered his foes by force and inaugurated a new era. But while Augustus brought an armistice to the weary world, he was unable to usher in *Saturnia regna,* the golden age. "The *homo imperiosus,*" Stauffer has said, "could bind the dragon; but he could not slay it."[1]

The second man—born in the troubled little land of Israel, where even the mighty Caesar was never able to bring complete peace—was *homo pacifer,* or *princeps pacis,* as Isaiah foresaw (Isa. 9:6). After having overcome the temptation to follow the path of *homo imperiosus,* He moved firmly and fearlessly to the conflict of the Crucifixion. There He would wrest the kingdom from the ancient Dragon and make it possible for earth's golden age, the messianic rule, to come in power and great glory. This man, the lowly issue of Mary and the Spirit, is in truth "The divine Caesar—and the Son of God." The path to earth's glorious day lies hard by the Cross—a path constructed by the suffering of the Stranger from the world beyond. Virgil's prophetic words had been startlingly fulfilled; the turning of the ages had come.

Calvary, then, is the hinge of history. It was there that the decisive conflict between *civitas dei* and *civitas terrena* occurred. It was there that the kingdoms of this world became indeed the kingdoms of God and His Messiah.

The birth, the Baptism, the Temptation, and the Transfiguration are steps along the way to the throne. Before the climax of Golgotha, there lay the high points of the Triumphal Entry and Gethsemane. The former event is the subject of this study.

Jesus entered Jerusalem amid the shouts of the multitudes, "Hosanna to the Son of David; blessed is He who comes in the name of the Lord; hosanna in the highest!" (Matt. 21:9). Yet few realized the significance of the hour. To most, the Triumphal Entry was not triumphal at all, but nevertheless it was eventful in the world of the spirit.

On the other hand, Isaiah's words still rang with truth, so far as God's people were concerned: "An ox knows its owner, and a donkey its master's manger, but Israel does not know, My people do not understand" (Isa. 1:3). They were, it almost seems, demoniacally determined to be the instrument for the fulfillment of one of Jesus' saddest words, "It cannot be that a prophet should perish outside of Jerusalem" (Luke 13:33).

Palm Sunday, then, was a day of "wild rapture of enthusiasm" and "the delirium of eager welcome"[2] but of little genuine spirituality. They, the people of Jerusalem, wished to see the King in His might but not as "just and endowed with salvation" (cf. Zech. 9:9). Their excitement was real but misguided, and George MacDonald's "That Holy Thing" has captured their mood effectively:

> They were all looking for a king
>   To slay their foes and lift them high:
> Thou cam'st, a little baby thing
>   That made a woman cry.

In Jesus' mind the Triumphal Entry was not a bid for popular sympathy, as Nietzsche imagined.[3] It was an acted parable of the type the prophets had known and practiced, and it had messianic significance. It was designed by Him to make it absolutely certain that no one should misunderstand that His kingdom was not simply an earthly monarchy but also "an empire of the spirit."[4]

Behind the events of the day was the Word, specifically the word of the prophet Zechariah: "Rejoice greatly, O daughter of Zion! Shout in triumph, O daughter of Jerusalem! Behold, your King is coming to you; He is just and endowed with salvation, humble, and mounted on a donkey, even on a colt, the foal of a donkey" (Zech. 9:9). "This prophecy Jesus now deliberately acted out. By His action He proclaimed in the very home and heart of Israel that He was the Messiah, but a Messiah without arms or an army, a Messiah who was riding 'in lowly pomp' that road of the spirit marked out for the Servant of the Lord, a road on which ever darker fell the shadow of a Cross."[5] He was coming as the Prince to "speak peace to the nations" (Zech. 9:10). Speaking of the consistency of this event with the history of Christ, Edersheim says, "It behoved [sic] Him so to enter Jerusalem, because He was a King; and as King to enter it in such a manner, because He was such a King—and both the one and the other were in accordance with the prophecy of old."[6]

The Triumphal Entry was the Lord's declaration of Himself. No longer was His messianic mission and royal dignity a secret. The ancient prophecy had been fulfilled, and not forever will David's throne be unoccupied. All the details unite to proclaim boldly and loudly to the daughter of Zion, "Behold your King!"

The Preparation for the Triumphal Entry (Matt. 21:1–5)

THE ARRANGEMENTS (21:1–3)

The night before the Triumphal Entry Jesus was in Bethany, and it was from this friendly place that the festive procession set out for Jerusalem and the feast. Gathering His Galilean followers together, He was soon with them at Bethphage, over against Bethany, and the Mount of Olives. It was fitting that He enter the city by way of the mount since it had messianic associations (2 Sam. 15:32; Ezek. 11:23; Zech. 14:4–11). From there it was thought that the Lord God would appear to establish the kingdom; from there the deliverance of Israel would take place.

From the Mount of Olives Jesus sent two disciples, asking them to go to the nearby village and procure two animals for the procession. Mark 11:2 and Luke 19:30 add the significant detail that the animal on which He was to ride was to be one on which no one had yet sat.[7] This messianic feature is sometimes overlooked. Commenting on this and the similar expression in John 19:41, Godet remarks, "These are providential facts which belong to the royal glory of Jesus. When a king is received, the objects devoted to his service are such as have never yet been used."[8] The Lord's intention that this be His royal entry is seen very clearly.[9]

THE ATTESTATION (21:4–5)

At this point in his narrative Matthew specifically commented on the spiritual significance of the arrangements. The purpose of the acquisition of the animals was to fulfill prophecy (John 12:14–15), and this, in turn, was a request for national acknowledgment of

Jesus' messiahship. As an illustration of how vapid interpretations may be, one might cite the viewpoint of a modern scholar who has said that Jesus rode the donkey into the city because He was tired and the road was uphill all the way.[10]

The riding of the donkey into Jerusalem not only fulfilled prophecy; it was also a giant object lesson designed to imprint the event on the minds of the viewers in the style of some of the acted messages of the prophets (cf. Jer. 19:1–13; Ezek. 4:1–3). Afterward the real meaning of the events would dawn on the disciples. In the meantime they had the visual aid on which they might meditate.

The Procession Toward Jerusalem (Matt. 21:6–9)

THE PROCESSION (21:6–8)

While the disciples went their way to complete the arrangements for the donkey and her colt, the Lord and His followers inched along the well-known caravan road from Jericho to the City of the Great King. Thoughts of the time of Jerusalem's visitation moved Him to deep agitation, an agitation that would break soon into sobs of lamentation over the city,[11] for He knew the response that awaited Him there.

At an unknown point along the way the disciples met Him with the animals. It seems that they were accompanied by many who had heard the news of Jesus' intention to enter the city in lowly splendor. The enthusiasm generated as the two groups of followers met seems to have arisen spontaneously and to have taken the disciples with Christ by surprise.[12] Perhaps the sight of the crowd from Jerusalem with their palm branches, the national emblem of Palestine, kindled their interest and fervor. At any rate, the garments were put on the colt, and they set Jesus on the colt (cf. Luke 19:35). And as they made their way to the city, the disciples, too, cut down branches from the trees along the way and spread[13] them as a rough matting before the coming King. Although this procession is hardly to be compared with the usual royal parade, it surely is the most impressive of the centuries.

One wonders at the ignorance of the disciples in failing to understand what they were doing, and particularly when they were the chief participants in this great drama. But as Edersheim points out,

> We are too apt to judge them from our standpoint, eighteen [now nineteen!] centuries later, and after full apprehension of the significance of

the event. These men walked in the procession almost as in a dream, or as dazzled by a brilliant light all around—as if impelled by a necessity, and carried from event to event, which came upon them in a succession of but partially understood surprises.[14]

And it must also be remembered that most of the pilgrims acclaiming Him were no doubt provincials, not the same crowd of city rabble that would soon shout, "Crucify Him." They regarded Him as a hero and a friend, even though their views of Him did not reach the plateau of His real nature and mission.

THE ACCLAMATION (21:9)

Gradually the long procession drew near, sweeping up and then beyond the ridge of the Mount of Olives down toward the city. The crowds, both preceding and following, were now in full sight of the southeastern corner of the city where ancient Mount Zion had been situated. At that time Herod's royal abode was located there, but his dwelling was supposed to be on the very spot where the palace of David had been. At this juncture, when the city of David first came into view, the multitudes broke into praise, rejoicing "with a loud voice for all the miracles which they had seen" (Luke 19:37).

The sight of the storied City of David awakened echoes of David's psalms and unitedly they shouted, "Hosanna[15] to the son of David; blessed is He who comes in the name of the Lord; hosanna in the highest!" The words are based on Psalm 118:25–26, but it is not certain that they were designed to be quotations. Yet, whether designed or not, they are fitting utterances; for the psalm was indeed messianic, although indirectly so; and numerous rabbinic citations support this view.[16] This wonderful psalm, called by one commentator, "a string of pearls, each verse being independent like a proverb,"[17] was sung at the Feast of Tabernacles and at the Feast of Passover. The Feast of Tabernacles was designed to celebrate typically the kingdom joy and rest of the nation; if this is in view, the use of the psalm is very fitting for Jesus' entry as King in the name of the Lord.[18]

Other factors suggest this is the sense of its use. First, the bundles of palm branches may have suggested the *lûlābîm*—bundles of palm, myrtle, and willow branches intertwined—which were carried at the Feast of Tabernacles and waved at the mention of the "hosanna" of Psalm 118 in the liturgy of the feast. Second, ὁ ἐρχόμενος (he who comes) was a well-known messianic title. In the Lucan account this meaning is confirmed, for he wrote that the crowds shouted, "Blessed is the King who comes in the name of the Lord" (Luke 19:38). Mark's addition, "Blessed is the coming kingdom of our father David" (11:10)—words that are not a citation from Psalm 118 or any other passage—further defines and interprets the significance of the occasion.[19] So, in summary, the use of Psalm 118, the palm branches, and the messianic title with its confirmation in the interpretive additions of Mark and Luke make it evident that the Triumphal Entry was the official presentation to Israel of her long-promised King by a faithful Scripture-fulfilling God.

"Hosanna in the highest," literally, "save now [O Thou who dwells] in the highest," is either the appeal for heavenly enablement, a prayer addressed to God by the theocratic people on behalf of its King Messiah, or simply an ascription of praise to Him, the Israelite equivalent of "God save the king." It is difficult to be sure of the precise meaning, but unfortunately they did not really understand what they were saying.

The Puzzlement of the City at the Entry

THE INTERROGATION (21:10)

As the milling multitude entered the city gates, their tramping feet and loud acclamations gained the attention of the entire city—men, women, and children. The Greek word rendered "was stirred" comes from the root that is related to the word for an earthquake, and the clause is therefore a strong one (cf. Matt. 2:3). This was the multitude that was soon to cry, "Crucify Him." Now, however, they were genuinely agitated as tremors of anxiety shook them. The worried question of identity, "Who is this?" circulated from person to person, but there was no wholehearted seeking after Him.

THE EXPLANATION (21:11)

The explanation offered is about as anticlimactic as it is possible for a response to be. It is not, This is Israel's great King Messiah! He is your Lord, worship Him, but "This is the[20] prophet Jesus, from Nazareth in Galilee" (cf. John 12:16). The Lord was silent, His face wet with tears. He sadly retraced His steps to Bethany. The die was cast.

Several pieces of evidence point overwhelmingly to the fact

that Jesus formally and officially offered Himself to the nation as its promised Sovereign.

First, the time was right, for Daniel, in the great prophecy Sir Edward Denny called "the backbone of prophecy," had said that sixty-nine weeks of years lay between "the issuing of a decree to restore and rebuild Jerusalem until the Messiah the Prince" (Dan. 9:25). That time was just now expiring, and so in fulfillment of the prophetic word the Messiah appeared.

Second, the Lord's actions indicate that He intentionally fulfilled Zechariah 9:9 because of its messianic implications. It was prophetic symbolism at its purest and best.[21]

Third, Matthew's comment in 21:4, and particularly his use of the perfect γέγονεν (took place), declare that he believed Jesus was the fulfiller of the prophecy.[22]

Fourth, the parabolic teaching that follows the event in the narratives of both Matthew and Mark assumes that the kingdom was presented to the nation and, in addition, that it would be rejected (cf. Matt. 21:33–46; Mark 12:1–12).

Fifth, the actions of the people indicate that they were celebrating the epiphany of their messianic King, though their understanding was severely limited. The use of the palms, the national emblem often found on the coins of the period, and the use of Psalm 118 confirm this. Even the children who shouted "Hosanna to the Son of David!" took part in the affirmation. In fact, if they had not affirmed His Davidic position, the stones on the ground would have (cf. Luke 19:40).[23]

But in spite of the overwhelming testimony the Messiah met with no response. As Stalker says, "The provincial recognition of His claims was insufficient to carry a national assent. He accepted the decision as final."[24] They stumbled at the Stone of stumbling. Expecting a king who would come "armed to the teeth or bestriding a war-horse,"[25] they failed to recognize the One who came on the lowly donkey, the symbol of peace. They did not know Him nor did they know their own great need. This King conquers by meekness and lowliness, not by force of brazen power. Israel waited for a Messiah "to slay their foes and lift them high," but He came meekly to die. They did not understand that He must do the work of the Servant of Yahweh in passion and blood before He sits in regal splendor and reigns. As He later chided His own disciples on the way to Emmaus, "Was it not necessary for the Christ to suffer these things and [then] to enter into His glory?" (Luke 24:26).[26]

The disciples' failure to understand explains the sobs of lamentation that issued from the Lord when He and the company moved through the last defile and over the final brow of Olivet to the point of the descent when the entire city came into view. He sobbed there (cf. Luke 19:41), and as "He saw the city," He said, "If you had known in this day, even you, the things which make for peace! But now they have been hidden from your eyes. For the days shall come upon you when your enemies will throw up a bank before you, and surround you, and hem you in on every side, and will level you to the ground and your children within you, and they will not leave in you one stone upon another, because you did not recognize the time of your visitation" (19:42–44). Because they would not have Him at His first coming in peace, peace would flee from them. Seeing the future discipline and chastening of the nation, He wept. Walking headlong to ruin, they would have to learn the sad lesson that the Triumphal Entry was not only the story of the nation's rejection of its King, but also of their King's rejection of them.

Yet, all is not lost. The future holds a glorious hope. The promises, unconditioned in their ultimate fulfillment, shall be realized. Israel may deny Him, crucify Him, and attempt to forget Him, but His Word is inviolable. Disobedience may thwart the enjoyment of the promises, but it cannot cancel title to them or the ultimate possession of them. The day is coming, as He Himself suggested a few days later, when Israel in full understanding will shout the acclamation again, as they see Him coming the second time for deliverance: "Blessed is He who comes in the name of the Lord" (Matt. 23:39). Then shall take place the entry that is truly triumphal (cf. Zech. 14:1–11). In the meantime their house, as history has proved, is desolate (Matt. 23:38).

The hymn writer has caught the mood of the genuine Christian lament for Israel and the mood of Israel to come, who shall in similar words cry:

> O come, O come, Immanuel,
> And ransom captive Israel,
> That mourns in lonely exile here
> Until the Son of God appear.
> —Latin hymn, 12th century
> Trans. John M. Neale

CHAPTER 10

Roman Law and the Trial of Christ

R. Larry Overstreet

Though it is readily admitted that the chronological order of
some details of Christ's arrest and trials is difficult to determine,
the general outline is well agreed on by many writers.[1]

T he trial of Jesus Christ preceding His death by crucifixion
has been the subject of many books and articles. Many of
them deal specifically and in great depth with the Jewish
trials of Christ, but few attempt to deal in any detail with the
Roman law aspect of Christ's trial before Pontius Pilate. The
chapter seeks to analyze Christ's trial in view of what is known
both of Roman law of that time and of the Roman governor
Pontius Pilate.

Though it is readily admitted that the chronological order of
some details of Christ's arrest and trials is difficult to determine,
the general outline is well agreed on by many writers.[1]

The Man Pontius Pilate

Some writers have attempted to develop from Pilate's name
some information related to his descent. The following quotation
is representative of this.

> The *nomen* Pontius indicates the stock from which Pilate was descended.
> It was one of the most famous of Samnite names. . . . The name is often
> met with in Rom [*sic*] history after the Samnites were conquered and
> absorbed. . . . The *cognomen* Pilatus indicates the *familia,* or branch of
> the *gens* Pontius, to which Pilate belonged. It has been derived from
> *pileus,* the cap worn by freedmen; this is improbable, as Pilate was of
> equestrian rank. It has also been derived from *pilum,* a spear. Probably
> the name was one that had descended to Pilate from his ancestors and
> had long lost its meaning.[2]

In relation to this quotation, it should be noted that there are
examples of freedmen's descendants achieving equestrian rank in
Rome.[3] Some even achieved the status of senator. It is possible,
therefore, that the derivation from *pileus* is accurate.

It is clear from historical records that Pilate was the fifth
procurator of Judea, that he was appointed by the emperor Tiberius,
that he was procurator *cum potestate* (having civil, military, and
criminal jurisdiction), that he held office for ten years (A.D. 26–36),

and that in some way, not clearly known, he was subject to the legate of Syria, which was not uncommon at that time.[4]

It is also known that Pilate created much antagonism between himself and the Jews on at least four occasions. The first of these was immediately after his being appointed governor when he and his soldiers brought their standards bearing the emperor's image into Jerusalem and placed them within sight of the temple. This so enraged the Jews, who regarded it as idolatry, that Pilate yielded to them and had the standards returned to Caesarea.[5] A second occasion is recorded in Luke 13:1, which states that Pilate apparently killed some Galileans while they were offering sacrifices.

On a third occasion he used revenues from the temple to construct an aqueduct. The Jews also objected to this sacrilege, but Pilate had his soldiers beat the complainers into subjection with staves.[6] On the fourth occasion he hung golden shields, apparently bearing the name of the emperor as a deity, in Herod's palace. The Jews objected so strenuously to this that the emperor himself rebuked Pilate and ordered them removed. This event has been dated A.D. 32.[7]

It can thus be seen that Pilate had yielded to Jewish pressures on at least one occasion, and that the emperor himself had intervened to reprimand Pilate on another occasion; this latter event carries special significance since it occurred only about a year before the death of Christ. These historical events form an important background for Pilate's relationship to Christ.

The Governor and Roman Law

Four factors have a bearing on Pilate's dealings with Christ: the relationship of Roman law to the local law of provincials, the rights of Roman citizens in a province contrasted to those of noncitizens, Pilate's authority, and the punishment for the crime of treason.[8]

LOCAL PROVINCIAL LAW

Generally speaking, Roman law allowed the local law of each province to be exercised without much interference. Kunkel has pointed out that "local administration, the administration of justice as between the natives of the provinces, and many other tasks were in general simply left to the political organs of the subject people."[9] One significant exception to this was jurisdiction on matters involving capital punishment, which was reserved to the procurator. "The Romans did, for example, reserve the right to impose capital punishment, as in the case of Christ, but the day to day administration was none of their concern."[10]

This particular exception is critically important in the trial of Christ before Pilate, since the Jews expressly declared, "We have a law, and by that law He ought to die because He made Himself out to be the Son of God" (John 19:7); but they also said, "We are not permitted to put any one to death" (18:31). While it is true that sometime later the Jews did exercise the power of capital punishment, illegally, in the stoning death of Stephen (Acts 7:58), there was a great deterrent in the case of Christ, and that was the involvement of Annas (John 18:13, 24). In A.D. 15, while Annas was the Jewish high priest, he led the Sanhedrin to violate this law when there was temporarily no procurator in Judea. That action resulted in his being deposed by Valerius Gratus that same year.[11] It seems reasonable that Annas would have had a great influence on the decision of Caiaphas, the high priest during Christ's trial, since he was Caiaphas's father-in-law, and the case of Christ was one that involved great popular opinion.

RIGHTS OF INDIVIDUALS

The rights of individuals within a province varied depending on whether the person was a Roman citizen or a noncitizen, an alien. Lyall explains the state of the noncitizen.

> The *peregrini* were subjects of Rome, but not Romans, because they were not citizens. They were not liable to military service, but were subject to supervision, and to the heavy burden of Imperial taxation. In terms of strict Roman law they were rightless and dutiless, existing as objects and not subjects of law.[12]

Garnsey has pointed out that citizens were distinguished from aliens in the matter of corporal punishment. "Corporal punishment was traditionally used against slaves and aliens. This was written into the laws from the early second century B.C., when a *lex porcia* granted to Roman citizens the right of appeal against beating as well as execution."[13]

The only time a Roman citizen was supposed to be subject to execution without a properly constituted trial was if he had been declared an enemy of the state.[14] In other instances the difference between aliens and citizens in the empire was clearly maintained. "Discrimination in favour of citizens as opposed to aliens was thus a permanent feature of the Roman judicial system. It was practised in all spheres of law where aliens were technically excluded, as from the *ius civile,* and where they were not, as in criminal law."[15]

However, it should also be noted that from the time of the Republic onward aliens were supposed to be allowed "natural principles of equity which are common to all nations."[16] It may be concluded then that aliens—and Christ was one of these in relation to Roman law—had no direct legal standing at all; however, ethically and morally the natural principles of equity should have been applied in His case, but there was no legal compulsion to do so.

AUTHORITY OF THE GOVERNOR

Since Judea as a province was subject to Rome, "the governor exercised the unlimited jurisdiction of the military *imperium.*"[17] The governor of a province like Judea exercised military, financial, and judicial functions.[18] In judicial matters he "exercised both civil and criminal jurisdiction among Roman citizens, and also among foreigners, so far as such cases came before him by virtue of the province's statute *(leges provinciae)* or by the operation of his discretion."[19] While it is clear that the governor's judicial activity would mainly concern Roman citizens, it is also clear that "if the interests of Roman sovereignty were involved, no doubt he would also at all times have summoned provincials to his court."[20]

The extent of the governor's authority is evident in the types of punishment he could legally mete. He had the power of capital punishment over noncitizens,[21] and he could also "execute humbler citizens or send them to the mines."[22] The evidence indicates that the governor could inflict capital punishment on any Roman citizen, but "custom seems to have directed that the governor should remit capital cases of Roman citizens to the home government."[23] It may be concluded, then, that the Roman governor had absolute legal authority to deal with noncitizens, such as Christ, and to prescribe the death penalty, without fear of having his authority challenged.

As for the procedure a governor would follow, he could "deal with crime inquisitorially, i.e., by investigating on his own initiative and by any means at his disposal."[24] It is clear that "judicial administration in the provinces was much less precise and technical than that which was required in Rome itself."[25] This fact provided for the flexibility and informality in Pilate's dealings with Christ. There was nothing improper or unusual about it.

CRUCIFIXION AS A PUNISHMENT

Since Christ was crucified as a result of Pilate's final decision, it is needful to examine this mode of punishment and the people on whom it was used. In general the mode of crucifixion was adopted by the Romans "to inflict the death penalty upon rebellious slaves and seditious provincials."[26] Concerning crucifixion, Garnsey wrote,

> Crucifixion was the standing form of execution for slaves. . . . Further-more, in the reign of Nero, Gessius Florus scourged and crucified some Jews in Jerusalem, including some equestrians. On other occasions, Jewish rebels suffered crucifixion. . . . A political charge was at least aired in the trial of Christ.[27]

The Gospels indicate that Christ was charged with sedition or treason (Luke 23:2; John 19:2). The law on treason was not specifically delineated but was capable of wide interpretation. In fact, in the time of the empire, "the law was extended not only to all attempts on the life of the reigning prince, but to all acts and words which might appear to be disrespectful to him,"[28] and it was regarded as a capital crime. In the case of Christ, He "was on trial for his life before the Roman governor and the basis of the prosecution was his danger to the Roman state. The very means of execution shows that Jesus died as an offender against Rome, not the Jewish nation."[29]

An Analysis of the Trial

The object here is to present an analysis of Jesus' trial from the viewpoint of Roman law to determine whether Pilate acted legally or illegally. It is readily admitted that the four gospels do not deal directly with this subject. Evidently they "are far more interested in Pilate's character than in the judicial principles by which the trial was conducted."[30]

Some writers maintain that Pilate acted illegally. Clark is a representative of this position.

> The trial before Pilate was illegal because it was an appeal and yet a new charge of treason was presented by the chief priests. At the beginning the trial was marked with regularity and solemnity. But when Jesus returned from Herod, Pilate became afraid of the people. He listened to the mob— there was no order and no regularity.[31]

In response to Clark's position it should be observed first that this was not an appeal. The Jews brought Christ to Pilate because they were forbidden by law to put Him to death themselves. Second, it should be remembered that a provincial governor had the legal freedom to conduct a trial as informally and with as little set procedure as he wished. Clark's objections may hold good in relation to twentieth-century American jurisprudence, but they completely miss the mark of Roman jurisprudence.

Several observations may be made concerning Pilate and the legality of the trial of Christ. First, since Pilate was governor of Judea and this was considered a capital offense, he was the proper person to conduct the trial. Second, Pilate was quite correct in initially declining to hear the case, since the first charge was so vague (see John 18:30). Third, he acted in accord with Roman law when an indictment for treason was leveled against Christ (Luke 23:2), and he questioned Christ privately concerning this matter, deciding He was innocent. At this point Pilate had the legal authority to release Christ, but he did not do so. Instead he once again went to the Jews, for which he has been criticized as acting illegally. However, when it is remembered that under Roman law a noncitizen, such as Christ, had no legal rights to begin with, then Pilate could not have acted illegally. He may be accused of being unethical or immoral (and rightly so), but he should not be accused of acting illegally under the Roman legal system. He had every legal authority to continue or not, as formally or informally as he pleased. Fourth, Pilate did not act in an unusual manner when he sent Christ to Herod (Luke 23:6–12). Greenidge has pointed out that a provincial governor had the power to ask anyone he wanted to be his adviser, and that "it was even possible in an important prosecution to summon expert advice from another province—nay, even a neighboring provincial governor himself."[32] Herod's refusal to try Jesus indicates that in his opinion Jesus was innocent; Pilate used this in his argument for Christ's release (Luke 23:15).

The remainder of Pilate's legal dealings with Christ may be considered from the basis of a noncitizen having no legal rights in Roman law.

An Evaluation of Pilate's Actions

Pilate did attempt to save Jesus from the cross by declaring Him innocent, by offering to chastise or scourge Him, and by offering to release Him as was the custom (but Barabbas was released instead). Indeed, it has been accurately said that Pilate "sent Jesus to the cross, but not before he had exhausted every expedient for saving Him, except the simple and straightforward one of dismissing the case."[33] Pilate persisted in trying to convince the Jews to let him release Jesus "till they threatened to implicate in the charge of rebellion against Caesar the governor himself, if he persisted in unwonted mercy."[34] This must have had a special effect on Pilate, since only a year before Jesus' crucifixion, which took place in A.D. 33,[35] Pilate had been rebuked by the emperor Tiberius concerning the shields that he had set up in Herod's palace, which had offended the Jews. Pilate obviously was in no frame of mind at this early time to risk another confrontation with the emperor if he thought it could be avoided.

Also, when Pilate delivered Christ to be crucified, he demonstrated "all the cowardice of the judge who thus declines to act as the protector of innocence,"[36] and the natural principles of equity that should have been allowed to an alien (although not required by Roman law) were denied. This action was unethical and immoral, even though it was not technically illegal.

What could Pilate have done instead of sending Christ to the cross? He could have displayed the fortitude to do what was morally and ethically right and then relied on the emperor's sense of justice if the matter had been brought before him. The proconsul of Achaia, Gallio by name, did this very thing when the apostle Paul was brought before him (Acts 18:12–17); he refused to hear the case and drove the complainers from his presence. Pilate could have done this, but instead he chose to follow what he thought was the politically expedient route and sent Christ to the cross.

Pilate's Later Life

Pilate was removed from his position as governor in A.D. 36. The event that led directly to this was his leading his troops against some restless Samaritans on Mount Gerizim and conducting a needless massacre. The Samaritans complained about this to Vitellius, the legate of Syria, who immediately deposed Pilate and sent him to Rome to answer the accusations before Tiberius. However, by the time Pilate had reached Rome, Tiberius was dead and Caligula was on the throne.[37] What happened to Pilate following this is a matter of some conjecture. Though there are many traditions, Eusebius stated that Pilate committed suicide.[38]

Conclusion

There was technically no breach of Roman law in Pilate's trial of Jesus in relation to the fact that Christ was a noncitizen. However, there was more than the purely legal aspect. Pilate certainly showed cowardice in the face of the clamoring Jews, and he acted in an unethical and immoral manner in that he did not release Christ even though he knew He was innocent.

Pilate's character is not to be envied; he appears as a vacillating, compromising individual more concerned with political expediency than with equity at Jesus' trial. His actions may not be condemned because they were illegal; however, his actions may justly be condemned because he acted against his own conscience (Matt. 27:24) and against what was morally and ethically correct.

CHAPTER 11

The Agony of Christ in Gethsemane

S. Lewis Johnson Jr.

*T*he Gathering Storm is the title of the first volume of Winston Churchill's memorable history of World War II. The title is admirably suitable as a description of the circumstances surrounding Jesus' last visit to Jerusalem. At His Transfiguration, Moses and Elijah spoke "of His departure which He was to accomplish at Jerusalem" (Luke 9:31). As He strode on toward Jerusalem, even the disciples, so often dull-witted and obtuse, seemed to sense that something was in the air. Mark put it this way in one of his most striking texts, a verse filled with "the sense of the numinous"[1] and the awe of the supernatural: "And they were on the road, going up to Jerusalem, and Jesus was walking on ahead of them; and they were amazed, and those who followed were fearful. And again He took the twelve aside and began to tell them what was going to happen to Him" (Mark 10:32). It was "the gathering storm."

If the Transfiguration and the immediately following events mark the gathering of the storm, then the agony in Gethsemane marks the fall of the first sheet of rain amidst the blustery winds. Not that Jesus now for the first time begin to think of His passion, though He now began to dwell on it more deeply and frequently. His life had certain peaks, and on these peaks He saw the Cross as the culmination of His ministry. Among these heights were the temptation in the wilderness, the marriage in Cana of Galilee when Mary so spoke to Him that He was stirred to look on to His "hour" (John 2:4), and the feeding of the five thousand when the multitude wished to make Him a king. When the mother of Zebedee's children came craving a lofty place for her sons, He was moved to speak of "the cup" and "the baptism," both figures of His death (Matt. 20:20–28). And when the Greeks asked to interview Him (John 12:20–21), the request brought home to Him the wider mission of the future, but it also reminded Him of what must precede it. He was visibly shaken. As Stalker comments:

Instead of responding to their request, He became abstracted, His face darkened, and His frame was shaken with the tremor of an inward conflict. But He soon recovered Himself, and gave expression to the thoughts on which in those days He was steadying up His soul: "Except a corn of wheat fall into the ground and die, it abideth alone; but if it die, it bringeth forth much fruit."[2]

In a moment He added, "Now My soul has become troubled; and what shall I say, 'Father, save Me from this hour'? But for this purpose I came to this hour" (John 12:27). Then there came the words the apostle said were descriptive of the death He would die: "And I, if I be lifted up from the earth, will draw all men to Myself" (v. 32). These were peaks in the greatest life, but the highest still lay in the future.

The Heidelberg Catechism says that he suffered "all the time that he lived on earth, but *especially* at the end of his life." It was not without reason that the Church spoke of the "passio magna" without wishing to minimize his sufferings before the last days of his life. In the *passio magna* we see the final and utmost concentration of his suffering, and Scripture shows us that this distinction is not without reason, for Christ said to his disciples, "With desire I have desired to eat this Passover with you before I *suffer*" (Luke 22:15).[3]

The grand events of Gethsemane and Golgotha are some of the most precious possessions of Christianity. "Unspeakably great as He always was, it may be reverently said that He was never so great as during those days of direct calamity."[4]

Of the historicity of the Gethsemane account there can be no question. Even Joseph Klausner, an arch foe of the true nature of Christianity, felt compelled to write, "The whole story bears the hallmark of human truth: only a few details are dubious."[5] He and others have often pointed out that neither the disciples nor the early church would ever have invented the account of the agony of Christ. It presented too many problems for them in its picture of a Savior almost too human and sadly tragic and of apostles sleeping when they should have been watching. It was this picture that the enemies of the faith, such as Celsus in the second century and Julian in the fourth, held up to contemptuous ridicule, comparing the seemingly cowardly Jesus with the brave and magnanimous Socrates and others. Obviously, then, the writers of the New Testament would not have created such difficulties for themselves. Surely the accounts are reliable and historically true to fact.

The First Petition in Gethsemane (Matt. 26:36–39)

There was an eerie, foreboding sense of stillness, not unlike that of Sodom before its destruction, floating like fog over the city that had killed the prophets and stoned them that had been sent to it. The spiritually perceptive may well have felt afraid and cried out, "How awesome is this place!" (Gen. 28:17). The hymn that concluded the Passover supper had been sung, the great high-priestly prayer had been offered, and Jesus and His little band had passed through the north gate, crossed the Kidron Valley, turned right to the little garden called Gethsemane, which means "oil press."[6] Edersheim refers to the quiet place for retirement and prayer as "the other Eden, in which the Second Adam, the Lord from heaven, bore the penalty of the first, and in obeying gained life."[7]

After exhorting the disciples to pray that they might not enter into temptation, Jesus, with Peter and the sons of Zebedee, went farther into the garden to pray. The general theme of Jesus' prayer had to do with the passion, and it arose out of the thoughts suggested by the Last Supper. The new covenant was soon to be inaugurated in blood, and now the cold flood of suffering was beginning to break at His feet. With each step forward the anguish increased, and the agitation was visible before He spoke. The Greek expressions that describe His emotions are exceedingly strong, seemingly used in crescendo-like fashion. He was "grieved" and "distressed" (Matt. 26:37), "very distressed" (Mark 14:33), "troubled" (Mark 14:33), and "deeply grieved" (Matt. 26:38; Mark 14:34).

Finally He found the place He was looking for and fell on His knees (Luke 22:41), but the kneeling quickly became unbearable and so, pressed down by His spirit, He fell on the dust of the oil press. There He lay, recalling the messianic text, "But I am a worm, and not a man" (Ps. 22:6). "He filled the silent night with His crying and watered the cold earth with His tears, more precious than the dew of Hermon, or any moisture, next unto His own blood, that ever fell on God's earth since the creation."[8]

In His prayer Jesus said, "My Father, if it is possible, let this cup pass from Me; yet not as I will, but as Thou wilt" (Matt. 26:39). The term "cup," with others such as "baptism" (Matt. 20:22 KJV), is a figure of His death and is to be related to the cup of the Lord's Supper (cf. vv. 27–28). Somewhere James Denney spoke of "the cup our sins had mingled"; he rightly saw the word "cup" as a figure of Jesus' sacrificial work on human behalf.

The meaning of Jesus' tortured petition has been the subject of much discussion, and some novel interpretations have been suggested to extricate Him from His seemingly strange fear of the onrushing death He Himself had been announcing. Schilder, for example, thinks that Christ's petition was to the effect that He would not die under Satan's assault before the cross. He points to the agonizing struggle in the garden and contrasts it with the triumphant attitude of the cross, when He, in full command of His senses, disposed of His responsibilities to the apostle John (John 19:25–27). To Schilder it seems that the real struggle was in Gethsemane, and his view approaches that of Adam Clarke, who once said, "Jesus paid more in the Garden than on the cross." Of course Schilder's view overlooks the agonizing aspects of the struggle of Golgotha, such as, for example, the awful cry of dereliction, "My God, My God, why hast Thou forsaken Me?" (Matt. 27:46). And it also appears to be dangerously close to the erroneous suggestion that the saving work of Christ was carried out in His life as well as in His death.[9]

A second novel interpretation was that suggested by Donald Grey Barnhouse, the late pastor of the Tenth Presbyterian Church of Philadelphia and a prince of biblical expositors in the first half of the twentieth century. He contended that Jesus could not have prayed that He might be delivered from death by the cross because He knew that He must die and had repeatedly announced His death to the disciples.[10] Therefore Barnhouse said Jesus prayed that He would not suffer eternal separation from God. His petition pertained not to physical death on the cross but to eternal separation of the second death. However, the same objection Barnhouse lodged against the traditional view that Jesus prayed that He might be allowed to escape the cross, but only within God's will, can be lodged against his view. He made much over the fact that Jesus could not have prayed such a prayer because He knew He must die and had known it from early times. But the New Testament also plainly states that Jesus knew He would rise from the dead. In other words, He knew and prophesied that His death would not be followed by eternal separation from the Father (16:21; 17:23; 20:19).

The traditional view—that Jesus prayed that *if it should be within the will of God,* the way of the cross might not be taken—is the only view that does justice to the text and the reality of the struggle that went on within the God-Man. Superficially considered, there seems to be a conflict between the will of Jesus and the will of God, and this has caused some interpreters to stumble. For example, even John Calvin erred in saying that Christ corrected and recalled a wish that had suddenly escaped Him.[11] But at the very moment the Lord distinguished His will from the Father's, He subjected His own.[12] There was testing, but there was no sin, and the writer of the Epistle to the Hebrews confirmed this in saying that Jesus was heard amid the strong crying and tears "in that he feared" (Heb. 5:7 KJV). That last phrase is the interpretation of the last clause of the Lord's petition, "yet not as I will, but as Thou wilt."

The Second Petition in Gethsemane (Matt. 26:40–42)

Much as the Lord desired the companionship and support of His friends, He could not count on them. Although near, they were nodding, and while He lay in the dust in prayer, they lay sleeping. His question to Peter as the representative of the Twelve must have reminded the leader of the apostles of his brash promise to die with the Lord.[13] After the mild rebuke, the Lord retreated and offered a second petition, only slightly altered from the first: "My Father, if this cannot pass away unless I drink it, Thy will be done."[14]

The Third Petition in Gethsemane (Matt. 26:43–46)

Verse 44 records that Jesus "prayed a third time, saying the same thing once more." On His return from the second prayer, He found that sleep had weighted their eyes, and they did not know how to answer Him (cf. Mark 14:40). So He left them and prayed another prayer that was identical with the second. On His final return to them, victory had come. As Edersheim says, "After three assaults had the Tempter left Him in the wilderness; after the threefold conflict in the Garden he was vanquished."[15] Let the disciples sleep on, for the battle had been won. After a brief period of rest, Jesus called them to go forth to meet the other eight disciples and the band of soldiers who were coming under the direction of Judas to take Him (vv. 45–46).

From this moment on Jesus seemed never to have wavered in His purpose to go to Calvary. His sense of triumphant joy, confirmed by the coming of the strengthening angel to Him (Luke 22:43), is clearly reflected in the calm command to Peter after the wounding of Malchus: "Put the sword into the sheath; the cup which the Father has given Me, shall I not drink it?" (John 18:11).

The agony had lasted just one short hour, but how significant an hour! And yet questions continue to pose themselves. The liturgy of the Greek Orthodox Church includes a remarkable expression, "thine unknown sufferings," and there are depths here that poor, frail mortals shall never fathom, for He was God's "unspeakable" gift. Watts was right in writing, "And all the unknown joys He gives were bought with agonies unknown."

One question frames itself to all who read this account: Why the agony? Or, why did the Lord of Glory shrink before the future, which He held in His hand? Why did He who promised peace seem so emotionally disturbed in this dark hour? How can one think of the Lord as a Man astonished, disturbed, and sore troubled?

Was the cause of the agony the grief of broken family ties? There can be little doubt that He felt these more deeply than any other person, for none ever honored father and mother as He did (John 19:25–27). But this grief cannot explain the depth of His agony.

Was the grief the result of the loneliness of fear and misunderstanding? Referring to this, Stalker said, "He was terribly alone. The whole world was against Him—Jerusalem panting for His life with passionate hate, the tens of thousands from the provinces turned from Him in disappointment."[16] Further, He knew they would soon be scattered, sunken in fear and misunderstanding of the entire messianic mission (Matt. 26:31). But that can hardly explain His agony.

Was it the shame of the Roman gibbet? He would be numbered with the transgressors (Mark 15:28) and then die a criminal's death (Phil. 2:8). But such shame, great though it was, cannot account for this agony of blood and tears.

Was His agony the hellish ordeal of demonic opposition (Matt. 26:41)? He did say, "this hour and the power of darkness are yours" (Luke 22:53). This opposition was fierce, but other forces were fiercer. Matthew reported that Jesus said, "My soul is deeply grieved, to the point of death" (26:38). "Deeply grieved" renders περίλυπος, a strong word. Is this a clue to the agony? Was it caused by the horror of contact with sin and death?

> Man's nature, created of God immortal, shrinks (by the law of its nature) from the dissolution of the bond that binds body and soul. Yet to fallen man Death is not by any means fully Death, for he is born with the taste

of it in his soul. Not so Christ. It was the Unfallen Man, dying; it was He, who had no experience of it, tasting Death, and that not for Himself but for every man, emptying the cup to its bitter dregs.[17]

Yes, this had much to do with the agony. For the first time this Holy One must identify Himself with unholiness. This is difficult to understand, but it was agony indeed. Imagine a pure young girl forced to enter a house of prostitution and live there; multiply that sense of revulsion to infinity and one would have a pale illustration of Christ's agony in identifying Himself with human iniquity. But even this does not give the full picture.

There is no explanation of His agony that satisfies unless one includes the agony of the anticipation of the divine condemnation for sin. The agony stems from the judicial penalty for sin—the curse of the broken Law. Only that can fully explain His agony. That curse included separation from the Father, excruciating agony for the Son of His love. The word "distressed" in 26:37 strikingly illustrates this aspect of the agony. The verb ἀδημονέω is related to the word ἀπόδημος, which means "away from home." From this there developed the meaning "to be sorely troubled," because physical derangement often leads to mental anxiety. If this is the force of the word in verse 37,[18] the meaning admirably suits the context. This away-from-homeness finds its completion in the desolating shriek, "My God, My God, why hast Thou forsaken Me?" (27:46). Clearly that utterance expresses the horror that comes from spiritual death. The agony, then, came preeminently from the anticipation of the presentation of the bill for human sins. As the hymnwriter put it, "Death and the curse were in our cup, O Christ! 'twas full for thee!"

As a necessary corollary of this, one sees the inadequacy of the view of Peter Abelard (1079–1142) on the Lord's sufferings. How can His dying be an example for humankind, for others have died much calmer than He? But all is understandable if the penal element is there. To some degree His suffering was exemplary (1 Peter 2:21), but this view cannot satisfy and solve the mystery of the agony in Gethsemane. This was more than example; it was penal substitution.

What is the application of this event to believers today? Four points may be suggested. First, Gethsemane points to the perfection of Christ, the believer's High Priest. This is the use the author of Hebrews makes of the event. The agony was a vital feature of the humanity of Jesus Christ, through which He might exercise a sympathetic priestly ministry on behalf of His own. By virtue of divine appointment and human experience, He is the One to whom believers may draw near with boldness for mercy and grace (Heb. 4:15–16; 5:7–10).

Second, His agony illustrates the power of prayer, for it was in this area that the victory of Gethsemane was gained (Matt. 27:41).

Third, the agony illustrates the pattern for success in the spiritual life. It lies in the obedience signified by the words, "not as I will, but as Thou wilt" (26:39). His shuddering human nature yielded to the indomitable will of the divine Father. Believers, too, must learn to pray, not some, but all of Jesus' prayer.

Fourth, Gethsemane sets forth the passion of the Lord for the souls of the unredeemed. The voice of Gethsemane sounds forth, "I am willing," while the voice from Calvary cries, "It is finished." Both illustrate how much He cared.

CHAPTER 12

The Savior's Sufferings in Life

Robert P. Lightner

Evangelicals are united in their agreement that Christ suffered in His life on earth. There is some disagreement, though, as to the purpose and the accomplishments of those sufferings. Did Christ's sufferings in life provide substitution for sin, as did His sufferings in death on the cross?

The Reality of His Life Sufferings

SUFFERING BECAUSE OF HIS HUMANITY

That the eternal Son of God became incarnate in human flesh and possessed a true human body is an evident fact of Scripture. The Savior's birth (Matt. 1:18), normal human life and growth (Luke 2:52), and the human names ascribed to Him provide evidence that He possessed a truly human nature. Too, Scripture states He had a body of flesh (1 John 4:2), a human soul (John 12:27), and a human spirit (13:21).

The union of God with man of necessity involved suffering that is associated with humanity. The physical properties common to humans were His also. He suffered pain, and He grew hungry, thirsty, and tired. As a vital part of His humiliation in His incarnation, He voluntarily subjected Himself to the limitations of humanity (Phil. 2:7–8). He was the sinless One among sinners, the obedient One among the disobedient.

To be sure, He obeyed every precept of the Mosaic Law. He was born under the Law (Gal. 4:4). He was without sin (Heb. 4:15) and was the end of the Law (Rom. 10:4) and came not to destroy the Law but to fulfill it (Matt. 5:17). The writer to the Hebrews said He "learned obedience from the things which He suffered" (Heb. 5:8). This is not to imply that at any time He was disobedient; rather, it means that in His humiliation He learned what obedience costs. In becoming human, He voluntarily subjected Himself to a role in relation to the Father that involved submission and obedience.

SUFFERING CAUSED BY SATAN

Scripture records that Jesus was "led up by the Spirit into the wilderness to be tempted of the devil" (Matt. 4:1). Though the Holy Spirit providentially arranged for His temptation in the wilderness, the Devil was the instrument used to do the testing. Also Matthew revealed that the Devil left Him as he found Him, the sinless, spotless Savior (cf. Matt. 4:11).

It is generally acknowledged that Christ did not sin when tested by Satan in that unique and peculiar experience nor on any other occasion, for that matter. There is difference of opinion, though, as to whether Christ could have sinned. Even though the Savior did not sin, *could* He have sinned? The answer to that question must be an emphatic no. He could not sin because He did not possess the Adamic fallen nature, which provides the possibility, propensity, and potentiality of sin.

Appeal to the First Adam as an illustration of one who sinned, though without a sin nature, will not do. Granted, Adam did not have a sin nature as he came from the hands of the Creator. Yet he sinned. The striking difference between the First and the Last Adams, in this regard, is that the Last Adam is more than human. He is the God-Man. Since He not only possessed a sinless human nature but also was God manifest in the flesh, He could not sin because God cannot sin. Therefore all the temptations Christ faced came not from within but from without.

Because Christ did not possess a sin nature and therefore could not sin does not mean the temptations of the Devil were not real. The New Testament indicates they were very real. Christ suffered at the hands of Satan. As God, He possessed the power to turn stones into bread, to make a public display of the Father's preservation over Him, and to accept all the glory of the world, which belongs to Him, but to do these things at the invitation of Satan would have been to sin.

SUFFERING AT THE HANDS OF HIS FOES

The very ones who would be expected to have received Christ are the ones who rejected and opposed Him most. The Sadducees and Herodians opposed Him by ignoring Him. As far as the news that one was claiming to be the Messiah was concerned, they were not greatly stirred because they interpreted the claim as one more fraud and as evidence of a popular interest in such a claim. They paid attention to Him only when His followers seemed to be threatening a political revolt. This, they feared, would attract the attention of the Romans and bring new restrictions and impositions on them.

The reaction of the scribes and Pharisees to Christ's claims differed from that of the Sadducees and Herodians. He suffered from the religious experts even more than from the Sadducees. The Pharisees did not ignore Him. Instead, they followed Him and His teaching with relentless persistence. These religious leaders were respected by the people as the orthodox religious spokesmen of the day. And yet the sad paradox is that these were the ones who rejected, repudiated, and eventually crucified the Lord of glory. Their sinful doubt had so blinded their spiritual eyes that they could not see Him as their Messiah even though they were students of the Old Testament Scriptures that clearly spoke of Him. This brought stupendous suffering and sadness to the Savior. These who should have been His friends were His fiercest foes.

SUFFERING AT THE HANDS OF HIS FRIENDS

Neglect and rejection of Christ could be expected from His foes. Those who refused to accept Him as Israel's Messiah would naturally spurn Him and bring heartrending suffering to Him by their rejection of Him and His claims. But as He lived His sinless life, the Savior also suffered sorely at the hands of His friends— the Twelve whom He had chosen for a unique ministry. In His parting words to His own, Christ told them, "You are My friends, if you do what I command you" (John 15:14). But they brought suffering to Him through withdrawal, denial, and betrayal.

The withdrawal of His own, which climaxed when they "all left Him and fled" (Matt. 26:56), started long before that awful moment became a reality. Even though they had forsaken all to follow Him, yet they often failed to exercise complete faith in Him. On one such occasion Jesus said the reason for their powerlessness in serving Him was because of their unbelief (17:20). They also were characterized by unconcern at times. At a most crucial moment when they should have been found in supplication, they were deep in slumber (26:40). While their Master agonized in prayer, they slept. Pride crept into their lives, too, on occasion. They sometimes evidenced an unholy ambition. Anticipating, as they did, the establishment of the messianic rule on earth and having heard the Savior say He would be killed and then raised from the dead, they evidently assumed He would then institute the kingdom promised to their ancestors. This caused them to dispute among themselves "which of them was the greatest" (Mark 9:34). Two of the disciples in particular gave vent to their unholy ambition. James and John asked to be especially favored by the Lord. They wanted to sit "one on Your right, and one on Your left" (Mark 10:37). This must have grieved the heart of the Son of God. Surely their unbelief, unconcern, and unholy ambition brought suffering to Him. No doubt the most severe suffering, however, came when after they all, along with Peter, said they would not deny Him (Mark 14:31), they then soon "left Him and fled" (14:50). Here was the climax. His own had withdrawn from Him.

Peter's particular denial of His Lord signals an event that brought extreme suffering to the Savior. The Lord knew it would come to pass, for He had predicted it (Matt. 26:34). Peter probably thought it impossible. How could he, the spokesman for the Twelve, ever do such a thing? And yet that is exactly what he did before individuals and the crowds that gathered to accuse the Savior (Matt. 26:69–75; Luke 22:58; John 18:25).

The startling and difficult words of Christ to His own, "Did I Myself not choose you, the twelve, and yet one of you is a devil?" (John 6:70), must have puzzled the Twelve. Who could it be? Speaking of the entire group, Peter had just said, "Lord, to whom shall we go? You have words of eternal life" (6:68). It seemed impossible that one of the Twelve would ever act as an adversary to the Savior. If he of whom Christ spoke was present, he was certainly silent when Peter gave his testimony. As history unfolded, however, that is precisely what took place. Through treachery and deceit, Christ was betrayed by one of His own followers, one whom He had chosen and loved. Just as His own nation, which He had come to exalt and over which He was to reign as King and for which He was to bring in everlasting peace and righteousness, had officially rejected Him, so now, one of that small, select company betrayed Him into the hands of His executioners (Matt. 26:47–56).

The suffering and agony in life that accompanied Christ's perfect humanity cannot be denied. The question remains, Why did He suffer in life? Of what value were His life sufferings? Were these ways by which Christ made atonement for sin?

The Reasons for His Life Sufferings

The query propounded by the psalmist and the prophet, Why do the righteous suffer? is never more demanding of an answer than when asked of the Lord Jesus Christ. That He suffered in life is as certain and undeniable as that He suffered in death. Truly He was "a man of sorrows, and acquainted with grief" (Isa. 53:3), and "He was pierced through for our transgressions" (v. 5).

Theologians are usually divided in their answer to the question, What was the purpose of Christ's sufferings in life? It is customary, too, to find that dispensationalists usually hold to one view and nondispensationalists to another. In fact, one's view of the value of Christ's life sufferings and obedience to the Law is directly related to one's acceptance or rejection of covenant theology.

If one believes, as covenant theology contends, that God made a covenant with Adam promising him eternal life for his obedience and if this covenant is the basis for all God's redemptive dealings with humankind for all ages, then belief in the substitutionary nature of Christ's sufferings in life is a natural corollary. This is because just as the First Adam represented his posterity, so Christ, the Last Adam, represented the same group. Because the First Adam sinned, he plunged the entire human race into sin and guilt. Christ, as the Last Adam, therefore, came to do for the race what the First Adam failed to do—obey God and thus fulfill his part of the covenant.

The question under consideration is not, Did Christ suffer in life and in death? but rather, Why did He suffer in life? What was the theological importance of all He endured before His death on the cross? Two views that represent answers to this question are the vicarious atoning view and the nonatoning view.

THE VICARIOUS ATONING VIEW

Those who hold Reformed, or covenant, theology subscribe to this position. Closely associated with this view is the classification of Christ's obedience into active obedience and passive obedience. While some distinction is made between these two by making the active refer to Christ's obedience in life and the passive to His obedience in death, it is often conceded that the two cannot be separated. "The two accompany each other at every point in the Saviour's life."[1]

Berkhof explains this view of the vicarious nature of Christ's life sufferings by seeking to show the relationship of the First Adam to Christ, the Last Adam.

> The first Adam was by nature under the law of God, and the keeping of it as such gave him no claim to a reward. It was only when God graciously

entered into a covenant with him and promised him life in the way of
obedience that the keeping of the law was made the condition of obtain-
ing eternal life for himself and his descendants. And when Christ voluntarily entered into the federal relationship of the Last Adam, the keeping
of the law naturally acquired the same significance for Him and for those
whom the Father had given Him.[2]

Charles Hodge states this view clearly as he seeks to explain
the meaning of Christ's being made under the Law: "This subjection
to the law was not only voluntary, but vicarious."[3]

Murray, a more contemporary proponent of this view, also
presents the idea that what Christ suffered in life was as vicarious
and substitutionary as what He endured on the cross. "Christ's
obedience was vicarious in the bearing of the full judgement of
God upon sin, and it was vicarious in the full discharge of the
demands of righteousness. His obedience becomes the ground of
the remission of sin and of actual justification."[4]

A classic orthodox writer on the Atonement gave clear expression
to this concept:

Most readers who merely read the narrative of Christ's life as they do a
common history see nothing more in these sufferings than the opposition
of ungodly men to the cause of God or limit the endurance of the curse
on the part of Jesus to the hours when He hung upon the cross. But the
curse-bearing career of Christ was by no means of that nature nor limited
to that time.[5]

In summary of this view, then, the following becomes evident:
Those who hold to this view make Christ's life sufferings as
substitutionary as His sufferings in death, though they insist that
the one would not be complete without the other. Too, the view is
normally associated with belief in a covenant of works that God is
said to have made with Adam, promising him eternal life in return
for obedience. Since Adam failed God in the covenant relationship,
Christ, the Last Adam, came to obey God's Law for human
beings; thus He gained for them eternal life by His acts of obedience
in life as well as by His death on the cross.

This view of the life sufferings of Christ bristles with biblical
and theological problems. The orthodoxy and sincerity of those
who subscribe to it are genuine and need not be questioned.
Espoused by sincere and orthodox believers, this view has serious
weaknesses that make it unacceptable.

First, the view fails to take into account that before the Fall,
Adam did not have a sin nature. Instead, it assumes that to be

rightly related to God, Adam and his posterity were required to render perfect obedience to the commands of God. As Boettner said, "We believe that the requirement for salvation now, as originally, is perfect obedience."[6]

This concept of the vicarious nature of Christ's active obedience in His life suffering rests primarily on the idea of the covenant of works. Since the supposed covenant promised eternal life for obedience and since Adam disobeyed and all his posterity in him, Christ, the Last Adam, came to accomplish what the First Adam failed to do.

The fact that Adam came from the hands of the Creator sinlessly perfect must not be overlooked. Thus the command of God to obey Him was not designed to produce eternal life in him or to relate him rightly to God. He already enjoyed a state of sinlessness and a proper relation to and right standing before his Creator. Contrary to the contention of covenant theologians, Scripture does not say that Adam would have inherited eternal life had he obeyed God. Human effort is never presented as a condition of salvation in Scripture for any dispensation; rather, the command of God to Adam was designed to demonstrate his submission to the authority of God.

Second, this view minimizes the work of Christ on the cross. This detraction from the death of Christ is also seen in the words of Berkhof.

> And finally, if Christ had suffered only the penalty imposed on man, those who shared in the fruits of His work would have been left exactly where Adam was before he fell. . . . By His active obedience, however, He carried His people beyond that point and gave them a claim to everlasting life.[7]

Thus, according to this view, the death of Christ on the cross was not the sole basis on which God provided redemption and everlasting life for humanity. If the life sufferings are viewed as substitutionary and vicarious, then the Savior's passive obedience in the shedding of His blood on the cross must be viewed as less than the total or complete means by which God through His Son atoned for sin. The blood shed at Calvary would then constitute only part of the payment for sin.

Third, the most serious weakness of this view is the stark fact that no Scripture assigns substitution to the life sufferings of Christ. On the contrary, Scripture abounds with evidence that through His substitutionary death on the cross, and through that alone, He took the place of sinners and died on their behalf (Isa. 53:6–7; Rom. 3:18, 24–25, 5:7–9; 2 Cor. 5:14–21; 1 Peter 2:24).

The defense of the vicarious nature of Christ's active obedience for His suffering in life is voluminous, but scriptural proof is conspicuous by its absence. A few passages are usually cited, however, to seek to give this view scriptural support (e.g., Matt. 3:15; 5:17–18; John 15:10; Gal. 4:4–5; Heb. 10:7–9). But no one of these passages, or any other passage, teaches or even implies that Christ's life sufferings were vicarious.

True, Christ submitted Himself to John in baptism to fulfill all righteousness (Matt. 3:15), and He came to fulfill the Law (5:17–18), but that He by these acts was being a substitute for sin is foreign to the Scriptures. He kept the Father's commandments (John 15:10), but He did not do so as an act of substitution in place of sinners. Galatians 4:4–5 does not say that Christ's obedience to the Law was vicarious; rather, it teaches that He was born under the economy of the Law in order to redeem those who were under the Law. Likewise, Hebrews 10:7–9 says nothing about Christ's life being substitutionary. In fact, the verses that follow make it clear that the one sacrifice for sin was the offering of His body (10:10–12).

THE NONATONING VIEW

Without in any way detracting from the reality or the intensity of Christ's sufferings in life or from the sinlessness of His person and His absolute obedience to the Law of God, this view denies that the active obedience of the Savior was in any way vicarious or atoning. Those who subscribe to this view hold that the substitutionary work of Christ was on the cross and only the cross. The blood He shed when He was circumcised and the blood He shed when He prayed in Gethsemane did not make an atonement for sin. Only as He became a curse as He hung on the tree and cried, "It is finished," did He become the full and final sacrifice for sin as He took the place of sinners. All the contradictions of sinners that the Savior endured in life were real and cannot be viewed lightly. But though genuine and without comparison, they were not vicarious.

What then did the Savior's suffering in life accomplish? Two things were provided: proof of His sinless character and preparation for His sacrificial death.

PROOF OF HIS SINLESS CHARACTER

Each Passover lamb was confined from the tenth day of the month until the fourteenth to prove that it was without blemish (Ex. 12:3, 6). During this time the lamb was not a sacrifice for sin, but the time was needed to demonstrate its qualifications as a sacrifice. Christ is the antitype of that Paschal lamb. His life of suffering demonstrated His eligibility as an offerer and as the offering for sin. His sufferings in life did not provide a sacrifice or even make Him eligible to offer one, but they did demonstrate His right to be the sacrifice. They proved He was eligible to offer the one eternal sacrifice for sin. Though tested often and "in all points" (Heb. 4:15 KJV), He remained the sinless, spotless Savior. Thus His sinless life of suffering was a natural and necessary part of His person and His work on the cross.

Peter discussed the relationship of the sufferings of Christ in His life and in His death. In a context dealing with the believer's responsibility to submit to human government rather than to misuse individual liberty (1 Peter 2:11–20), the example of Christ is brought to the fore (vv. 21–25). In His life "Christ also suffered for you, leaving you an example for you to follow His steps, who committed no sin, nor was any deceit found in His mouth" (vv. 21–22). When on the cross "while being reviled, He did not revile in return; while suffering, He uttered no threats, but kept entrusting Himself to Him who judges righteously" (v. 23). It was there alone that "He Himself bore our sins in His body on the cross, that we might die to sin and live to righteousness; for by His wounds you were healed" (v. 24).

The sufferings of Christ in life proved and demonstrated His impeccability. Through them all He "committed no sin, nor was any deceit found in His mouth." In the midst of all the sin and corruption about Him, His sinless person was preserved though often offended.

PREPARATION FOR HIS SACRIFICIAL DEATH

One small infraction of the Law would have disqualified Christ as the Sin-bearer. His death would then not have availed as a sacrifice. Like the priest under the Levitical system, He would have had to provide a sacrifice for Himself before He could have offered one for sinners. Furthermore, He would have had to repeat the sacrifice continually as those priests did. In fact, His sacrifice would have been no different from theirs. In contrast to the repeated sacrifices of the old economy and in contradiction of the view that His life sufferings were vicarious, Peter declared, "Christ also died for sins once for all, the just for the unjust, in order that He might bring us to God, having been put to death in the flesh, but made alive in the spirit" (3:18).

Again the Scriptures provide the relationship between the Savior's sinless life and His sacrificial death. Paul put it this way: "He made Him who knew no sin to be sin on our behalf, that we might become the righteousness of God in Him" (2 Cor. 5:21). True, He knew no sin—He obeyed the Law perfectly—but His sinless life was not the sacrifice for sin. The context of this passage bears abundant testimony to the fact that through death alone (vv. 14–15) He was made to be sin. In death He was so closely identified with sinners and the guilt of their sin that the Father viewed His death as the sin offering.

Conclusion

True to the prophecy of Isaiah, the Savior "was despised and forsaken of men, a man of sorrows, and acquainted with grief; and like one from whom men hide their face, He was despised, and we did not esteem Him. Surely our griefs He Himself bore, and our sorrows He carried" (Isa. 53:3–4; cf. Matt. 8:17). However, it was only when He was "stricken, smitten of God, and afflicted" that He was "pierced through for our transgressions" and was "crushed for our iniquities." Only in death did the Lord cause "the iniquity of us all to fall on Him" (Isa. 53:4–6).

CHAPTER 13

The Death of Christ

S. Lewis Johnson Jr.

If there is one thing about the death of Jesus Christ that is prominent, it is this: It was a very strange exodus. In some memorable words Helmut Thielecke stated that Jesus did not die a martyr's death, like radiant Stephen under a hail of stones, nor like the noble Socrates in "scornfully superior resignation." Rather, His dying was with "a helpless despairing cry in the most terrible isolation."[1]

How may such a death be explained? Why do Christians revere it and Him so? When referring to his fruitful ministry in their city, Paul reminded the Corinthians, "For I determined to know nothing among you except Jesus Christ, and Him crucified"[2] (1 Cor. 2:2). And, when nearing the end of his sustained spiritual and emotional appeal in the epistle to the Galatians, the apostle cried out, "But may it never be that I should boast, except in the cross of our Lord Jesus Christ, through which the world has been crucified to me, and I to the world" (Gal. 6:14). It is evident that Paul regarded the death of Jesus Christ as a matter of the most signal importance. He was followed in this by Martin Luther, who wrote somewhere, "theologia crucis—theologia lucis" (The theology of the cross— the theology of light). And not surprisingly, even non-Christians have sensed that the Cross of Christ has a certain paramount relevance to the human story. The Unitarian Sir John Bowring, in a hymn Christians often sing, "In the Cross of Christ," wrote:

> In the cross of Christ I glory,
> Towering o'er the wrecks of time;
> All the light of sacred story
> Gathers round its head sublime.

A satisfying solution to the enigma of this strange event is to be found in that helpless, despairing shriek the Savior uttered on Mount Golgotha. And it seems likely that the early church also thought this cry of dereliction one of His most trenchant utterances.

113

The evidence for this is to be found in the seven utterances of the dying Lord. Three of the utterances—the first, second, and seventh—are found only in Luke 23, while three others—the third, fifth, and sixth—are found only in John 19. The central utterance, the fourth, the cry of dereliction, "My God, My God, why hast Thou forsaken Me?" is found in both Matthew and Mark (Matt. 27:46; Mark 15:34). Since Matthew and Mark were written before Luke and John, it is evident that this cry of desolation was the only dying utterance of Jesus Christ the early church had in written form for some time. It is as if they thought that cry set forth the preeminent revelation, the supreme doctrine, the foremost lesson of the Savior's death. Without question this pristine judgment was eminently correct.

The Circumstances of the Fourth Utterance From the Cross (Matt. 27:45)

THE PLACE OF THE UTTERANCE

Matthew stated that Jesus was brought to a skull-shaped mound known as Golgotha, or "the Skull"[3] (27:33). Many Bible scholars feel that Gordon's Calvary, located to the north of the city and outside the ancient walls, is likely the place of the Crucifixion. Others believe that the Church of the Holy Sepulchre, located in the city, was the place of His sacrifice and burial. The Old Testament typology, which put the offering of the bullock of the sin offering outside the camp of Israel (cf. Lev. 4:12), would seem to be more compatible with the Garden Tomb, as Gordon's Calvary is now known.

THE TIME OF THE UTTERANCE

Since the Lord was placed upon the cross at nine o'clock in the morning (Mark 15:25) and remained there until three in the afternoon, He was in agony for six hours.

THE ATMOSPHERE OF THE UTTERANCE

As often seen in the critical events of Jesus' life, the natural or physical circumstances seem intentionally to reflect the spiritual import of the events. A star, symbol of light from heaven, appeared at the birth of the One who came from above. An undying angel is prominent in the accounts of the Resurrection. And so here the darkness reflects the spiritual significance of the Crucifixion. In fact, the cry gives the meaning of the darkness, and the darkness elucidates the significance of the cry. It is manifest that the darkness, often figurative of sin and judgment in the Bible, clearly indicated that Jesus' death had an intimate connection with the curse of sin.

The Invocation in the Fourth Utterance From the Cross (Matt. 27:46a)

When one approaches the study of passages pertaining to the Atonement, two extremes must be avoided. On the one hand some wrongly contend that little or nothing at all can be known about the Atonement, since it is a mystery. Sometimes a verse is cited to substantiate this view, such as 1 Corinthians 13:12: "For now we see in a mirror dimly, but then face to face; now I know in part, but then I shall know fully just as I also have been fully known." On the other hand others confidently claim to be able to elucidate thoroughly the intricacies of the theology of the Atonement. They feel there is no mystery whatsoever. It is all bound up in the penal substitutionary theory of the Atonement reflected in verses like Isaiah 53:6: "All of us like sheep have gone astray, each of us has turned to his own way; but the LORD has caused the iniquity of us all to fall on Him."

Of course any acceptable theory of the Atonement must include within it the genuine features of the penal substitutionary theory. Yet does this theory exhaust the significance of His sublime redemptive work? Probably not. In fact it seems that when the Cross is pondered most deeply and earnestly, it is inevitable that one should still cry out with Paul, "Oh, the depth of the riches both of the wisdom and knowledge of God! How unsearchable are His judgments and unfathomable His ways" (Rom. 11:33). Some things can be known and some things cannot be known about the death of the Son of God.

In the suffering Savior's fourth utterance from the cross, He cried out, "Eli, Eli[4] lama sabachthani," which means, "My God, My God, why has Thou forsaken Me?" It is significant that He addressed the Father as "My God, My God." Its significance is seen in view of the terms used in the other utterances from the cross and in the terms in the Lord's prayers elsewhere.

In His first utterance Jesus said, "Father, forgive them; for they do not know what they are doing" (Luke 23:34). In the seventh utterance He said, "Father, into Thy hands I commit My spirit"

(23:46). In His opening and closing words He said, "Father," but in the central utterance, the fourth, He said, "My God, My God."

Jeremias has pointed out several significant facts related to Jesus' language when He spoke to God the Father.[5] First, He spoke of God as "Father" in the Gospels about 170 times. And yet at the time of Jesus' ministry, Palestinian Judaism was reluctant to speak of God as Father. Second, though no one has produced a single instance in which God was addressed as "my Father" by an individual, Jesus, however, spoke of God as "My Father." He almost always used those words in His prayers—for a total of twenty-one times. There is only one instance in which Jesus addressed God without the title "My Father." That occasion, of course, was His fourth utterance from the cross. There can be only one explanation: He regarded His relationship to God at this precise moment as being a judicial one not a paternal one. In other words, He saw Himself primarily as a human being before God, not as the eternal Son before His Father.

Yet it must not be overlooked that He addressed God as "My God, My God." As Pink has written, "It was a cry of distress but not of distrust."[6] Spurgeon agreed, for he said about this cry, "It shows manhood in its weakness, but not manhood in revolt."[7] Even in the midst of the awful desolation of divine judgment the trust of the perfect human never wavered. He was sifted and found to be all wheat, and in this He stands out in "majestic dissimilarity"[8] from all mere humans. In trials and tragedies people often turn to others rather than to God, and they cry out in unbelieving accents, "In the light of this, can there be a God?" or, "If there is a God, why does He permit this?" However, Jesus turned to His God and, with the words of Holy Scripture given Him by God, offered His petition to the One who seemed to have forsaken and forgotten Him. He implicated His God in His dereliction and in so doing He gained His release. Soon He was saying, "Father, into Thy hands I commit My spirit."

The Interrogation in the Fourth Utterance From the Cross (Matt. 27:46b)

The answer to the question "Why hast Thou forsaken Me?" involves one in the continuing discussion of the Atonement. There are three well-known theological answers to the question of Christ's atonement. The first is the theory of Peter Abelard, best known as the subjective, or moral influence, view. The Cross reveals the love of God and produces faith and love in believers, which is the basis of the forgiveness of sins. This theory finds a measure of support from 1 Peter 2:21: "For you have been called for this purpose, since Christ also suffered for you, leaving you an example for you to follow in His steps." This, however, has nothing to do with the forgiveness of sins, and this is the weakness of Abelard's view.

A second answer is the theory that Aulén called "the 'classic idea' of the atonement."[9] This view, probably first suggested by Ignatius, sees the Atonement as a conflict between God and Satan with humankind in the middle. Christ defeated Satan on the cross by dying for sin and thus freed human beings from bondage to Satan, who held humankind captive as a result of sin. The Bible does place emphasis on this view. For example John wrote, "The Son of God appeared for this purpose, that He might destroy the works of the devil" (1 John 3:8; cf. Col. 2:15; Heb. 2:14–15). And furthermore it is prominent in the first promise of redemption in the Bible, the *protoevangelium* of Genesis 3:15 (the penal satisfaction theory is also suggested in Gen. 15:20–21). It is not saying too much to contend that the basis of Christ's atonement is the vindication of God in His victory over sin and Satan. But this view does not include all there is to say about atonement.

A third answer was that of Anselm of Canterbury, the so-called objective, or satisfaction, view. In his famous *Cur Deus Homo,* he pointed out that Christ made satisfaction to God for human sin by offering Himself as a substitutionary sacrifice for human beings. Anselm's view finds expression in many biblical passages and is probably the most popular view among evangelicals. Jesus set forth this view in these words: "For even the Son of Man did not come to be served, but to serve, and to give His life a ransom for many" (Mark 10:45; cf. Rom 3:24–25). While there is a measure of truth in each theory (and quite a bit of error in Abelard's), and while it is honest also to admit that no one theory does full justice to the transcendent greatness of the atonement of Christ, yet a biblical theory of the Atonement must stress the features of Anselm's view. A solution to the meaning of Jesus' cry of desolation is to be found along the lines of Anselm's penal satisfaction theory.

THE INTERROGATION: "WHY?"

Jesus' question did not stem from unbelief. Rather it was a request on the level of His genuine humanity for more information regarding the experience of the desolate judicial separation from God the Father that He was undergoing for humankind's sins. It represented one of the many features of the "perfection" of the incomparable Redeemer (Mark 13:32; Luke 2:40, 52; Heb. 2:10; 5:7–10).

THE EXPLANATION: "FORSAKEN"

The word *forsaken* is the clue to the meaning of the Cross. It expresses in the most direct and forthright manner the separation of God the Father from Jesus of Nazareth. That separation is spiritual death, and it represents the penalty for sin that Jesus paid. That this separation must have been substitutionary, that is, for others, is indicated by answers to the following questions:

Would a loving God forsake the only good human being who ever lived (Matt. 3:17; Ps. 37:25)? The answer to that question must be no. Then Jesus, the only good human being who ever lived, must have been forsaken for others.

Would a loving God injure the only innocent human being who ever lived? The answer must be the same, with the same conclusion. There is no question that this involves an offense to human self-righteousness, but Cranfield addresses this point.

> Various attempts have been made to get rid of its offence: e.g., it has been suggested that Jesus had the whole psalm [Ps. 22] in mind and that therefore the saying was really an expression of faith cut short by physical weakness which prevented him from quoting more; or that Jesus felt forsaken but was not really forsaken. But such softening explanations are unsatisfactory. Rather is the cry to be understood in the light of Mark 14:36, 2 Cor. 5:21, Gal. 3:13. The burden of the world's sin, his complete self-identification with sinners, involved not merely a felt, but a real, abandonment by his Father. It is in the cry of dereliction that the full horror of man's sin stands revealed. But the cry also marks the lowest depth of the hiddenness of the Son of God—and so the triumphant τετέλεσται ["It is finished"] of John 19:30 is, paradoxically, its true interpretation. When this depth had been reached, the victory had been won."[10]

In view of this it is difficult to understand how a leading Protestant can write, in the light of the clear teaching of the New Testament (Gal. 3:13; 2 Cor. 5:21), "If God dealt with Him as if He were a sinner and the greatest sinner, then we must say of God (as a cynical Frenchman did say of God of these penal theologies): 'Your God is my devil.'"[11] True to the Scriptures was the statement James S. Stewart of the University of Edinburgh made in the Stone Lectures at Princeton Theological Seminary:

"This is the heart of the atonement: Jesus Christ stood in the stead of others."[12]

THE NECESSITY OF SUBSTITUTION

The necessity for substitution in the Atonement is bound up in the demands of the holy God, who must have His righteousness and justice satisfied in order to be legally free to extend His love to the lost. The good pleasure of God to save sinners, founded in His love and justice, has expressed itself in the sacrificial work of Jesus Christ. As Paul put it, "He made Him who knew no sin to be sin on our behalf, that we might become the righteousness of God in Him" (2 Cor. 5:21). And "Christ redeemed us from the curse of the Law, having become a curse for us—for it is written, 'Cursed is everyone who hangs on a tree'" (Gal. 3:13).

The cry of dereliction, then, was occasioned by the atonement. It vividly expressed the unknown sufferings of the vicarious Sufferer as He bore the guilt and penalty of sin for sinners at the hands of a loving but holy God. As a stanza from a hymn puts it,

> He pleads His passion on the tree,
> He shows Himself to God for me.

This truth was expressed in the Old Testament in various ways, including the sin offering of Leviticus, the ordinance governing the cleansing of the leper, the experience of the brazen serpent, and others. It is found implicitly in the very psalm Jesus cited. The psalmist, after uttering his complaint in Psalm 22:1–2, then cried out, "Yet Thou art holy, O Thou who art enthroned upon the praises of Israel" (v. 3). That pointed clause, "Yet Thou art holy," vividly denotes the necessity of atonement. And since this was the only way redemption could be secured, God took the initiative and carried it out, so that the prophet's words are wonderfully true, "But the LORD was pleased to crush Him" (Isa. 53:10).

The Triumphant Conclusion

If the Savior was perplexed, it was only for a moment, because He soon was heard shouting, "It is finished!" (John 19:30) and commending His spirit to the Father (Luke 23:46). And now as a direct result of Jesus' having been forsaken on Golgotha, the author of Hebrews stated confidently that Jesus confirmed the Old Testament promise, "I will never desert you, nor will I ever forsake you" (Heb. 13:5).

The fourth utterance from the cross, then, gives a satisfying rationale for the comprehension of the Cross and the Atonement. It enables believers to understand the compelling appeal it had for the first Christians.

> Well might the sun in darkness hide
> And shut his glory in,
> When Christ, the Mighty Maker, died
> For man the creature's sin.
>
> —Isaac Watts

The picture in this august incident on the cross contains implicitly a solemn warning. The death He died opens a window on the terrible consequence of eternal death. If it produced from Him, the only sinless human being, this agonizing cry in the midst of such utter desolation, what must it portend for those who shall for their own sin fully and justly suffer what Paul called, "eternal destruction, away from the presence of the Lord" (2 Thess. 1:9)?

This utterance from the cross helps believers understand better the apostle's majestic utterance, "Great is the mystery of godliness" (1 Tim. 3:16). Who can fully comprehend the Cross? Yet who, touched by God's Spirit, can fail to appreciate it? Henry C. Mabie, missionary diplomat and author of several books on the Cross, used to tell of the Gospel being preached to a South African tribe. The chief of the tribe listened intently and then asked that the missionary repeat the story of the cross. While the missionary was again lifting up his Savior, the chief rushed forward, crying, "Hold on! Hold on! Take Jesus Christ down from the cross. Take Him down, I say. Jesus Christ does not belong on that cross—I belong on that cross."

Luther was right: The theology of the Cross is the theology of light.

> In perfect love He dies;
> For me He dies, for me.
> O all-atoning sacrifice,
> I cling by faith to Thee.

CHAPTER 14

The Resurrection and Ascension of Christ

Edward Robinson

The great fact of the resurrection of Jesus Christ from the dead, by which He "was declared the Son of God with power" (Rom. 1:4) and in which God fulfilled "the good news of the promise made to the fathers" (Acts 13:32–33), stands out everywhere prominently on the pages of the New Testament as one of the cardinal doctrines of the Christian faith and the earnest of each believer's future resurrection. The burden of Paul's preaching was "that Christ died for our sins according to the Scriptures, and that He was buried, and that He was raised on the third day according to the Scriptures" (1 Cor. 15:3–4). The apostle strongly affirmed that "if Christ has not been raised, then our preaching is vain, your faith also is vain. Moreover we are even found to be false witnesses of God, because we witnessed against God that He raised Christ, whom He did not raise, if in fact the dead are not raised" (15:14–15).

Yet with all this certainty as to the great fact itself, it is also true that in respect to the circumstances connected with this important event, difficulties are presented to the mind even of the sincere inquirer by the different ways in which the four Evangelists have recorded these circumstances. Not that the facts recorded by them are in a single instance inconsistent with each other, but the main difficulty lies in harmonizing the four accounts in such a way as to bring out a full and complete order and sequence of the events, so natural and consistent as to commend itself to the understanding of all. To do this in any good degree, something of a hypothesis must be introduced. Certain things must be assumed as links, to connect facts otherwise isolated. Hardly any two interpreters have followed precisely the same track in harmonizing the four narratives of the sacred writers. Also, more of these apparent difficulties are found in this short section of the gospel history than in almost all the rest.

One fruitful source of apparent or alleged difficulty is to assume that each Evangelist would naturally present an account of all the circumstances accompanying and following the Lord's resurrection. If this is granted, there would indeed be obstacles next to insurmountable in the way of harmonizing the various narratives, to say nothing of the entire incompatibility of such a view with any and every idea of inspiration on the part of the sacred penmen. For this reason, apparently, it has been a favorite position with the opponents of inspiration and of Christianity in general to represent the Evangelists as following different and uncertain traditions and each as having recorded all that he knew, and then to press the difficulties and discrepancies arising from this hypothesis as sufficient not only to disprove inspiration, but also to overthrow the credibility of the gospel records.

Yet to show that this position is wholly untenable, it is necessary simply to inspect the sacred pages. The writers of the Gospels, acting under the guidance of the Spirit of God, did not record all the deeds and sayings of the Lord. Each has selected those appropriate for the specific object he had in view. Also the first three Evangelists recorded, for the most part, only the acts and discourses of Jesus in Galilee and wrote solely of one visit to Jerusalem, on the occasion of His last Passover, while John described chiefly His visits and teachings at or near the holy city. Similarly, in their narratives of the scenes of the resurrection each writer followed his own method, recording what pertained to his own particular purpose or experience. Thus Matthew spoke only of a single appearance of the risen Lord at Jerusalem, namely, to the women, which is not referred to by any of the other Evangelists, while he mentions but one in Galilee. Mark enumerated three other appearances at Jerusalem but said nothing of Galilee, though he recorded the charge of the angel to the disciples to go to Galilee. Luke also spoke of three appearances (one of them different) at Jerusalem, but he too included not a word of Galilee. John reported likewise three appearances at Jerusalem (one of them still different) and described another interview with the disciples on the shores of the Lake of Tiberias. And what is even perhaps more remarkable, only Mark and Luke made any allusion whatever to the Lord's ascension.

The purpose of this study is not to discuss every cavil that the acuteness of unbelief may raise in regard to this portion of the gospel records but rather to suggest and elucidate what seems to be the natural order of the events and to dwell only on those difficulties that present themselves to the mind of the sincere inquirer after truth. These arise from the brevity of the sacred writers, who in their narration of facts have not seen fit to introduce all the minor connecting circumstances, without which present-day readers, distanced in time, are unable to gain a complete and connected view of the whole.

In perusing the following pages, readers will find it advantageous to have before them a Greek harmony of the four gospels or at least to make constant reference to their Greek Testaments.

The Time of the Resurrection
(Matthew 28:1–2; Mark 16:2, 9; Luke 24:1; John 20:1)

That the resurrection of the Lord took place before full daylight on the first day of the week follows from the unanimous testimony of the Evangelists regarding the visit of the women to the sepulcher. But the exact time He rose is nowhere specified. According to the Jewish mode of reckoning, the Sabbath ended and the next day began at sunset, so that had the Resurrection occurred even before midnight, it would still have been on the first day of the week and on the third day after the Lord's burial. An earthquake had occurred and the stone had been rolled away before the arrival of the women, and so far as the immediate narrative is concerned, there is nothing to show that all this might not have happened some hours earlier. Yet the words of Mark render it certain that there could have been no great interval between these events and the arrival of the women, since Mark affirmed in 16:9 that Jesus "had risen early [πρωΐ] on the first day of the week," and in verse 2, he reported that the women went out very early (λίαν πρωΐ). While the women returned to the city, the guards no doubt were on their way to inform the chief priests what happened (Matt. 28:11). After having been terrified by the earthquake and the appearance of an angel, they would hardly have waited any longer before sending information to their employers. The body of Jesus had therefore probably lain in the tomb not less than about thirty-six hours.

The Holy Spirit has not seen fit to disclose the actual scene of the Resurrection. The circumstances of that awful moment, so fraught with importance to angels and humans, remain shrouded in darkness. The sacred writers have narrated only what they saw after the sepulcher was empty. When Jesus called Lazarus

forth out of his tomb, "he who had died came forth, bound hand
and foot with wrappings; and his face was wrapped around with
a cloth" (John 11:44). But when the Lord Himself arose, no
voice of power thus called Him forth, bound hand and foot. In
the dark recesses of the sepulcher, through almighty power,
His spirit revived, unseen and unknown to every mortal eye.
Angels ministered to Him and opened before Him the door of
the tomb. Here was no struggle, no agony, no confused haste,
but on the contrary "the linen wrappings [were] lying there, and
the face-cloth, which had been on His head [was] not lying with
the linen wrappings, but [was] rolled up in a place by itself"
(John 20:6–7). Since His own garments had been parted by lot
among the soldiers, who furnished the risen Lord with raiment?
Who stanched the wound in His side, which was probably
intended to pierce His heart? Faith answers these and all such
questions without difficulty: To that Omnipotence that raised
Him from the dead, to the angels who thus attended on Him in
the Resurrection, it would be a light thing indeed to minister to
these physical needs.

The Women Visit the Sepulcher
(Matthew 28:1–8; Mark 16:1–8; Luke 24:1–11; John 20:1–2)

The first notices of the Lord's resurrection are connected with
the visit of the women to the sepulcher on the morning of the first
day of the week. According to Luke the women who had stood by
the cross went home and rested during the Sabbath (23:56); Mark
added that after the Sabbath was ended, that is, after sunset and
during the evening, they prepared spices for embalming Him.
They were either not aware of the previous embalming by Joseph
and Nicodemus or else they also wished to show their respect and
affection to their Lord by completing more perfectly what before
had been done in haste (John 19:40–42).

THE TIME

All four Evangelists stated that the women went out very early
to the sepulcher. Matthew's expression is "as it began to dawn."
Mark's words "very early" are less definite but are appropriate to
denote the same point of time (cf. "in the early morning," Mark
1:35). Luke has the more poetic term of "early dawn." John's
language is also definite: "early . . . while it was still dark." All
these expressions fix the time at what is called early dawn, or

early twilight, after the break of day but while the light is yet struggling with darkness.

Thus far there is no difficulty, and none would ever arise had not Mark added the phrase ἀνατείλαντος τοῦ ἡλίου, which must be translated, "the sun being risen," or "when the sun had risen." At first these words seem to be in direct variance both with the words "very early" by Mark himself and with the language of the other Evangelists. Interpreters have attempted to harmonize this apparent discrepancy in one of three ways.

1. Some say the words "very early" refer to the time when the women set off from their homes. However, this would include a longer interval of time than could well have been occupied in going from the city to the sepulcher, unless they loitered by the way, which is not likely. Besides, the language of Luke and John, and most naturally that of Matthew, seems to relate the "early dawn" to the *arrival* of the women at the place. Also in Mark the two phrases, λίαν πρωΐ ανδ ἀνατείλαντος τοῦ ἡλίου both qualify the clause ἔρχονται ἐπὶ τὸ μνημεῖον (coming to the sepulcher), one just as much as the other. It therefore seems impossible to say they refer to different points of time.

2. The Greek Codex Bezae has ἀνατέλλοντας, a present participle, "rising," and a few manuscripts insert ἔτι (still) before the aorist participle ἀνατείλαντος. However, the whole weight of textual authority is the other way, and no editor of the New Testament has ever ventured to adopt either of these readings. Both are regarded as obviously mere expedients to get rid of the difficulty. But they do not remove the problem because the insertion of ἔτι is incompatible with the aorist form of the verb, while the present ἀνατέλλοντος, so far as it marks only the rising of the sun above the horizon, is itself just as inconsistent with the preceding "early dawn." It matters very little here whether the sun was in the act of rising or had already just risen.

3. Hengstenberg, J. D. Michaelis, and others have suggested that the idea of sunrise is a relative one. The sun is already risen, when as yet it is not visible in the heavens, for the morning dawn proceeds from it. This may contain the germ of the true solution.

Since Mark first specified the point of time by λίαν πρωΐ, a phrase sufficiently definite in itself and supported by all the other Evangelists, one must conclude that when Mark added ἀνατείλαντος τοῦ ἡλίου, he did not mean to contradict himself. Instead he used this latter phrase in a broader and less definite sense. As the sun is the source of light and of the day and as its earliest rays produce the contrast between darkness and light, between night and dawn, so the term *sunrising* might easily be a metonymy of cause for effect, used for the sun's earlier interval when its rays, still struggling with darkness, do nevertheless usher in the day.

Such a popular usage prevailed among the Hebrews. Zebul told Abimelech to lie in wait with his people in the field during the night. Then he added, "And it shall come about in the morning, as soon as the sun is up, that you shall rise early and rush upon the city" (Judg. 9:33). The Septuagint has the same use of the aorist and the same juxtaposition of πρωΐ and ἅμα τῷ ἀνατεῖλαι τὸν ἥλιον. Yet one cannot for a moment suppose that Abimelech was to wait until the sun actually appeared above the horizon before he made his attack. Speaking of young lions that by night roar after their prey, the psalmist added, "When the sun rises they withdraw, and lie down in their dens" (Ps. 104:22). Again the Septuagint has the aorist ἀνέτειλεν ὁ ἥλιος. But wild animals do not wait for the actual appearance of the sun before they shrink away to their lairs; the break of day, the dawning light, is the signal for their retreat. (Also see the Septuagint of 2 Sam. 23:4 and 2 Kings 3:22.) In all these passages the language parallels that of Mark; they serve to illustrate the principle that the rising of the sun is used in a popular sense as equivalent to the rising of the day or "early dawn."

THE NUMBER OF THE WOMEN

Matthew mentioned Mary Magdalene and the other Mary (Matt. 28:1). Mark referred to Mary Magdalene, Mary the mother of James, and Salome (Mark 16:1). Luke wrote of Mary Magdalene, Joanna, Mary the mother of James, and others with them (Luke 24:10). John spoke of Mary Magdalene alone and said nothing of any other (John 20:1). The first three Evangelists are in accord with respect to the two Marys but no further, while John differed from them all. Is there a discrepancy here?

No. Though John, in narrating circumstances with which he was personally connected, saw fit to mention only Mary Magdalene, it does not at all follow that others were not present. Nor did Matthew, writing only of the two Marys, mean to exclude the presence of others. Indeed the very words John put into the mouth of Mary Magdalene (οὐκ οἴδαμεν, "we do not know," John 20:2) presuppose the fact that others had gone with her to the tomb.

That there was something with respect to Mary Magdalene that gave her a peculiar prominence in these transactions may be inferred from the fact that not only did John mention her alone, but also the other Evangelists named her first.

This parallels that of the demoniacs of Gadara and the blind men at Jericho; in both cases Matthew wrote of two persons, while Mark and Luke mentioned only one (Matt. 8:28; 20:30; Mark 5:2; 10:46; Luke 8:27; 18:35). Something peculiar in the station or character of one of the persons rendered him in each case more prominent and led the other two Evangelists to speak of him particularly. But their language was not exclusive nor is there in it anything that contradicts the statements of Matthew.

In 1824 Marquis de Lafayette, friend of George Washington, revisited the United States. Everywhere he was received with joyous welcome, and his progress through the country resembled a public triumph. Cities and states and the Congress of the nation vied with each other in the honors and pageants showered on the nation's guest. Historians will record these events as a noble incident in the life of a public man. But if other writers, entering more fully into detail, were to narrate this visit as made not by Lafayette alone but by Lafayette and his son and that both shared in the honors and hospitalities so lavishly proffered, would there be any contradiction between the statements of the two classes of writers? Or should still another class relate the same general facts as having occurred in respect to three persons, Lafayette, his son, and his secretary, would there even then arise any contradiction? Certainly no one would even think of bringing such a charge.

THE ARRIVAL AT THE SEPULCHER

According to Mark, Luke, and John, the women, on reaching the tomb, found the great stone with which it had been closed already rolled away. Matthew, on the other hand, after narrating that the women went out to see the sepulcher, proceeded to mention the earthquake, the descent of the angel, his rolling away the stone and sitting on it, and the terror of the watch, as if all these things took place in the presence of the women. Such at least is the usual force of ἰδού. The angel too (Matt. 28:5) addressed the women as if he were still sitting on the stone that had been rolled away.

The apparent discrepancy, if any, arises simply from Matthew's brevity in omitting to state in full what his own narrative presupposes. According to verse 6, Christ was already risen, and therefore the earthquake and its accompaniments must have taken place earlier, to which the sacred writer returned in his narration. And though Matthew did not say the women entered the sepulcher, yet in verse 8 he spoke of them going out of it (ἐξελθοῦσαι) so that their interview with the angel took place not outside the sepulcher but in it, as narrated by the other Evangelists. When therefore the angel said to them, "Come, see the place where He was lying" (v. 6), this was not spoken outside the tomb to induce them to enter but within the sepulcher, just as in Mark 16:6.

THE VISION OF ANGELS IN THE SEPULCHER

Of this John wrote nothing. Matthew and Mark referred to one angel; Luke referred to two. Mark said he was sitting; Luke spoke of them as standing (ἐπέστησαν). This difference in respect to numbers is parallel to the case of the women. The other alleged difficulty as to the position of the angels also vanishes when ἐπέστησαν in Luke 24:4 is understood in its appropriate and acknowledged meaning "to appear suddenly" without reference to its etymology.

Some diversity also exists in the language addressed to the women by the angels. Matthew and Mark recorded the angels' charge to tell the disciples to depart into Galilee (Matt. 28:7; Mark 16:7). In Luke this is not referred to, but the women were reminded of the Lord's declaration that He would rise again on the third day. Neither of the Evangelists here professed to report all that was said by the angels, and so there is no room for contradiction.

The Women Return to the City and the Lord's First Appearance (Matthew 28:7–10; Mark 16:8; Luke 24:9–11; John 20:1–2)

John, speaking only of Mary Magdalene, said that having seen that the stone was taken away from the sepulcher, she went in haste to tell Peter and John. He said nothing of her having seen the angels nor of her having entered the sepulcher. The other Evangelists, speaking of the women generally, related that they entered the tomb, saw the angels, and then returned into the city. On their way Jesus met them. They recognized Him, fell at and embraced His feet, and received His charge to the disciples. Was Mary Magdalene now with the other women? Or did she enter the city by another way? Or had she left the sepulcher before the others?

It is evident that Mary Magdalene was not with the other women when Jesus met them. Her language to Peter and John forbids the supposition that she had already seen the Lord: "They have taken away the Lord out of the sepulcher, and we know not where they have laid Him" (John 20:2). She therefore must have entered the city by another path and gate or else she left the sepulcher before the others or possibly both these positions may be true. She bore her tidings expressly to Peter and John, who would seem to have lodged by themselves in a different quarter of the city, while the other women went apparently to the rest of the disciples. But this supposition of a different route is essential only if it is assumed that she left the tomb with the other women.

That, however, she actually departed from the sepulcher before her companions would seem more probable for several reasons. (a) She spoke to Peter and John only of the absence of the Lord's body. (b) She said nothing in this connection of a vision of angels. (c) When, after returning again to the tomb, she saw the angels, it was evidently for the first time. (d) She repeated to them that the cause of her grief was her complaint about the disappearance of the body (John 20:12–13). She may have turned back from the tomb without entering it at all, as soon as she saw that it was open. She may have inferred from the removal of the stone that the sepulcher had been rifled. Or she may first have entered with the others when, according to Luke, "they did not find the body of the Lord Jesus" and "were perplexed about this" (Luke 24:3–4) before the angels became visible to them. The latter supposition seems best.

As the other women ran to tell His disciples, "behold, Jesus met them and greeted them. And they came up and took hold of His feet and worshiped Him. Then Jesus said to them, 'Do not be afraid; go and take word to My brethren to leave for Galilee, and there they shall see Me'" (Matt. 28:9–10). The women had left the sepulcher "with fear and great joy" (v. 8) after the declaration of the angels that Christ was risen, or, as Mark put it, "trembling and astonishment had gripped them" (Mark 16:8). Jesus met them with words of gentleness to quiet their terrors: "Do not be afraid." He permitted them to approach and embrace His feet, and to express their joy and homage. He reiterated the message of the angels regarding to His "brethren," the eleven disciples (Matt. 28:10).

This appearance and interview is narrated only by Matthew; none of the other Evangelists give any hint of it. But Matthew stopped short. Mark simply related that the women fled from the tomb; "they said nothing to anyone, for they were afraid" (Mark 16:8). This of course can only mean that on their way to the city they spoke to no one about what they had seen, for the very charge of the angels, which they went to fulfill, was that they should "go, tell His disciples" (v. 7). Luke narrated more fully that "they returned from the tomb and reported all these things to the eleven, and to all the rest. . . . And these words appeared to them as nonsense, and they could not believe them" (Luke 24:9, 11). Perhaps one reason the other Evangelists omitted mentioning this appearance of the Lord is that the disciples disbelieved the report of the women that they had seen Jesus. Later they also disbelieved Mary Magdalene's report (Mark 16:11). They were ready, it would seem, to admit the testimony of the women about the absence of the body and their vision of the angels but not their testimony about the resurrection of Jesus and His appearance to them (Luke 24:21–24). And later when the Eleven had become convinced by the testimony of their own senses, those first two appearances to the women became of less importance and were less regarded. Hence the silence of all three Evangelists as to the one, of two writers as to the other, and of Paul as to both (1 Cor. 15:5).

Peter and John Visit the Sepulcher and Jesus Appears to Mary Magdalene
(Mark 16:9–11; Luke 24:12; John 20:3–18)

The full account of these two events is given solely by John. Matthew said nothing of either events, Luke merely mentioned in general that Peter, on the report of the women, went to the tomb, while Mark spoke only of the Lord's appearance to Mary Magdalene, which he seems to represent as His first appearance.

According to John's account Peter and the beloved disciple, excited by the tidings of Mary Magdalene that the Lord's body had been taken away, hurried to the tomb. They ran; John outran Peter, arrived first at the tomb, and, stooping down, saw the grave-clothes but did not enter. The other women were no longer at the tomb nor had the disciples met them on the way. Peter then came up, entered the tomb, and saw the graveclothes lying and the napkin that was about His head not lying with the rest but wrapped together in a place by itself. John then entered the sepulcher, "and he saw, and believed" (John 20:8).

What was it that John believed? Was it the report of Mary Magdalene that the body had been removed? He could have believed her report at the moment he stooped down and looked into the tomb without having entered. His belief must have been of something more and greater. The graveclothes lying orderly in their place and the napkin folded together by itself made it evident that the sepulcher had not been rifled nor the body stolen by violent hands. These garments and spices would have been of more value to thieves than merely a naked corpse; at least, they would not have taken the trouble to fold them together. The same circumstances showed also that the body had not been removed by friends, for they would not have left the graveclothes behind. All these considerations produced in the mind of John the germ of a belief that Jesus was risen from the dead. John believed (ἐπίστευσε) because he saw, "for [γάρ] as yet they did not understand the Scripture" (v. 9). He now began more fully to recall and understand the Lord's repeated declaration that He was to rise on the third day (e.g., Matt. 16:21; 17:23; Luke 9:22; 24:6–7), a declaration on which the Jews had already acted in posting guards at the tomb (Matt. 27:63–66). In this way the difficulty that is sometimes expressed that there is no connection between John 20:8 and 20:9 disappears, for the word ἐπίστευσε is left in the signification of a religious belief, its usual meaning in John's gospel. In this chapter it refers more particularly to a belief in the Lord's resurrection (vv. 8, 25, 27, 29). To understand it in verse 8 as simply a belief in the tidings of Mary Magdalene, without some definite adjunct to show that it is to be thus limited, would be a departure from the customary usage of the word by John.

The two disciples then went to their homes. Mary Magdalene, who had followed them back to the sepulcher, remained, weeping. While she wept, she too, like John, "stooped and looked into the tomb; and she beheld two angels in white sitting, one at the head, and the other at the feet, where the body of Jesus had been lying" (John 20:11–12). To their question as to why she wept, her reply was the same report she had given to the two disciples: "Because they have taken away my Lord, and I do not know where they have laid Him" (v. 13). Of these angels nothing further is known. This narrative seems to show clearly that Mary had not before seen the angels and also that she had not before been told that Jesus was risen. Otherwise she was in a most unaccountably obtuse and unbelieving frame of mind, which seems contrary to fact. If she had earlier informed the two disciples of a vision of angels and of Christ's resurrection, it is difficult to see why John would fail to mention this circumstance, so important and so personal to himself.

After replying to the angels, Mary turned herself about and saw
a person standing near, whom she took to be the keeper of the
garden. He too inquired why she wept. Her reply was the same as
before, except that she, not unnaturally, supposed him to have
been engaged in removing the body, which she wanted to recover.
He simply uttered in reply, in well-known tones, the name "Mary!"
and the whole truth flashed on her soul. Doubt was dispelled, and
faith triumphed. She exclaimed, "Rabboni!" that is, "My dearest
Master!" and apparently, like the other women (Matt. 28:9), she
fell at His feet to embrace and worship Him. This Jesus forbade
her to do, in these remarkable words: "Stop clinging to Me [μή
μου ἅπτου], for I have not yet ascended to the Father; but go to
My brethren, and say to them, 'I ascend to My Father and your
Father, and My God and your God'" (John 20:17).

At first it is difficult to see why Jesus told Mary Magdalene not
to touch Him, when He had just before permitted the other women
to hold Him by the feet and when also the same evening He told
His disciples to touch and see Him for themselves, while showing
them His hands and His feet. Interpreters have attempted to solve
this difficulty in various ways.

First, Chrysostom and Augustine take ἅπτου figuratively, giving
the verse this sense: "Regard not this my earthly manifestation,
for I am yet to be glorified in heaven." This is not, in itself,
inappropriate, and is followed by Calvin, Beza, Grotius, and
others. But this use of ἅπτου is exceedingly harsh and without
example in Greek nor is the subsequent οὔπω ἀναβέβηκα (I have
not yet ascended) compatible with such an explanation.

Second, others suppose Mary to have been uncertain whether
what she saw was a real body or a mere illusion, and she wished to
touch Jesus to decide this point. This Jesus forbade, asserting that
He was yet in His earthly body, which would be changed at His
ascension into a glorified body. But this hypothesis does not touch
the difficulty stated above, for on this supposition why would the
Lord not have given the same prohibition in the case of the other
women and the disciples? Besides, such an unwillingness to be
touched could only have increased in Mary's mind the suspicion
that what she saw was a mere fantasy.

Third, a common view is that Jesus intended to prevent Mary
from delaying and wasting time in embracing Him; instead He
wanted her to hasten to the disciples and make known the joyful
tidings. But it is not easy to see why such great haste was necessary

in the case of Mary Magdalene more than in that of the other women who were charged with a similar message to the disciples. If this were the meaning, one would expect the present tense, "I do not yet ascend." Further, the meaning here assigned to ἅπτω, "to cling to, to delay," cannot be supported.

Fourth, another explanation is based on the peculiar character of Mary Magdalene. She had been distinguished for her devotedness to the Lord and to His teaching during His ministry; she had stood by His cross along with His mother and the beloved disciple, from whose lips she had doubtless heard a report of those last discourses, so full of tenderness and pathos, that Jesus held with the Twelve the same night in which He was betrayed; she was now among the first to visit His sepulcher and was weeping bitterly because His body was no longer to be found. When therefore Jesus spoke to her and she recognized Him as her Lord and Master, now risen from the dead, in joyful surprise and triumphant faith she recurred to those promises contained in His last discourse (John 14:18, 28–29; 16:16, 19–20, 22, 28) and beheld in Him the ascended Savior, the already glorified Redeemer, who had returned from heaven to fulfill His promise made to His disciples. Jesus corrected this impression by urging her not to embrace Him under such misapprehension, "for I have not yet ascended to the Father."

Mark 16:9 seems to represent this appearance of Jesus at the tomb to Mary Magdalene as His first appearance: "After He had risen early on the first day of the week, He first [πρῶτον] appeared to Mary Magdalene." In attempting to harmonize this with Matthew's account of the Lord's appearance to the other women on their return from the sepulcher, several methods have been adopted.

Some have assumed that the other women, after returning to the city to deliver the message of the angels to the disciples, went a second time to the sepulcher, after Peter, John, and Mary Magdalene had already departed from it, and that they were now on their second return to the city when Jesus met them. The objection to this view is its complexity, in a matter where the language of Matthew is so very direct and explicit: "And they departed quickly from the tomb with fear and great joy and ran to report it to His disciples. And [as they went to tell His disciples] behold, Jesus met them" (Matt. 28:8–9). The inference seems unavoidable that the interview took place on their way to the city, after they first left the sepulcher, even if the words in brackets be omitted, as is the case in some manuscripts.

Others have suggested that the women, after leaving the tomb to return to the disciples, had a long distance to go in order to find some of them, inasmuch as the disciples had all been scattered on the death of their Lord and were lodging in different parts of the city or perhaps in Bethany. Jesus appeared first to Mary Magdalene and afterwards to the rest while they were on their way to some of the more distant disciples. This solution is still more artificial and less probable than the preceding one.

Still others have proposed that the appearance to Mary Magdalene and to the other women were the same; that what John and Mark related of Mary Magdalene in particular, Matthew in his brief and general way attributed to all the women. So Luke, it is said, apparently narrated that Peter ran to the sepulcher after hearing the report of all the women (Luke 24:12), while John said that he and Peter went there after hearing from Mary Magdalene alone. To this view there would perhaps be less objection were the circumstances in the two cases similar. But they are not. In fact they are so diverse that it is quite evident that they belong to different occasions. In the one case Jesus appeared to the women as they were returning to the city, He permitted them to embrace His feet, and He sent a message to the disciples to go into Galilee. In the other instance He appeared to Mary Magdalene alone at the tomb, He forbade her to touch Him, and His message to the disciples was that He was to ascend to His Father and their Father.

More to the purpose is the view that regards πρῶτον in Mark 16:9 not as absolute but as relative. Mark narrated only three appearances of the Lord; of these three the one to Mary Magdalene took place first and the one to the assembled disciples the same evening occurred last (ὕστερον, v. 14). In any succession of events where πρῶτον and ὕστερον are employed, whatever may be the number of intervening terms, πρῶτον marks the first of the series and ὕστερον the last of the same series and of no other. So here in Mark, ὕστερον is put with the third appearance narrated, but had four been mentioned, ὕστερον could not have stood with the third but would have been used with the fourth or last, and so in every case. (For other examples of this use of ὕστερον, see Matt. 21:37; 22:27; and 26:60.) Hence as ὕστερον is here put relatively and therefore does not exclude the subsequent appearances of the

Lord to Thomas and in Galilee, so too πρῶτον stands relatively
and does not exclude the previous appearance to the other women.
A similar example occurs in 1 Corinthians 15:5–8, in which Paul
enumerated those to whom the Lord showed Himself after His
resurrection, namely, to Peter, to the Twelve, to five hundred
brethren, to James, to all the apostles, and "last of all" (ἔσχατον
πάντων) to Paul also. Now if Paul had written "he was seen first
of Cephas" (ὤφθη πρῶτον Κηφᾷ), assuredly no one would ever
have understood him as asserting that the appearance to Peter was
the first absolutely. Similarly, when John declared that Jesus
showed Himself to His disciples by the Sea of Galilee for the *third*
time after He was risen from the dead (John 21:14), this is said
relatively to the two previous appearances to the assembled
apostles. It does not exclude the four earlier appearances, to Peter,
to the two at Emmaus, to Mary Magdalene, and to the other
women—one of which John himself related in full.

So after her interview with Jesus, Mary Magdalene returned to
the city and told the disciples she had seen the Lord and He had
spoken these things to her. According to Mark 16:10–11 the
disciples were "mourning and weeping," and when they heard
that Jesus was alive and she had seen Him, they did not believe.

Jesus Appears to Two Disciples and to Peter
(Mark 16:12–13; Luke 24:13–35; 1 Corinthians 15:5)

Jesus' appearance on the way to Emmaus is related in full only
by Luke. Mark merely noted the fact, while the other two
Evangelists and Paul (1 Cor. 15:5) made no mention of it.

On the afternoon of the same day the Lord arose, two of His
disciples, one of them named Cleopas (Luke 24:18),[1] were
walking to Emmaus, a village seven-and-a-half Roman miles
from Jerusalem—a walk of two or two-and-a-half hours. They
had heard the news brought by the women and also by Peter and
John that the tomb was open and empty and that the women had
also seen a vision of angels, who said that Jesus was alive.
Probably they had also heard the reports of Mary Magdalene and
the other women, that Jesus Himself had appeared to them, but
they did not regard or mention them (v. 24) because they, like
the other disciples, had looked on them as "nonsense, and they
would not believe them" (v. 11). As they went, they were sad
and talked together of all the things that had happened. After
some time, Jesus Himself drew near and went with them. But

they did not recognize Him. Mark said He was in another form, ἐν ἑτέρᾳ μορφῇ (Mark 16:12), and Luke affirmed that "their eyes were prevented from recognizing Him" (Luke 24:16). Was there in this anything miraculous? His garments of course were not His former ones, and this was probably one reason Mary Magdalene had earlier taken Him for the keeper of the garden. Also perhaps these two disciples had not been intimately acquainted with the Lord. He had arrived at Jerusalem only six days before His crucifixion, and these might possibly have been recent converts who had not before seen Him. To them, the change of garments and the unexpectedness of the meeting would render a recognition more difficult, nor could it be regarded as surprising that under such circumstances they would not know Him. Still all this is hypothesis, and Luke's statement that "their eyes were prevented from recognizing Him" and the manner of the Lord's parting from them afterwards seem more naturally to imply that the idea of a supernatural agency, affecting not Jesus Himself but the eyes or minds of the two disciples, was in the mind of the sacred writer.

Jesus inquired about the cause of their sadness, He chided them for their slowness of heart to believe what the prophets had spoken, and then He expounded to them "the things concerning Himself in all the Scriptures" (v. 27). They felt the power of His words, and their hearts burned within them. By this time they came near the village, it was toward evening, and the day was far spent. Their journey was ended, and Jesus was about to depart. In accord with oriental hospitality they constrained Him to remain with them. He consented and as He sat at meat with them, He took bread, blessed it, broke it, and gave it to them. At that moment their eyes were opened, they knew Him, and He vanished away from them, ἄφαντος ἐγένετο ἀπ' αὐτῶν (v. 31). Here the question is raised whether the language necessarily implies anything miraculous. Some say the Emmaus disciples simply did not see Him, using Luke 4:30, John 8:59, and Acts 8:39 to illustrate the idea. However, Luke's wording most naturally expresses the idea of supernatural agency.[2]

Full of wonder and joy, the two disciples left the same hour for Jerusalem. They found the Eleven and other disciples assembled, and as they entered they were met with the joyful exclamation, "The Lord has really risen, and has appeared to Simon" (Luke 24:34). They then rehearsed what had happened to themselves, but according to Mark the rest did not believe them. As with the women, so here too there seems to have been something in the position or character of these two disciples that led the others to give less credit to their testimony than to that of Peter, one of the leading apostles.

This appearance to Peter is mentioned by no other Evangelist, and nothing is known of the particular time or the attending circumstances. It would seem to have taken place either not long before or else shortly after the Lord's appearance to the two disciples. It had not happened when they left Jerusalem for Emmaus or at least they had not heard of it. It had occurred when they returned, and it was long enough before to have been fully reported to all the disciples and believed by them. Perhaps this appearance occurred about the time the two disciples left, or shortly afterward.

Paul, in enumerating those by whom the Lord was seen after His resurrection (1 Cor. 15:5), mentioned Peter first. He probably passed over Jesus' appearances to the women and to the two disciples because they did not belong among the apostles.

Jesus Appears to the Ten and Afterward to the Eleven (Mark 16:14–18; Luke 24:36:48; John 20:19–29; 1 Corinthians 15:5)

The narrative of Jesus' first appearance to the apostles is most fully given by Luke; John added a few circumstances; Mark and Luke have preserved the first charge given privately to the apostles to preach the Gospel in all the world—a charge afterwards repeated in a more public and solemn manner on the mountain in Galilee. When Paul said the Lord appeared to the Twelve, he obviously employed this number as the usual designation of the apostles and probably included both the occasions narrated in this section. Mark and Luke spoke of the Eleven, yet John wrote that Thomas was not at first among them so that only ten were actually present.

According to Mark, the disciples were at their evening meal, which implies a not very late hour. John said the doors were shut (κεκλεισμένων) because of the disciples' fear of the Jews (John 20:19). While the two who had returned from Emmaus were still recounting what had happened, Jesus Himself "came and stood [ἦλθε καί ἔστη] in their midst and said to them, 'Peace be with you' " (v. 19). Was this entrance of the Lord miraculous? No one doubts that it could have been. He had walked on the water, and

He had just been risen from the dead, so He might have presented Himself to His followers in some miraculous way in spite of bolts and bars.

But does the language here necessarily imply a miracle? The doors indeed were shut, but the word "shut" does not of itself signify that they were bolted or fastened. The object no doubt was to prevent access to Jewish spies or also to guard themselves from the danger of being arrested, and both these objects might perhaps have been effectually accomplished by a guard at the door. Nor do the words used of the Lord strictly indicate anything miraculous. The word commonly employed to express the sudden appearance of angels is ἐφίστημι, but that is not used here. Instead John wrote that He "came and stood in their midst," implying nothing more than the ordinary mode of approach. There is in fact nothing in the whole account to suggest a miracle except John's remark about the doors, and as this circumstance is not mentioned either by Mark or Luke, it may be doubted whether it necessarily means the mode of the Lord's entrance was miraculous.

The disciples had disbelieved the reports of most of those who said they had seen the Lord, and now they could hardly believe their eyes. They were terrified and frightened; they supposed they had seen a spirit (Luke 24:37). The Lord reassured them, showed them His hands and His feet to convince them that it was He Himself, and He called for food and ate before them (vv. 39–43). He upbraided them for their unbelief regarding His resurrection (Mark 16:14). Then, too, He opened their minds so they could understand the Scriptures, showing them that Christ was to suffer and to rise from the dead the third day (Luke 24:45–46). He then said they were appointed to preach the Gospel not to Jews alone but to all the world (Mark 16:15). As a symbol of this commission and of the power they would soon receive, "He breathed on them, and said to them, 'Receive the Holy Spirit'" (John 20:22). This action was in recognition of the gracious promise He made before in the Upper Room (14:26; 16:7), which was to be fulfilled on the Day of Pentecost.

At this interview Thomas was not present. On his return the other disciples told him what happened. But Thomas now disbelieved the others, as they before had disbelieved the women. His reply was, "Unless I shall see in His hands the imprint of the nails, and put my finger into the place of the nails, and put my hand into His side, I will not believe" (20:25). Eight days later, when the disciples were again assembled and Thomas was with them, Jesus came as before, stood in their midst, and said, "Peace be with you." He permitted Thomas the test he had demanded and charged him to believe. Thomas, convinced and abashed, exclaimed in the fullness of faith and joy, "My Lord and my God!"—Jesus' divine nature manifested in the flesh. The Lord's reply to Thomas is strikingly impressive. "Because you have seen Me, have you believed? Blessed are they who did not see, and yet believed" (20:29). He and the other disciples who were to be the heralds of the Lord's resurrection and of the Gospel refused to believe except on the evidence of their own senses. Yet all others after them who have borne the Christian name have believed this great fact of the Gospel solely on their testimony. God had overruled their unbelief for good in making it a powerful argument for the truth of their testimony on behalf of this great fact, which they themselves were so slow to believe.

Jesus Appears in Galilee
(Matthew 28:16–20; John 21:1–24; 1 Corinthians 15:6)

It appears from the narrative in Matthew that while the disciples were still in Jerusalem, Jesus had appointed a time when He would meet them in Galilee on a certain mountain (Matt. 26:32). They therefore left Jerusalem after the Passover, probably soon after the interview at which Thomas was present, and returned to Galilee. While waiting for the appointed time, they engaged in their usual occupation of fishing. One day toward evening seven of them, including Peter, Thomas, and the sons of Zebedee, were fishing on the lake with their net, but during the night they caught nothing (John 21:2–3). At early dawn Jesus stood on the shore near them and told them to cast their net on the right side of the boat. They did so "and then they were not able to haul it in because of the great number of fish" (21:6). Recognizing in this miracle their risen Lord, they pressed around Him. Peter with his characteristic ardor jumped into the water to reach Him sooner. At their Lord's command they prepared a meal from the fish they had taken. "Jesus came and took the bread, and gave them, and the fish likewise" (v. 13). This was His third appearance to the Eleven, or rather to a large number of them together. On this occasion after their meal the Lord put to Peter the touching and thrice-repeated question, "Do you love Me?"

At length the set time arrived, and the eleven disciples went away "to the mountain which Jesus had designated" (Matt. 28:16). It would seem most probable that this time and place had been set by the Lord for a solemn and more public interview not only with the Eleven, whom He had already met, but with all His disciples in Galilee. Therefore on this occasion, "He appeared to more than five hundred brethren at one time" (1 Cor. 15:6). That the interview was not confined to the Eleven alone would seem evident from the fact that "some were doubtful" (Matt. 28:17), for this could hardly be true of any of the Eleven after what had already happened to them in Jerusalem and in Galilee and after they had been appointed to meet their risen Lord at this very time and place. The appearance of the 500 must have occurred in Galilee, for even after the Lord's ascension, the believers who were gathered in Jerusalem totaled about 120 (Acts 1:15). Thus it may be suggested that the appearances described by Matthew and Paul were identical. It was a great and solemn occasion. Jesus had directed that the Eleven and all His disciples in Galilee should convene on the mountain. It was the closing scene of His ministry in Galilee. Here His life had been spent. Here most of His mighty works had been done and His discourses presented. Here His followers were most numerous. He therefore left those among whom He had lived and labored longest. And He repeated to all His disciples in public the solemn charge He had already given in private to the apostles: "Go therefore and make disciples of all the nations . . . and lo, I am with you always, even to the end of the age" (Matt. 28:19–20). This was doubtless His last interview with His disciples in that region, His last great act in Galilee.

Jesus' Further Appearances at Jerusalem and His Ascension (Acts 1:3–12; Luke 24:49–53; 1 Corinthians 15:7)

In Acts 1:3 Luke related that Jesus showed Himself alive to the apostles, "after His suffering, by many convincing proofs, appearing to them over a period of forty days, and speaking of the things concerning the kingdom of God." This would seem to imply interviews and communications, one of which may have been Jesus' appearance to James, mentioned only by Paul (1 Cor. 15:7), subsequent to that to the five hundred brethren. This probably occurred in Jerusalem after the apostles returned from Galilee. This James was probably the Lord's half brother, who was highly esteemed in the church and is often simply so named without any special designation (e.g., Acts 12:17; 15:13; 21:18; Gal. 2:9, 12). At the time when Paul wrote, the other James, "the brother of John," as he was called, was already dead (Acts 12:1).

After appearing to James, the Lord was seen by "all the apostles" (1 Cor. 15:7). This too was apparently an appointed meeting and was doubtless the same of which Luke spoke as occurring in Jerusalem immediately before Jesus' ascension. This, of course, was the Lord's last interview with His apostles. He repeated to them the promise of the baptism with the Holy Spirit, which would soon take place, and He charged them not to depart from Jerusalem until this was accomplished (Acts 1:8; Luke 24:48–49). Strange as it may seem, the Twelve in this last solemn moment put to Him the question, "Lord, is it at this time You are restoring the kingdom to Israel?" (Acts 1:6). Their darkened minds, not yet enlightened by the baptism of the Spirit, still clung to the idea of a temporal Prince and Savior who would deliver His people not from their sins but from the galling yoke of Roman dominion. The Lord dealt gently with their ignorance and lack of faith: "It is not for you to know times or epochs, . . . but you shall receive power when the Holy Spirit has come upon you; and you shall be My witnesses . . . even to the remotest part of the earth" (vv. 7–8).

During this discourse or in immediate connection with it, Jesus led the Eleven "out as far as Bethany [ἕως εἰς Βηθανίαν], and He lifted up His hands and blessed them. And it came about that while He was blessing them, He parted from them" (Luke 24:50– 51). His ascension, then, took place at or near Bethany. However, in Acts 1:12 the same writer, Luke, related that after the ascension the disciples "returned to Jerusalem from the mount called Olivet." Luke obviously did not mean to contradict himself. The most this expression can be made to imply is that in leaving Bethany, which lies on the eastern slope of the Mount of Olives a mile or more below the summit of the ridge, the disciples returned to Jerusalem by a path across the mount. Yet from this remark in Acts arose, probably early in the fourth century, the legend that fixed the place of the ascension on the reputed summit of the Mount of Olives. If that was the true spot, then the Lord ascended from it in full view of all the inhabitants of Jerusalem. But that circumstance was not hinted at by Luke nor would it have been in accord with the life and character of the Savior.

As these disciples stood gazing and wondering, and while a cloud received their Lord out of their sight, two angels stood by them in white apparel. They announced that this same Jesus, who was thus taken up from them into heaven, will return (Acts 1:9–11). This annunciation concludes the written history of the Lord's resurrection and ascension.

Summary

At early dawn on the first day of the week the women who had attended on Jesus—Mary Magdalene, Mary the mother of James, Joanna, Salome, and others—went out with spices to the sepulcher to embalm the Lord's body. They inquired among themselves who would remove the stone that closed the tomb. On their arrival they found the stone already taken away, for there had been an earthquake, and an angel had descended and rolled away the stone and sat on it, so that the frightened guards became like dead men. The Lord had risen.

The women, knowing nothing of all this, were amazed; they entered the tomb, and not finding the body of the Lord, they were perplexed. At that time Mary Magdalene, impressed with the idea that the body had been stolen, left the tomb and the other women and ran to the city to tell Peter and John. The others remained in the tomb, and immediately two angels appeared who announced to them that Jesus was risen from the dead and told the women to tell His disciples. The women left quickly for the city to make this known to the disciples. On the way Jesus met them, permitted them to embrace His feet, and told them to go tell His disciples. The women related these things to the disciples, but the disciples did not believe them.

Meanwhile Peter and John had run to the tomb and, entering in, had found it empty. But the orderly arrangement of the graveclothes and of the napkin convinced John that the body had not been removed either by violence or by friends. The germ of a belief that the Lord had risen arose in his mind. The two then returned to the city. Mary Magdalene had returned to the tomb, having followed them, and remained standing and weeping before it and looking in she saw two angels sitting. Turning around, she saw Jesus, who told her to tell His disciples too.

The resurrected Lord's appearances to His disciples and others, as recorded by the Evangelists and Paul, may be arranged as in the following list.

1. To the women returning from the sepulcher, reported only by Matthew
2. To Mary Magdalene at the tomb, reported by John and Mark
3. To Peter, perhaps early in the afternoon, reported by Luke and Paul
4. To the two disciples going to Emmaus, toward evening, reported by Luke and Mark
5. To the apostles (except Thomas) assembled at evening, reported by Mark, Luke, John, and Paul
   (These five appearances all took place at or near Jerusalem on the first day of the week, the same day on which the Lord arose.)
6. To the apostles, Thomas being present, eight days later in Jerusalem, reported only by John
7. To seven of the apostles on the shore of the Lake of Tiberias, reported only by John
8. To the Eleven and to five hundred other brethren, on a mountain in Galilee, reported by Matthew and Paul
9. To James, probably at Jerusalem, reported only by Paul
10. To the Eleven at Jerusalem immediately before the Ascension, reported by Luke in Acts and by Paul

CHAPTER 15

Pauline Theology Relative to the Death and Resurrection of Christ

Charles L. Feinberg

The theology of Paul has been the subject of much controversy. The apostle has been accused of formulating a speculative system that was the product of his own fertile imagination and wholly devoid of historical basis. Some scholars assert that Paul perverted the simple message of Christ concerning the approaching kingdom into a theology inconsistent with the mind and purpose of Christ. Some claim Paul was the destroyer of the Christianity of Christ.[1] Their cry is "Back to Christ," and their work is professedly "a quest for the historical Jesus." It is maintained further that "it was not his religious beliefs, but his religious experience, which was of supreme importance to him."[2] In other words, Paul's experiences are the abiding values, but his terminology must be relegated to the past.

What the apostle did, it is argued, was to destroy the simplicity of the gospel message and to substitute in its place a series of doctrines concerning the way of salvation. In refutation of these contentions it can be affirmed, first, that Paul was warranted in emphasizing the death and resurrection of Christ because Christ Himself attached great importance to these facts. Second, Paul's doctrines were not based on some mental aberrations but on demonstrable historic facts and events. Third, the church in its early history did not regard Paul as an innovator, nor did the intimate friends and apostles of Christ. Fourth, the apostle always regarded himself as a true disciple of Christ, never intimating by so much as a word that he disagreed with any of Christ's teaching or commandments. Fifth, one must certainly hold a low view of the inspiration of the Scriptures if one doubts Paul when he wrote, "For I would have you know, brethren, that the gospel which was preached by me is not according to man. For I neither received it from man, nor was I taught it, but I received it through a revelation of Jesus Christ" (Gal. 1:11–12). Who can deny these words and still maintain a consistent belief in the inspiration of Scripture? The alleged discrepancy between Paul and Christ and the extended controversy over it appear, then, to be products of the minds of the objectors to the theology of the apostle.

What was Paul's teaching concerning Christ? In Romans 2:16 the apostle called his teaching "my gospel." Later, in exhorting and encouraging Timothy in his work of the ministry, Paul again labeled his doctrine as "my gospel" (2 Tim. 2:8). When Paul wrote of his preaching, he was referring to all that he had taught. The apostle explains exactly what is meant by the phrase "my gospel" when he succinctly declared, "Now I make known to you, brethren, the gospel which I preached to you, which also you received, in which also you stand, by which also you are saved, if you hold fast the word which I preached to you, unless you believed in vain. For I delivered to you as of first importance what I also received, that Christ died for our sins according to the Scriptures, and that He was buried, and that He was raised on the third day according to the Scriptures" (1 Cor. 15:1–4). At the basis of Paul's theology, then, lies his gospel, which embodies the death, burial, and resurrection of the Lord Jesus Christ. This discussion seeks to show what part these events in the life of the Lord played in the theology of Paul and what God through the apostle would have believers learn from each event.

The Death of Christ

The early disciples of the Lord Jesus Christ had conceived of the death of their Messiah as a most calamitous event. When Peter first heard of it, he was quick to rebuke the Lord, saying, "God forbid it, Lord! This shall never happen to You" (Matt. 16:22). The Emmaus disciples also saw only disappointment in the crucifixion of their Lord, for they sorrowfully related, "But we were hoping that it was He who was going to redeem Israel" (Luke 24:21). After the resurrection of Christ the disciples were reconciled to the fact of His death, but it was Paul who, far from conceiving of the death of Christ as an untimely end of His work, showed that it was the consummation of all God's purposes for the salvation of humankind. Paul sought to demonstrate that Christ's death was the crowning achievement of Christ's work on earth. Paul called his preaching the preaching of the Cross (1 Cor. 1:18), declaring, "But may it never be that I should boast except in the cross of our Lord Jesus Christ, through which the world has been crucified to me, and I to the world" (Gal. 6:14). And Paul continued to preach this "wisdom of God," even though it was a stumbling block to the Jews and merely foolishness to the Greeks (1 Cor. 1:21, 23). Paul's "Christology is accordingly an interpretation of the historic Jesus, and more particularly of His death, from the viewpoint of one who believed that He had not only died, but had risen again, and who had entered on the experience of a life that flowed from the Crucified and Risen One."[3] According to Paul the death of Christ was the supreme manifestation of the love of God the Father and of God the Son. The Father had truly shown His love to Abraham when He unconditionally gave him such great promises. David had experienced the warmth of God's love when blessing after blessing, undeservedly to be sure, were showered on him. Of Solomon it was said, "and the LORD loved him" (2 Sam. 12:24). God was under no obligation to do so; He was not responsible for the breach between Himself and humankind. It was wholly of His love that He gave His Son for the world. Truly, "God demonstrates His own love toward us, in that while we were yet sinners, Christ died for us" (Rom. 5:8). In spite of the infinite cost, God "did not spare His own Son, but delivered Him up for us all" (8:32).

Numerous benefits accrue to believers because of Jesus' death. First, the Cross manifests His love toward humankind. Paul wrote, "I have been crucified with Christ; and it is no longer I who live, but Christ lives in me; and the life which I now live in the flesh I live by faith in the Son of God, who loved me, and delivered Himself up for me" (Gal. 2:20). For the joy set before Him of bringing many into glory, Christ endured the cross and despised the shame (Heb. 12:2). In truth, when Christ was in the form of God, He thought it not a prize to be snatched at to be equal with God, but He made Himself of no reputation and humbled Himself because of His great love, becoming obedient to death, even the ignominious and shameful, yet glorious, death of the cross (Phil. 2:6–8). How could God's love and that of Christ be more fully or effectively expressed?

Second, positional sanctification has been procured by the death of Christ. All who believe in the Lord Jesus Christ are said to be in Christ, accepted in the Beloved. Just as Christ was sanctified and set apart to the will and work of the Father, so are all believers by virtue of His efficacious death. "We have been sanctified through the offering of the body of Jesus Christ once for all" (Heb. 10:10). There is nothing lacking in this sanctification; nothing need be added to it. But it must be understood that this is not (as some have erroneously supposed and contended for) practical or experimental sanctification. This sanctification is wholly that of position and not of state. It is the common heritage of all Christians.

It is almost hard to conceive of a church with more grave error, sin, and dissent than the Corinthian church. There was unspeakable immorality in the form of incest ("immorality of such a kind as does not exist even among the Gentiles," 1 Cor. 5:1), party spirit leading to dissenting groups, error regarding the Lord's Supper resulting in dishonor to this ordinance, and disbelief in the resurrection of believers. In spite of all this, however, Paul asserted, "you were washed, . . . sanctified, [and] justified in the name of the Lord Jesus Christ, and in the Spirit of our God" (6:11). This is both possible and true, because every believer has "put on the new self, which in the likeness of God has been created in righteousness and holiness of the truth" (Eph. 4:24). The blessing of this forensic truth is alone made possible through the death of Christ.

Third, Satan met his defeat at the Cross of Calvary. When Adam fell in his disobedience to the command of God, he became defective in his whole moral, physical, and spiritual being. He came under the bondage and yoke of Satan. But through Christ humankind was delivered and is free (potentially, of course), for He said, "Concerning judgment . . . the ruler of this world has been judged" (John 16:11). Paul said that when Christ "disarmed the rulers and authorities, He made a public display of them, having triumphed over them through Him" (Col. 2:15). The writer of Hebrews stated that through death Christ rendered "powerless him who had the power of death, that is, the devil; and [delivered] those who through fear of death were subject to slavery all their lives" (Heb. 2:14–15). Believers in Christ need live under fear no longer, for Satan's power has been broken, and he is now a defeated usurper—all through the death of Christ.

Fourth, the ground for the exercise of God's grace was laid in the death of Christ. Grace has often been confused with love and mercy. Because of the use of these terms in such close proximity in Ephesians 2:4–6, many have thought they are synonymous. God has always loved humankind and there was a time (in the case of Adam before the Fall) when He did not need to display His mercy. Mercy is called forth when the object of love is needy. But God could desire to be both loving and merciful when the way for Him to be gracious was not provided. When it is provided, then grace is present. What then is the righteous ground of the exercise of God's grace?

In eternity past, before God created the earth or humankind, the triune God—Father, Son, and Holy Spirit—existed in eternal bliss. God's attributes were in full and blessed harmony with one another. When sin entered into the world by one man and universal death entered by that sin, immediately these attributes in God were pitted against one another. God's holiness demanded the just and full payment for sin, while His love sought to express itself to sinners but was hampered because the full penalty for sin had not been paid. What a different picture this is from what is usually thought of in the Fall: the curses on the ground, the decree that man should earn his bread by the sweat of his brow, the pronouncement that woman would know pain and sorrow in childbirth, the sentence of universal death. But what of God? Does this whole question not concern Him infinitely more than it did humankind? God needed infinite satisfaction for the breach against His infinite holiness. And He never had it until the Lord Jesus Christ forsook heaven's glory and humbled Himself and willingly gave Himself to be placed on a cross to die as the Substitute for sinful humans. Then and only then was God's infinite holiness completely and perfectly satisfied.

In view of the death of Christ, God could now not only love sinners, but He could freely exercise His grace. What had been accomplished by this fact? First, there was the removal of all condemnation. Before the Cross, people walked under the death sentence and all the condemnation and judgment of God was on them. When it fell in all its awful force on Christ, it was forever removed from humans. People could appropriate by faith this work done for the sake of their reconciliation. God was now rendered propitious toward them, because the Just had taken the place of the unjust, thus bringing them to God (1 Peter 3:18). God could remain just and in addition be the Justifier of anyone who believes in Jesus (Rom. 3:26), because the Cross had removed all objectionable things from the sight of God. Second, there was the imputation to the sinner of all merit, no less than the righteousness of God in Christ. God had made Christ to be sin for the sinner that the sinner in turn might be made the righteousness of God in

Christ (2 Cor. 5:21). What an ineffably glorious exchange! Now sinners are not only rid of their sin, but have something positive placed to their account before God—the righteousness of Christ. These two factors in the exercise of God's grace are nowhere pictured in the Scriptures with more prominence and force than in the offerings of Leviticus—the sweet savor and the nonsweet savor offerings. The nonsweet savor offerings—the sin and trespass offerings—were fulfilled in Christ when He secured the forgiveness of God for sinners. The sweet savor offerings—the burnt, meal, and peace offerings—speak of Christ offering His full perfection to the Father that it might be imputed to believers, thus procuring justification for them. In the nonsweet savor offerings, wherein God's holiness is satisfied, condemnation is subtracted from believers; in the sweet savor offerings justification is added. In a word, then, "grace is the limitless, unrestrained love of God for the lost, acting in full compliance with the exact and unchangeable demands of His own righteousness through the sacrificial death of Christ."[4] It is God's limitless love expressed toward humankind in infinite goodness, because it is not hindered or stayed by the righteous demands of God's awful holiness.

What is the relationship of the death of Christ to the sins of Old Testament saints like Abraham, Jacob, David, and Moses? God was not acting on the basis of judgment with these people but was continually dealing with them by acts of mercy and kindness. Of Noah, the Word states that he "found favor in the eyes of the LORD" (Gen. 6:8). What was done with their sins? The Scriptures reveal that the method of atoning for sins was by the sacrifice of animals. This procedure sufficed only to "cover" (the literal meaning of *atone*) their sins from the sight of God. "For it is impossible for the blood of bulls and goats to take away sins" (Heb. 10:4). Someone has aptly put it, "The blood of animals could not take away sins, because they are non-moral; the blood of men could not take away sins, for they are immoral; only the blood of Christ can take away sins, because He alone is moral."

In speaking of these Old Testament times Paul declared that God "overlooked the times of ignorance" (Acts 17:30). From the very nature of the case God could not always deal this way with sin and still maintain His righteous character in human eyes or, more importantly, satisfy the demands of His infinite holiness. Therefore Paul, in the book of Romans, set forth God's method. Paul showed the utter depravity and moral degradation of the heathen. Next he brought to light the condemnation of the Gentiles. Finally then, he pointed out the guilt and sin of the Jews. Having concluded all three classes under sin, Paul announced the remedy in Christ, "whom God displayed publicly as a propitiation in His blood through faith. This was to demonstrate His righteousness, because in the forbearance of God He passed over the sins previously committed; for the demonstration, I say, of His righteousness at the present time, that He might be just and the justifier of the one who has faith in Jesus" (Rom. 3:25–26). This, then, was God's plan: the sins of Old Testament saints were to be covered and their penalty to be rolled forward to the time when Christ died for all the sin and sins of the world, whereby God could vindicate His justice and holiness in past dealings with sin and also be able to justify anyone who would believe in Jesus. What an all-sufficient death was that of the blessed Savior!

Fifth, Christ's death brought about the end of the Law. Paul wrote in Romans 10:4, "For Christ is the end of the law for righteousness to every one who believes." What did Paul mean by this statement? The apostle had just pointed out that Israel failed to submit themselves to the righteousness of God because they were engaged in seeking a righteousness of their own (v. 3). They had viewed the Law as a means whereby through their own works they could attain to a righteousness that would please and satisfy God's demands. But they were ignorant of the nature of the Law, "for if a law had been given which was able to impart life, then righteousness would indeed have been based on law" (Gal. 3:21). The Law was incapable of either giving people life or enabling them to procure the righteousness of the Law. No one had kept the Law sufficiently to warrant his attaining this legal righteousness. Every Israelite had failed to keep some particular requirement of the Law. Therefore they were all under the curse. "For as many as are of the works of the Law are under a curse; for it is written, 'Cursed is everyone who does not abide by all things written in the book of the law, to perform them' " (3:10). Christ bore "the curse of the Law, having become a curse for us—for it is written, 'Cursed is everyone who hangs on a tree' " (3:13). Moreover, Christ fulfilled all the requirements of the Law, for He was the only Jew ever to keep the whole Law, and thus He was able to pay humankind's debt of obedience to it. Furthermore "the law, since it has only a shadow of the good things to come and not the very form of things, can never by the same sacrifices year by year, which they offer continually, make perfect those who draw near" (Heb. 10:1). The shadow was done away with in the death of the Lord Jesus Christ.

Sixth, the sum total of what Christ accomplished on the cross when He said, "It is finished," is included in the three terms of *redemption, reconciliation,* and *propitiation.*

Redemption is always toward sin in the sense of a release effected by a payment of a ransom. Christ paid the penalty for sin, for it is written, "being justified as a gift by His grace through the redemption which is in Christ Jesus" (Rom. 3:24). He is the One in whom "we have redemption through His blood, the forgiveness of our trespasses, according to the riches of his grace" (Eph. 1:7). Christ paid the ransom for the penalty of sin and has thus freed people from ever having to suffer the penalty of their own sin.

Reconciliation is toward human beings. Unregenerate, carnal man is not subject to God, nor can he be. His sin separates him from God. When satisfaction has been made for the objectionable barrier to the favor of God, then one is said to be reconciled. The difference between God and man has been satisfactorily adjusted. How is this done? Paul answered, "we were reconciled to God through the death of His Son" (Rom. 5:10). "Now all these things are from God, who reconciled us to Himself through Christ, and gave us the ministry of reconciliation, namely, that God was in Christ reconciling the world to Himself, not counting their trespasses against them, and He has committed to us the word of reconciliation" (2 Cor. 5:18–19). Christ has made such an adequate reconciliation that God is no longer imputing people's trespasses to them and has also given believers this message to tell to others who can be reconciled in the same way as they were—by faith in Christ's reconciling work.

Propitiation is toward God. Just as the blood of the expiatory victim was sprinkled on the mercy seat on the Day of Atonement to render God favorable and propitious by the fulfillment of the demands of His awful holiness, so the blood of the Lord Jesus rendered God favorable toward humans. God's favor has been eternally won through Christ, "whom God displayed publicly as a propitiation in His blood through faith . . . that He might be just and the justifier of the one who has faith in Jesus" (Rom. 3:25–26). No child of God need now pray to God, "God be merciful to me a sinner." This has already been accomplished once for all by the Cross of Christ.

That death is the outcome of sin is the clear and united testimony of the Scriptures. How then could the eternal God the Son, who had never sinned, hang on a tree, dying a shameful malefactor's death? There is but one answer: He is taking someone else's place; He is dying instead of another—a vicarious and substitutionary death. No sin or guilt of Christ (for He had none) entered into the transaction of the death of Christ. It was all for those who believe. In the fullest sense of the word, "Christ died for us" (Rom. 5:8), because God "made Him who knew no sin to be sin on our behalf, that we might become the righteousness of God in Him" (2 Cor. 5:21).

The Resurrection of Christ

No less important in Paul's theology than the death of Christ is the resurrection of Christ. The resurrection of Christ involves, among other things, the inspiration of the Scriptures, for the raising of Christ from the dead was predicted in the Old Testament. Paul said in Pisidian Antioch,

> And we preach to you the good news of the promise made to the fathers, that God has fulfilled this promise to our children in that He raised up Jesus, as it is also written in the second Psalm, "Thou art My Son; today I have begotten Thee." And as for that fact that He raised Him up from the dead, no more to return to decay, He has spoken in this way: "I will give you the holy and sure blessings of David." Therefore He also says in another Psalm, "Thou wilt not allow Thy Holy One to undergo decay." For David, after he had served the purpose of God in his own generation, fell asleep, and was laid among his fathers, and underwent decay; but He whom God raised did not undergo decay (Acts 13:32–37).

In his epistles, Paul fully developed his teaching concerning Jesus' resurrection. He related the Resurrection, first, not only to the work of Christ, but to His person as well, for the simple reason that His work gains its significance from the character of His person. What He does is of vital importance to human salvation because of who He is. What light then does the Resurrection throw on the person of Christ? It shows Him to be the eternal Son of God; every claim of deity is here established and proved. "It removed misgivings, because it cancelled the misleading impressions created by a Son of God in weakness."[5] Paul wrote that Christ "was declared the Son of God with power . . . according to the Spirit of holiness, Jesus Christ our Lord" (Rom. 1:4). Whereas Paul wrote in the previous verse that Christ was "born of a descendant of David according to the flesh," speaking of His limitation, humiliation, and weakness, now he proclaimed that Christ was proved to be very God with power, because He is holy and was raised from the dead. Indeed, Christ is He whom God raised up again, "putting an end to the agony of death, since it was impossible for Him to be held in its power" (Acts 2:24).

As with the death of Christ, so with His resurrection, believers enjoy several marvelous spiritual benefits. First, His resurrection makes it possible for the believer to enjoy experiential sanctification. Through the death of Christ positional sanctification was effected for all believers; through the resurrection experimental sanctification was made possible. In His death, Christ died not only for sin, but He died to sin as well. He made it possible for believers to have dominion over the power of sin. After Paul discussed in Romans 5 the benefits of salvation and the federal headship of the old creation and that of the new, he concluded, "But where sin increased, grace abounded all the more" (Rom. 5:20). Then he asked whether this grace of God is to be license for believers to do whatever they please and to continue in sin. His answer in 6:4–5 was, in essence, "We have been crucified with Christ and are dead to sin; we have been resurrected with Him to walk in newness of life."

Many have wrongly deduced that Paul was teaching expressly what he was forbidding. One writer claims, "There was no one-sidedness about our Lord's teaching which might lead to Antinomianism, as actually happened in the case of the teaching of St. Paul."[6] This has always been the contention of those who do not understand Paul's lofty and divine principle of grace. Paul did teach that whereas the sin nature has been condemned in the flesh, still it is not destroyed but brings forth its fruit, sins. Therefore the apostle declared that believers are to consider themselves "dead to sin, but alive to God in Christ Jesus" (6:11). They are to yield themselves to God as those who are "alive from the dead" (6:13). They are to cleanse themselves "from all defilement of flesh and spirit, perfecting holiness in the fear of God" (2 Cor. 7:1). They are to walk in the Spirit and "not carry out the desire of the flesh" (Gal. 5:16). Through the Spirit they are to put to death the deeds of the body and live (Rom. 8:13). They are to recognize that they have crucified the flesh with the affections of lust. They are to "lay aside the old self, which is being corrupted in accordance with the lusts of deceit," being "renewed in the spirit of [their] mind, and put on the new self, which in the likeness of God has been created in righteousness and holiness of the truth" (Eph. 4:22–24). They are to "live sensibly, righteously and godly in the present age, looking for the blessed hope and the appearing of the glory of our great God and Savior, Christ Jesus" (Titus 2:12–13). Does this testimony of Paul intimate in any way a leaning toward antinomianism? Do these exhortations of Paul contain any such teaching as antinomianism? Any such suggestion is a travesty on the true doctrine of Paul. But on the other hand all the blessings contained in these exhortations are made available to believers on the basis of Christ's death and through the power of His resurrection life.

Second, Jesus' resurrection guarantees the believer's justification. Many are of the opinion that Christ was raised from the dead to accomplish justification for the believer. It is more correct to speak of the Resurrection as the guarantee of the justification Christ wrought by His death. The resurrection of Christ proves beyond a doubt that God has accepted His death for humankind as the full satisfaction of His claims for human justification. Christ "was delivered up because of our transgressions, and was raised because of [lit., 'on account of'] our justification" (Rom. 4:25). Just as Christ was delivered up on account of people's offenses, because they had grievously offended the holiness of God, just so was He raised to show that His death had fully and completely availed for believers and that now they stand in the presence of God the Father justified from all things.

Third, Jesus' resurrection makes available to believers His own resurrection life. How true are the blessed words, "I am the resurrection and the life" (John 11:25). Throughout the New Testament this great truth of the believer's identification with the Lord Jesus Christ is stressed. From their risen Lord and Savior believers receive their spiritual sustenance. In this sense the resurrection "is the means by which they are made recipients of the gifts which the Death secured."[7]

Paul wrote in Romans 6:3–14,

> Or do you not know that all of us who have been baptized into Christ Jesus have been baptized into His death? Therefore we have been buried with Him through baptism into death, in order that as Christ was raised from the dead through the glory of the Father, so we too might walk in newness of life. For if we have become united with Him in the likeness of His death, certainly we shall be also in the likeness of His resurrection, knowing this, that our old self was crucified with Him, that our body of sin might be done away with, that we should no longer be slaves to sin;

for he who has died is freed from sin. Now if we have died with Christ, we believe that we shall also live with Him, knowing that Christ, having been raised from the dead, is never to die again; death no longer is master over Him. For the death that He died, He died to sin, once for all; but the life that He lives, He lives to God. Even so consider yourselves to be dead to sin, but alive to God in Christ Jesus.

Therefore do not let sin reign in your mortal body that you should obey its lusts, and do not go on presenting the members of your body to sin as instruments of unrighteousness; but present yourselves to God as those alive from the dead, and your members as instruments of righteousness to God. For sin shall not be master over you, for you are not under law, but under grace.

This passage clearly states the principle on which the new life is to be lived for and unto righteousness: by union with Christ in His resurrection life. How clear are these truths that speak of the great power and unsearchable riches that have come to believers by virtue of the life He now lives, for just as He "lives to God" (v. 10), so can believers also live in and through Him. It can truthfully be said, "if any man is in Christ, he is a new creature; the old things passed away; behold, new things have come" (2 Cor. 5:17). The things that are new are just as literal and actual as were the old things. The spiritual resurrection life of the believer is the immediate counterpart of Christ's resurrection.

In Colossians 2:10–13 Paul affirmed, "and in Him you have been made complete, and He is the head over all rule and authority; and in Him you were also circumcised with a circumcision made without hands, in the removal of the body of the flesh by the circumcision of Christ; having been buried with Him in baptism, in which you were also raised up with Him through faith in the working of God, who raised Him from the dead. And when you were dead in your transgressions and the uncircumcision of your flesh, He made you alive together with Him, having forgiven us all our transgressions." And in Ephesians 2:6–7 Paul wrote that God "raised us up with Him, and seated us with Him in the heavenly places, in Christ Jesus, in order that in the ages to come He might show the surpassing riches of His grace in kindness toward us in Christ Jesus." God did for the Christian exactly what He did for Christ. No wonder Paul exclaimed, "Blessed be the God and Father of our Lord Jesus Christ, who has blessed us with every spiritual blessing in the heavenly places in Christ" (1:3). Many other passages could be cited that mention the reality and blessedness of this life Christ came to bestow.

Fourth, another important result of Christ's resurrection is His priestly work. When Christ as High Priest offered Himself up on the cross as the sacrifice for sins, He effected forgiveness and justification, but He did not complete His high priestly work. There remained yet His work as Advocate and Intercessor. "And if anyone sins, we have an Advocate with the Father, Jesus Christ the righteous" (1 John 2:1). When a believer falls into sin, Satan, the ever-ready accuser of believers (Rev. 12:10), accuses him of sin before the Father. Then Christ, the believer's great Advocate and Helper, sets forth the propitiation for his sins that He has made and gains the believer's acquittal. (Confession, of course, restores fellowship, which is lost through the believer's sin.) Paul did not write of the advocacy of Christ, but he did speak of His intercessory work: "Christ Jesus is He who died, yes, rather who was raised, who is at the right hand of God, who also intercedes for us" (Rom. 8:34). And Hebrews 7:25 states, "He is able also to save forever those who draw near to God through Him, since He always lives to make intercession for them." Christ ever praying and interceding for the believer—what a reassuring and comforting thought.

In His earthly ministry Christ said to Peter, "Simon, Simon, behold, Satan has demanded permission to sift you like wheat; but I have prayed for you, that your faith may not fail" (Luke 22:31–32). In His intercessory prayer Christ prayed, "I do not ask Thee to take them out of the world, but to keep them from the evil one" (John 17:15). Christ is now continuing to pray this prayer for believers. "The lesson constantly enforced in" the Epistle to the Hebrews "is that the high priesthood of Christ is 'fulfilled' by His work in heaven; that only after His Resurrection is He in a position to exhaust the functions of that office; and that His offering does not reach its culminating point until, within the heavenly sanctuary, He presents Himself to the Father in all that perfection of service which the Father claims."[8]

> The priesthood of Christ transcends all other because it is exercised in the heavenly sphere. It is a permanent priesthood. It possesses all the value and effectiveness which only such conditions can give. As high priest in the heavenly sphere, the exalted Christ exercises a twofold function in behalf of His redeemed community on earth: toward God He intercedes; toward man He confers help and strength. These functions acquire their effectiveness through Christ's resurrection and exaltation in the heavenly sphere.[9]

Fifth, the resurrection of Christ also has made possible His exaltation. In this exalted sphere He became and still is the Head of the body which is His church and bride. Paul showed that Christ is not only the humbled and suffering Savior, but also the exalted and glorified Lord. On behalf of the Ephesians the apostle prayed:

> that you may know what is the hope of His calling, what are the riches of the glory of His inheritance in the saints, and what is the surpassing greatness of His power toward us who believe. These are in accordance with the working of the strength of His might which He brought about in Christ, when He raised Him from the dead, and seated Him at His right hand in the heavenly places, far above all rule and authority and power and dominion, and every name that is named, not only in this age, but also in the one to come. And He put all things in subjection under His feet, and gave Him as head over all things to the church, which is His body, the fulness of Him who fills all in all (Eph. 1:18–23).

God not only raised Christ from the dead, but He also enthroned Him in unique authority as Head of the church.

Sixth, the resurrection of Jesus Christ guarantees that every believer will some day be raised from the dead. "If the Spirit of Him who raised Jesus from the dead dwells in you, He who raised Christ Jesus from the dead will also give life to your mortal bodies through His Spirit who indwells you" (Rom. 8:11). "For our citizenship is in heaven, from which also we eagerly wait for a Savior, the Lord Jesus Christ; who will transform the body of our humble state into conformity with the body of His glory, by the exertion of the power that He has even to subject all things to Himself" (Phil. 3:20–21).

Other references of a similar nature are included in the Scriptures (e.g., Rom. 8:29; 1 Cor. 6:14; 2 Cor. 4:14; 1 Thess. 4:14), but the most extended discussion of this vital truth is in 1 Corinthians 15. The fact to be borne in mind in this chapter is that Paul was not trying to argue the resurrection of Christ; that was taken for granted among the believers to whom he was writing. Instead he was defending the resurrection of Christians, which some at the church in Corinth were denying. Paul, proceeding on the basis of the resurrection of Christ and its apparent implications for those who are in Him, pointed out that the resurrection of believers is certain and secure. First, he said there is such a thing as resurrection from the dead because Christ was raised (1 Cor. 15:12–13). Second, he considered the utter absurdity of the thought that

Christ had not been raised (vv. 14–19). Then he stated, "But now Christ has been raised from the dead, the first fruits of those who are asleep. For since by a man came death, by a man also came the resurrection of the dead. For as in Adam all die, so also in Christ all shall be made alive" (vv. 20–22). Third, Paul terminated his argument with a discussion of the nature of the resurrection body. There will be those who have "fallen asleep" (died) in Jesus and whose bodies have seen corruption; in this case the corruption will put on incorruption. There will be those who have not "fallen asleep" (died) at the coming of the Lord and their mortal bodies will put on immortality (vv. 35–53). First Corinthians 15 definitely shows that the redemption of God extends to spirit, soul, and body. Believers will be redeemed completely. "The resurrection of Christ is not only a prophecy of our resurrection, but its guarantee, its earnest and pledge, its first fruits."[10]

Conclusion

Paul presented the death of Christ as having six marvelous benefits and the resurrection of Christ as also having six remarkable effects. Obviously, then, the death and resurrection of Christ are preeminently important and occupy an all-essential, vital, and indispensable place in Paul's thinking and writing.

CHAPTER 16

The Glorified Christ on Patmos

Robert L. Thomas

The significance of symbolic language in the Apocalypse has been the subject of debate in the church almost since its inception. Differences of opinion have arisen because of different hermeneutical principles, with some commentators prone to press the symbols of the book to unreasonable extremes while others are unnecessarily literal in their interpretation.

Another common error is to overlook the relationship between John's language and the Old Testament source of his terminology. A highly significant passage where this tendency can be seen is the writer's description of the glorified Christ found in Revelation 1:13–16. The various aspects of the Lord's appearance are, for the most part, derived from the Jewish Scriptures, yet there exists a great diversity of opinion regarding the significance of each part, a difference that is due largely to a lack of attention to this relationship.

Beckwith's remarks are to the point here.

> Christ appears, portrayed in traits taken chiefly from descriptions of God and an angelic being given in the Old Testament, which are meant to picture him in dazzling glory and majesty, vv. 13–16. A symbolic meaning is not to be sought in the details, except so far as they form traits in a picture of resplendent glory, and contain current terms used in expressing divine activities.[1]

Beckwith also writes, "It is important to determine the meaning which the author attached to the symbols used and to avoid fancifulness to which they easily lend themselves—a most common source of misinterpretation."[2]

To illustrate, one might survey several commentaries and find that the words "His head and His hair were white like white wool, like snow" (1:14) are taken to mean anything from beauty to suffering, with various other alternatives such as sinlessness, authority, maturity, or wisdom.[3] If a sane approach to exegesis is followed, the interpreter understands that the Lord wished to convey to John one major idea, and not six, by this particular feature of the vision.

A careful examination of the vision, therefore, should disclose in what character the risen Christ wished to reveal Himself to the apostle, and hence to the churches, for the purpose of conveying the remaining content of the book.

Turning around, John saw in the middle of the seven lampstands one whom he chose to describe by ten distinguishing characteristics.

First, He was "like a son of man" (1:13). These words are derived from Daniel 7:13, which states that one like a son of man appeared in order to receive earthly dominion. The comparison sets forth essentially the human appearance, and thus the humanity, of the one whom John saw. In omitting the definite article before "son," the author agreed with the Septuagint version of Daniel. From this fact and from the use of ὅμοιον (like) before the words, it is apparent that the messianic title "Son of Man," found so frequently in the Gospels, is not intended here. Nevertheless there can be no disputing the fact that this personage is identical with the Messiah, who is pictured in Revelation 19:11–16 as coming triumphantly. The strong impression on the author at this point, however, is His human appearance.

Second, He was "clothed in a robe reaching to the feet" (1:13). In the Greek Old Testament such language is used to depict part of the high priest's apparel,[4] but the same is true in an even more striking manner in Ezekiel 9:2. There both Greek words found in Revelation are applied to the man charged with setting a mark on some of the Jerusalemites before the others are destroyed.[5] Of these two possible emphases, a priestly ministry and one of mercy in the face of impending judgment, the latter is the more likely choice, since nowhere else in the book does Christ appear in a priestly capacity.[6] On the other hand one of the principal thrusts of the visions is His activity in extending mercy to those exempted from the punishments that are about to fall. The man in Ezekiel is associated with six others whose office is to smite the sinful inhabitants of the city while passing by those who are grieved over the city's abominations. Herein lies the similarity to Christ's future ministry of administering mercy in the midst of God's wrath on the world (Rev. 7:2–3; 9:4).

Third, He was "girded across His breast with a golden girdle" (1:13). Again the terminology seems to be suggested by an Old Testament expression, one from Daniel 10:5, where the main difference is in the location of the girdle. In Daniel's vision the girdle was about the loins, but in the Patmos experience it was about the breast. The resemblance between these two visions is nevertheless more pronounced than that between Christ and the priest, as some have suggested.[7] Though this was characteristic of priestly dress, it was not the priests' habit exclusively.[8] Apparently the high girding normally accompanied any garment "down to the feet."[9]

This aspect of Christ's dress more probably bears a closer relationship to the angels of the seven last plagues (Rev. 15:6). Though the wording is not identical, it is close enough to warrant this association. So this part of John's vision must have come to suggest Jesus' part in the climactic outpouring of God's wrath, which these seven plagues or bowls depict.

Fourth, "His head and His hair were white like white wool, like snow" (1:14). The terminology in this case is drawn from Daniel 7:9, where one called "the ancient of days" is similarly described. The title, reserved for God alone, places particular emphasis on the preexistence of the One so named. To interpret the symbolic appearance further and say that the hair is white because of suffering[10] or to say that the emphasis on whiteness brings out the concept of sinlessness[11] seems to press the figure to undue extremes. A more sound exegetical procedure limits each feature of the vision to one principal idea.

Fifth, "His eyes were like a flame of fire" (Rev. 1:14). This aspect of the vision relates to Daniel 10:6. Such language has reference to the surpassing intelligence of the one so described. In Daniel's prophecy it is intelligence about future events, for the stated purpose of the man's coming to Daniel is to make him understand what would befall Israel in the latter days (Dan. 10:14). The Revealer of the Apocalypse also had a knowledge of the future that He was to share with John.

Sixth, "His feet were like burnished bronze, when it has been caused to glow in a furnace" (Rev. 1:15). The exact nature of the metal called χαλκολίβανον is impossible to ascertain. Most linguists say it refers it to a "mixed metal of great brilliance," a burnished brass or bronze.[12] The purity of the metal is emphasized by its shining or glowing quality and by its comparison to a furnace in which impurities are removed from molten metal. Figuratively, then, it is a picture of moral purity. Insofar as the feet are concerned, in the New Testament they quite often signify a person in motion

(Luke 1:79; Acts 5:9; Rom. 3:15; 10:15; Heb. 12:13). Such a thought completes the picture of moral purity moving among the churches.

Seventh, His voice was "like the sound of many waters" (Rev. 1:15). Apparently John was likening the voice to the endless pounding of the shore by waves of the Aegean Sea, a suggestion of a powerful force (Ps. 93:4; Isa. 17:13). But the specific source of the phrase is the prophetic experience of Ezekiel when the prophet saw and heard the glory of the God of Israel returning to the temple in Jerusalem (Ezek. 43:2).[13] So the apostle was identifying this personage with God and the power of His utterance as He returned to dwell with His people.

Eighth, "in His right hand He held seven stars" (Rev. 1:16). According to verse 20 the stars represented angels or messengers.[14] Whether they are angelic or human, this divine Figure exercises complete control over them. In thinking of the stars as symbolic of the seven churches, some have seen the added thought of safekeeping in this expression (cf. John 10:28).[15] But since the churches are symbolized by the lampstands, the stars are best limited to the messengers. In this case the Lord's hold on them connotes His absolute control. When He thus controls the messengers of the churches, readers are assured of His right to speak authoritatively to the churches themselves.

Ninth, "out of his mouth came a sharp two-edged sword" (Rev. 1:16). Like the previous detail, this one is not derived directly from an Old Testament source; however, an indirect relationship to smiting the earth "with the rod of His mouth" from Isaiah 11:4 seems possible. In keeping with the use of this terminology in Revelation 2:16 and 19:15, the principal thought is the punishing power of Christ's word.[16] It is a picture of the Son's defeat of His enemies and His pronouncement of judgment on them.[17]

Tenth, His face was "like the sun shining in its strength" (1:16). In this last notation the terminology is derived from Judges 5:31, a portion of the song of Deborah and Barak, in which the phrase describes those who love the Lord. Undoubtedly, however, the apostle's thoughts immediately went back to his unforgettable experience with the Lord on the Mount of Transfiguration. On that occasion Christ's "face shone like the sun" (Matt. 17:2) in an anticipatory glimpse of the glory to be manifest in His second coming to the earth. Now the aged apostle was given the unique privilege of a second foreview of that glory. The quality of the brightness is heightened through the addition of the words "in its [or, his] strength"; there are no clouds or mist to diminish the intensity of the sun's rays. This word on the glory of the person addressing John climaxes the series of descriptive phrases, bringing the seer to the ground at the feet of his divine companion (Rev. 1:17).

Because of the number of points of contact between the first vision on Patmos and the figure described in Daniel 10:5–6, there is some merit in Bullinger's statement that the purposes of the two appearances are the same. As the one in Daniel came to make the prophet understand what should befall Israel in the latter days (10:14), so the appearance of Christ helped make John understand the same thing.[18] Yet this opinion is somewhat narrow since it does not allow for similarities to other prophetic passages.

Instead, Christ was presenting Himself to John in a way that would prepare the apostle for various aspects of the visions to follow. A brief suggestion in summary of the vision will show how this purpose was realized:

1. His human form sets the stage for His appearance as the seed of David (Rev. 5:5).
2. His garment down to His feet anticipates His protection of the 144,000 in the midst of God's wrath (7:2–3; 9:4).
3. His high girding is a foreview of His part in inflicting wrath (6:16).
4. His white hair recalls His fitness to participate in the consummation because of His part in the origin of the world (1:11, 17–18; 2:8; 3:14; 21:6; 22:13).
5. His eyes like a flame of fire relate to His activity in opening the seals and thus unveiling the future (6:1, 3, 5, 7, 9, 12; 8:1).
6. His feet like burnished brass impress the churches with the high standard of purity that characterizes His judgment (21:8).
7. His voice like the sound of many waters is the mighty voice of God heard as He makes His abode with His choice witness (14:2).
8. His grip on the seven stars is suggestive of the right He has, as Head of the church, to address these seven churches (2:1).
9. The sword out of His mouth looks forward to the conquest over His enemies at the time of His second advent (19:15).
10. The brightness of His countenance typifies the glory of His future reign (21:23).

CHAPTER 17

The Present Universal Lordship of Christ

John F. Walvoord

Different points of view in eschatology have had an unfortunate effect on the proper statement of the present lordship of Christ. If amillennialism and postmillennialism are correct that Christ in the present age must fulfill promises of universal rule over the earth by means of the church and the preaching of the Gospel, this would contradict the concept that He is now seated at the Father's throne waiting for that future time when He will return to earth in power and glory to set up His earthly rule. The premillennial position is fully in harmony with the scriptural revelation given concerning the present universal lordship of Christ and relieves much of the confusion that occurs when attempts are made to see millennial prophecies fulfilled in the present age.

A study of the passages dealing with the lordship of Christ provides additional evidence for the validity of the premillennial interpretation. Scriptures pertaining to this subject reveal a threefold division of the subject: the present position of Christ at the right hand of the Father, the extent of His present authority, and the expectation of Christ as revealed in the Scriptures that anticipate a future aspect of His lordship.

The Present Position of Christ

Some scholars tend to neglect what the Scriptures say about the present position of Christ at the right hand of the Father, mentioned in many Scriptures (Ps. 110:1; Matt. 22:44; 26:64; Mark 12:36; 14:62; 16:19; Luke 20:42; 22:69; Acts 2:33–34; 5:31; Rom. 8:34; Eph. 1:20; Col. 3:1; Heb. 1:3, 13; 8:1; 10:12; 12:2; 1 Peter 3:22).

This position of being seated at the right hand of the Father is obviously one of highest possible honor and involves possession of the throne without dispossession of the Father. The implication is that all glory, authority, and power is shared by the Father with the Son. The throne is definitely a heavenly throne, not the Davidic throne and not an earthly throne. It is over all the universe and its creatures.

One of the assumptions of postmillennial and amillennial interpreters is that the throne Christ now occupies is the throne of David. However, an examination of the New Testament discloses that not a single instance can be found where the present position of Christ is identified with David's throne. In view of the many references to the fact that Christ is now seated at the right hand of the Father, it is inconceivable that these two positions are identical, as none of the twenty passages uses the expression "throne of David" as a proper representation of the present position of Christ. If Christ is now on the throne of David, it is without any scriptural support whatever.

The impossibility of David's throne and the Father's throne being one and the same is readily demonstrated by the simple question of whether David could sit on the Father's throne. The answer is obvious. David's throne pertained to the earth, to the land of Israel, and to the people of Israel. It never contemplated any universality, and it was never anything more than an earthly throne.

The description of the throne of David in the Old Testament makes this clear. David's throne had to do with his rule over the people of Israel during his generation. That it was promised that it would continue was interpreted by the Jews as a promise of a future earthly kingdom. By contrast, every reference to the throne of the Father pictures it as in heaven. The throne of the Father is eternal, that is, it existed long before David was born or his kingdom or throne began. In all these points there is dissimilarity between the throne of David and the throne of God the Father.

The distinction between the two thrones is also brought out by examination of their characteristics. The throne in heaven on which Christ is now seated is obviously one of supreme honor, glory, victory, power, and authority. No power on earth or in heaven could possibly have a higher position nor could there be one of more honor and privilege than what the Lord Jesus Christ now possesses. The throne of God is in keeping with the divine attributes of the eternal God and is supported by infinite power and authority in keeping with the position and work of the second person of the Trinity. Because He is on the throne in glory, saints are able to have victory in this world and can be assured that though the power of Satan and the temptations of this world are real and though they experience weakness because of their sin nature, it is still true that Christ is on the throne and thus He is able to sustain them in their hour of need.

The position of Christ on the throne is also theoretically important because it reveals the present position of the body of Christ. The church is in Christ and therefore is positioned where Christ already is located, namely, in the presence of God. The locality of Christ in heaven on the throne does not interfere with His divine omnipresence. At the same time He can be on the throne on behalf of believers and be in communion with believers on earth. His presence on the throne, however, guarantees that believers will be with Christ bodily in heaven after the resurrection and translation of the church and will reign with Him (Rev. 3:21).

By contrast, these factors cannot be said of the throne of David. The church has no relationship to the throne of David nor was the throne of David one of infinite power and authority. Conceivably it could be lost and destroyed, though David was assured that it would not be. To confuse such dissimilar positions is to bring confusion to the Word of God.

The Present Authority of Christ

The present authority of Christ is over the old creation. Though it is not always evident because of the presence of sin and rebellion against God, the Scriptures make it clear that eventually all opposing forces to Christ will be put down. This is the plan of God and it will be brought to fruition. In the sovereign wisdom of God, He has permitted sin and rebellion to continue in order to permit a further display of His grace and an extension of time for the lost to hear and believe the Gospel. The ultimate victory, however, is assured because it is based on the triumph of Christ on the cross and the authority of Christ as the One seated at the right hand of God the Father. In one sense Christ has the absolute authority over the old creation, but in keeping with the purposes of God, He is waiting to manifest His authority when He has put down all evil.

A major passage in the New Testament revealing the extent of His present lordship is 1 Peter 3:22, which describes Jesus Christ as being seated "at the right hand of God, having gone into heaven, after angels and authorities and powers had been subjected to Him." In contrast to prophetic passages such as Isaiah 9:6–7 that refer to His future lordship over the earth, the passage in Peter specifically speaks of His present authority. The reference to angels is undoubtedly to the holy (unfallen) angels though, ultimately, fallen angels also will come under His authority. The superiority and authority of Christ over angels is revealed in Hebrews 1:4–14, which affirms that He has a more excellent name than the angels, that He is the Son of God, that angels worship Him, that His throne is forever, that His position is in contrast to the servant character of the angels, that He has existed from eternity long before the angels were created, and that to Him alone is the invitation given to sit at the right hand of the Father until His enemies are made His footstool.

In 1 Peter 3:22 the word translated "authorities" (ἐξουσιῶν) refers to "rulers and functionaries of the spirit world."[1] It apparently refers to angelic beings, whether holy angels or fallen. The word "powers" (δυνάμεων) has the same idea but with the added thought of inherent power. Arndt and Gingrich define *power* as "a personal supernatural spirit or angel."[2] Thayer gives a more specific definition: "inherent power, power residing in a thing by virtue of its nature, or which a person or thing exerts and puts forth."[3] The three words together reveal that Jesus Christ in His position at the right hand of the Father has lordship over all created beings superior to human beings and specifically over angels, whether fallen or unfallen. It is important to observe that while Christ has authority over this area of creation He manifestly is not exerting it to the full; He is permitting evil forces to continue their domination over the world while Satan, "the god of this world" (2 Cor. 4:4), is yet unbound.

Another important passage bearing on the subject is Ephesians 1:19–23, which reveals that the present authority of Christ stems from His resurrection. Paul prayed that the Ephesian church might know "the surpassing greatness of His power toward us who believe. These are in accordance with that working of the strength of His might which He brought about in Christ, when He raised Him from the dead, and seated Him at His right hand in the heavenly places, far above all rule and authority and power and dominion, and every name that is named, not only in this age, but also in the one to come" (vv. 19–21). Then in verses 22–23 Paul added the climax to the whole concept of Christ's authority: "And He put all things in subjection under His feet, and gave Him as head over all things to the church, which is His body, the fulness of Him who fills all in all." This statement indicates that Christ's power extends to all creatures and all aspects of the universe. The word translated "rule" in verse 21 (ἀρχῆς) literally means "first place," revealing that Christ is first before all others. Added to the meaning of this word is the phrase "far above," indicating not only supremacy but also that Christ is infinitely above any others who might be considered, such as angels or human beings. The words "authority" and "power" are the same words used in 1 Peter 3:22 (ἐξουσίας and δυνάμεως), though they are singular here instead of plural.

Another word is introduced, however, in Ephesians 1:21: "dominion" (κυριότητος). Literally this means lordship, coming from κύριος. It indicates that Christ is Lord over all other lords, that He is Lord of lords. Paul put a final superlative touch on his description of the authority of Christ in stating that the rule, authority, power, and dominion of Christ are far above "every name that is named, not only in this age, but also in the one to come." There is no competition whatever to the present position and lordship of Christ. He is supreme now and He always will be. The word "age" (αἰῶνι) represents a time idea. In the present time as well as in the future, Christ is supreme in power and authority.

The concluding statement of Ephesians 1:22 is that God "put all things in subjection under His [Christ's] feet." This expression is probably derived from Psalm 8:6, "Thou dost make him to rule over the works of Thy hands; Thou hast put all things under his feet." Because Psalm 8 deals with God's commission to the "son of man" (v. 4), the implication is that Christ will rule over the earth as the ideal Man. In creating humankind, God gave Adam the responsibility of exercising authority over the earth. This was spoiled by the entrance of sin into the human race. Now Christ, as the second Adam, is qualified by His perfect life, His victory over death and sin, and His resurrection to rule over the earth. This is the ultimate intent of God, namely, that His Son should rule, as indicated in Psalm 2:8–9. Though today this authority is not fully manifested in the present evil world, Christ nevertheless has power and authority to put down evil and is waiting for the proper time for the consummation of the present age to fulfill this purpose of God. The expression "put in subjection" (ὑπέταξεν) is a positional ingressive aorist, that is, it indicates that Christ has come into this position where all things are in subjection under

Him. Other Scriptures clearly show that the realization of absolute subjection of all creation is a part of God's future program (1 Cor. 15:25). At the present time, however, Christ is exercising His lordship over the church and this ultimately will be extended to the entire universe.

Much has been made of the fact that in the philosophic consideration of Christianity, that the present world is not a good world in many respects. Some philosophers therefore consider it an irresolvable problem that if God were both omnipotent and good, He would not permit an evil world. Both attributes, according to this point of view, could not be true. Therefore they choose a finite God but one who is good, a God who cannot control the universe but desires to bring good into it.

The solution to this problem lies in the fact that the Bible clearly recognizes the present age, judged by present standards, as not necessarily good. No book in all the world more frankly faces the sinfulness of the human heart and the evil and sorrow of life than the Bible. The solution is resolved, however, in that the Bible anticipates that ultimately sin will be judged and righteousness will triumph, and with it the omnipotence and goodness of God will both fully be demonstrated.

In keeping with this truth Christ is shown in Psalm 110:1 as seated at the right hand of God awaiting the subjugation of His enemies: "The LORD says to my Lord: 'Sit at My right hand, until I make Thine enemies a footstool for Thy feet.'" According to Hebrews 10:13, this is a position characterized by rest rather than by activity: "Waiting from that time onward until His enemies be made a footstool for His feet." While Christ in His present position has authority and power to do everything necessary to put down evil and is assured of ultimate victory, it is also evident that the present exercise of this power is being withheld to some extent to permit a future consummation of His universal rule over creation. The Scriptures represent the present age, therefore, as a period of waiting for a future display of the power of Christ. This is precisely what is anticipated in the premillennial interpretation of Scripture. The present church age is a parenthesis in the program of God, in which the ultimate domination of Christ over the earth, as its supreme Ruler, is withheld in some aspects so that God might fulfill His present purpose of calling out of the world a heavenly people.

The present age, however, is not one of complete inactivity, as is clear from 1 Corinthians 15:24–28. The program leading to the ultimate subjugation of His enemies is underway, but the final triumph will not come until the end, as there is rebellion even at the end of the Millennium against the government of Christ. Meanwhile, however, Christ is seated at the right hand of the Father awaiting His hour of triumph in which history will come to its close, and the power, sovereignty, and majesty of Christ will be obvious to every creature.

Chapter Notes

Chapter 1

1. Benjamin B. Warfield, "Person of Christ," in *International Standard Bible Encyclopaedia*, 4 (1939): 2342–43.
2. Ibid., 2338–39.

Chapter 3

1. Joseph Klausner, *Jesus of Nazareth: His Life, Times, and Teaching*, trans. Herbert Danby (New York: Macmillan, 1946), p. 377.
2. Ibid., p. 379.
3. Ibid., p. 342.
4. W. A. Visser't Hooft, *The First Assembly of the World Council of Churches* (New York: Association, n.d.), p. 197.
5. John A. T. Robinson, *Honest to God* (Philadelphia: Westminster, 1963), pp. 72–73.
6. L. Harold DeWolf, *The Case for Theology in Liberal Perspective* (Philadelphia: Westminster, 1959), p. 71.
7. Nels F. S. Ferré, *The Finality of Faith* (New York: Harper and Row, 1963), pp. 48–49.
8. Edward W. Bauman, *The Life and Teaching of Jesus* (Philadelphia: Westminster, 1960), p. 201.
9. Robinson, *Honest to God*, p. 70 (italics his).
10. C. Milo Connick, *Jesus: the Man, the Mission, and the Message*, p. 311.
11. Ibid., p. 313.
12. Cecil John Cadoux, *The Historic Mission of Jesus* (New York: Harper, 1943), pp. 27, 103.
13. Paul B. Kern, *The Basic Beliefs of Jesus* (Nashville: Cokesbury, 1935), p. 223.
14. Vincent Taylor, *The Names of Jesus* (New York: St. Martins, 1953), p. 65.
15. Geerhardus Vos, *The Self-Discovery of Jesus* (New York: Doran, 1026).
16. Rudolf Bultmann, *Jesus and the Word*, trans. Louise Pettibone Smith and Erminie Huntress Lantero (New York: Scribner, 1958), p. 9.
17. Bultmann, *Theology of the New Testament*, trans. Kendrick Grobel, 2 vols. (London: SCM, 1952, 1955), 1:26.

18. Ernest Cadman Colwell, *An Approach to the Teaching of Jesus* (New York: Abingdon & Cokesbury, 1947), pp. 74–75.
19. Bertram Lee Woolf, *The Authority of Jesus and Its Foundation* (London: Allen & Unwin, 1929), pp. 233–34.
20. Martin Dibelius, *Jesus,* trans. Charles B. Hedrick and Frederick C. Grand (Philadelphia: Westminster, 1949), p. 13.
21. A. T. Robertson, *Word Pictures in the New Testament,* 6 vols. (Nashville: Broadman, 1933), 5:158–59.
22. Marvin R. Vincent, *Word Studies in the New Testament,* 4 vols. (Grand Rapids: Eerdmans, 1946), 2:197.
23. Bauman, *Life and Teaching of Jesus,* pp. 201–202 (italics his).
24. Vos, *Self-Disclosure of Jesus,* p. 142.
25. Kern, *Basic Beliefs of Jesus,* p. 227.

Chapter 4

1. Charles Hodge, *Systematic Theology,* 3 vols. (London: Clarke, 1960), 2:464.

Chapter 5

1. Alfred Edersheim, *The Life and Times of Jesus the Messiah* (Grand Rapids: Eerdmans, 1962), p. 285.
2. John made it plain that the Baptist saw the vision, but there is no evidence that he heard the voice. If the reading σὺ εἶ is original, as McNeile thinks possible, it is even more plausible that Jesus alone heard the voice. In that event He may well have given the disciples the full story on the occasion of the incident mentioned in Matthew 20:20–28. In that passage the term "baptism" is given its most illuminating exposition (Alan Hugh McNeile, *The Gospel according to St. Matthew* [London: Macmillan, 1915], pp. 35–36).
3. G. Campbell Morgan, *The Crises of the Christ* (New York: Revell, 1903), p. 86.
4. Alfred Plummer, *A Critical and Exegetical Commentary on the Gospel according to St. Luke,* 6th ed. (New York: Scribner's Sons, 1903), p. 79.
5. Morgan, *Crises of the Christ,* p. 90.
6. For details on His appearance and early years see Ethelbert Stauffer, *Jesus and His Story,* trans. Richard and Clara Winston (New York: Knopf, 1959), pp. 43–61.
7. B. F. Westcott, *The Gospel according to St. John* (1892; reprint, Grand Rapids: Eerdmans, 1954), p. 118.
8. Archibald M. Hunter, *Introducing New Testament Theology* (London: SCM, 1957), p. 10.
9. The word διεχώλυεν is intensive, and the imperfect is conative (cf. McNeile, *St. Matthew,* p. 30).

10. "Der Widerspruch des Täufers ist überwunden" (Theodor Zahn, *Das Evangelium des Matthäus*, p. 144).
11. Σχιζομένους (Mark 1:10).
12. Ἔδωκα τὸ πνεῦμά μου ἐπ᾿ αὐτόν (LXX).
13. G. R. Beasley-Murray, *Baptism in the New Testament* (New York: St. Martin's, 1962), p. 61. He points out that viewing His baptism as only the first step in the *via dolorosa* is misleading.
14. Hunter, *Introducing New Testament Theology*, p. 15.
15. Ibid.
16. Morgan, *The Gospel according to Matthew*, p. 28.
17. Cf. Beasley-Murray, *Baptism in the New Testament*, p. 64.
18. G. C. Berkouwer, *The Person of Christ*, trans. John Vriend (Grand Rapids: Eerdmans, 1954), p. 246.
19. The word πρέπον is suggestive. Baptism is not a commandment of the Law, but it is a duty. The word means "to be proper, right" (William F. Arndt and F. Wilbur Gingrich, *A Greek-English Lexicon of the New Testament and Other Early Christian Literature* [Chicago: University of Chicago Press, 1957], p. 706.)

Chapter 6

1. For a defense of the deity of Christ over against the charge of docetism, see Nigel Turner, *Grammatical Insights into the New Testament* (Edinburgh: Clark, 1965), pp. 13–17.
2. Cf. Richard Chenevix Trench, *Studies in the Gospels*, 6th ed. (London: Kegan Paul, Trench, Trübner, 1896), p. 29.
3. William G. T. Shedd, *Dogmatic Theology*, 3 vols. (Grand Rapids: Zondervan, n.d.), 2:332. His famous illustration of the iron wire and the iron bar should be read.
4. B. Harvie Branscomb, *The Gospel of Mark* (New York: Harper & Brothers, n.d.), p. 22.
5. T. W. Manson, *The Servant-Messiah: A Study of the Public Ministry of Jesus* (Cambridge: University Press, 1953), p. 55.
6. Hunter, *Introducing New Testament Theology*, p. 15.
7. T. W. Manson, *The Servant-Messiah: A Study of the Public Ministry of Jesus* (Cambridge: University Press, 1953), p. 56.
8. W. Graham Scroggie, *The Gospel of Mark* (London: Marshall, Morgan & Scott, n.d.), pp. 29–30.
9. The dependent clause is a first-class condition, a condition of assumed reality. Satan accepted the title of Son of God for purposes of argument. Often this type of condition is translated by *since,* but this is unnecessary because the English *if* may have and often does have the force of *since,* like the Greek εἰ. For example, if one were to say, "I am going to town," the hearer might respond by saying, "If (= since, for I am assuming the reality of the statement) you are going to town, would you run an errand for me?" This type of *if* is found in verse 3. The anarthrous υἱός is

correctly rendered "the Son" in accord with Colwell's rule. Cf. James Hope Moulton, *A Grammar of New Testament Greek,* vol. 3: *Syntax,* by Nigel Turner (Edinburgh: Clark, 1963), p. 83.

10. P. T. Forsyth, *The Person and Place of Jesus Christ,* 5th ed. (London: Independent, 1950), p. 35.

11. G. Campbell Morgan, *The Crises of the Christ* (Grand Rapids: Kregel Publications, 1989), p. 131.

12. James Denney, *Jesus and the Gospel* (London: Hodder & Stoughton, 1908), p. 189.

13. Helmut Thielecke, *Between God and Satan,* trans. C. C. Barber (London: Longmen, 1958), p. 2.

14. Manson, *The Servant-Messiah,* p. 57.

Chapter 7

1. It is now widely recognized that the whole of Mark relates to Jesus' temptation narrative. See, for example, E. Best, *The Temptation and the Passion: The Markan Soteriology* (Cambridge: Cambridge University Press, 1965); William L. Lane, *The Gospel according to Mark* (Grand Rapids: Eerdmans, 1974), p. 206; and Walter W. Wessel, "Mark," in *The Expositor's Bible Commentary,* 12 vols. (Grand Rapids: Zondervan, 1984), 8:623.

2. See B. Gerhardsson, *The Testing of God's Son (Matt 4:1–11 & Par): An Analysis of an Early Christian Midrash* (Lund: Gleerup, 1966), pp. 36–38; and W. D. Davies and D. C. Allison, *A Critical and Exegetical Commentary on the Gospel according to Saint Matthew,* International Critical Commentary (Edinburgh: Clark, 1988), 1:355.

3. Lane, *Mark,* p. 59.

4. C. K. Barrett, *The Holy Spirit and the Gospel Tradition* (London: SPCK, 1947), p. 49.

5. G. H. P. Thompson, "Called-Proved-Obedient: A Study in the Baptism and Temptation Narratives of Matthew and Luke," *Journal of Theological Studies* n.s., 11 (1960): 9.

6. Ibid.

7. See W. R. Stegner, "Wilderness and Testing in the Scrolls and in Matthew 4:1–11," *Bible Review* 12 (1967): 18–27, who shows that the wilderness, as a concept, is correlated with the motif of trial, testing, and temptation. Cf. W. Marxen, *Mark the Evangelist: Studies on the Redaction History of the Gospel* (Nashville: Abingdon, 1969), pp. 26–28; and U. W. Mauser, *Christ in the Wilderness: The Wilderness Theme in the Second Gospel and Its Basis in the Biblical Tradition* (London: SCM, 1963), p. 14.

8. Davies and Allison, *Critical and Exegetical Commentary,* 1:354.

9. See B. Byrne, *"Sons of God"—"Seed of Abraham": A Study in the Idea of the Sonship of God of All Christians in Paul against the Jewish Background* (Rome: Biblical Institute Press, 1979), pp.

9–78; E. Lövestam, *Son and Saviour: A Study of Acts 13:32–37.*
With an Appendix: "Son of God" in the Synoptic Gospels (Lund:
Gleerup, 1961), pp. 88–112; M. Hengel, *The Son of God: The*
Origin of Christology and the History of Jewish-Hellenistic
Christianity (London: SCM, 1976), pp. 41–56; S. Schechter,
Aspects of Rabbinic Theology (reprint, New York: Schocken, 1961),
pp. 46–64; G. F. Moore, *Judaism in the First Centuries of the*
Christian Era, 3 vols. (Cambridge, Mass.: Harvard University Press,
1927–1930), 2:201–11; and Herman L. Strack and Paul Billerbeck,
Kommentar zum Neuen Testament aus Talmud und Midrasch
(Munich: Beck, 1922–1956), 1:219–20, 392–96; 3:19–22.

10. Gerhardsson, *The Testing of God's Son,* p. 21.
11. See R. T. France, *Jesus and the Old Testament: His Application of*
Old Testament Passages to Himself and His Mission (Downers
Grove, Ill.: InterVarsity, 1971), p. 53.
12. Lane, *Mark,* p. 59; cf. D. Hill, *The Gospel of Matthew,* New
Century Bible (London: Marshall, Morgan & Scott, 1972), p. 99.
13. These are too complex to discuss here. See, among many, Barrett,
Gospel Tradition, pp. 25–45; and J. D. G. Dunn, *Baptism in the*
Holy Spirit (London: SCM, 1970), pp. 23–37.
14. See Thompson, "Called-Proved-Obedient," p. 8; and L. Goppelt,
Typos: The Typological Interpretation of the Old Testament in the
New (Grand Rapids: Eerdmans, 1982), pp. 97–98.
15. Psalm 80:17 calls Israel "the man of Thy right hand." The term
"the man" (μΤΝΠ = ὁ ἄνθρωπος) recalls the same in the Septuagint
of Genesis 1–3, where it refers to Adam.
16. Isaiah 13:21; 34:14; Matthew 12:43; Luke 8:29; 11:24; Revelation
18:2; cf. Mark 5:5. See Gerhard Kittel, "ἔρημος," in *Theological*
Dictionary of the New Testament 2 (1964): 657; Best, *The*
Temptation and the Passion, p. 5; Mauser, *Christ in the Wilderness,*
pp. 100–101; Marxen, *Mark the Evangelist,* p. 47; Strack and
Billerbeck, *Kommentar zum Neuen Testament aus Talmud und*
Midrasch, 4:515–16; and H. A. Kelly, "The Devil in the Desert,"
Catholic Biblical Quarterly 26 (1964): 194–95.
17. Also see J. Pedersen, *Israel, Its Life and Culture,* 2 vols. (reprint,
London: Cumberlege, 1946), 1:453–70; Mauser, *Christ in the*
Wilderness, p. 37, n. 2; Davies and Allison, *Critical and Exegetical*
Commentary, 1:354; and Lane, *Mark,* p. 61.
18. See E. Fascher, "Jesus und die Tiere," *Theologische Zeitschrift* 90
(1965): 561–70; W. A. Schulze, "Der Heilige und die wilden Tiere:
Zur Exegese von Mc. 1,13b," *Zeitschrift für die neutestamentliche*
Wissenschaft 46 (1955): 280–83; A. Feuillet, "Le récit Lucanien
de la tentation (Lc 4,1–13)," *Biblica* 40 (1959): 617–28; P. Pokorny,
"The Temptation Stories and Their Intention," *New Testament*
Studies 20 (1973–74): 120–22; Davies and Allison, *Critical and*
Exegetical Commentary, 1:356–57; R. A. Guelich, *Mark 1:1–8:26,*
Word Biblical Commentary (Dallas: Word, 1989), p. 38; C. S.

Mann, *Mark,* Anchor Bible (Garden City, NY: Doubleday, 1986), pp. 203–4; Goppelt, *Typos,* p. 98; Best, *The Temptation and the Passion,* p. 8; Barrett, *Gospel Tradition,* pp. 49–50; and J. T. Milik, *Ten Years of Discovery in the Wilderness of Judea* (London: SCM, 1959), p. 115.

19. Guelich, *Mark 1:1–8:26,* p. 39; cf. W. Grundmann, "σύν-μετά," in *Theological Dictionary of the New Testament* 7 (1971): 796–97; and Milik, *Ten Years of Discovery in the Wilderness of Judea,* p. 115.

20. Guelich, *Mark 1:1–8:26,* p. 30.

21. On the equation of "Son of Man" with "Son of God," see S. Kim, *The "Son of Man" as the Son of God* (Tübingen: Mohr, 1983).

22. See J. H. Eaton, *Kingship and the Psalms* (London: SCM, 1976), pp. 146–49.

23. See Davies and Allison, *Critical and Exegetical Commentary,* 1:358–59.

24. The denial of the connection with Israel by Kittel, "ἔρημος," (2:658), and Best *(The Temptation and the Passion,* pp. 5–6) neglects the symbolic significance of the number forty as well as the typological links between Jesus and Israel throughout the Gospels. That Jesus' forty days is not Israel's forty years is not really important, because the Gospels speak of a complex of exodus/wilderness imagery that does not depend on a strictly one-for-one correspondence between the respective elements. Typology is normally looser than many are willing to allow; what is important is the conviction that there is an overall consistency of divine activity in salvation history whereby God's acts in the Old Testament set in motion a rhythmic pattern that is brought to a climax in the New Testament. As Dupont puts it, the parallelism consists not simply in words but in the situations of Israel and Jesus respectively (J. Dupont, "L'arrier-fond biblique du récit des tentations de Jesus," *New Testament Studies* 3 [1956–1957]: 289). Also there is the Old Testament principle that days correspond to years (Num. 14:34; Ezek. 4:5). Cf. Gerhardsson, *The Testing of God's Son,* pp. 42–43.

25. Mauser, *Christ in the Wilderness,* p. 99.

26. Davies and Allison, *Critical and Exegetical Commentary,* 1:360; Barrett, *Gospel Tradition,* p. 51; and Robert H. Gundry, *Matthew: A Commentary on His Literary and Theological Art* (Grand Rapids: Eerdmans, 1982), p. 55.

27. Davies and Allison, *Critical and Exegetical Commentary,* 1:360.

28. T. L. Donaldson, *Jesus on the Mountain: A Study in Matthean Theology* (Sheffield: JSOT, 1985), p. 91. In addition, see Lövestam, *Son and Savior,* pp. 94–101.

29. Gundry, *Matthew,* p. 58. Theissen has argued that the temptation of Jesus to prostrate Himself (προσκυνέω) in exchange for the kingdoms of the world reflects the absolutist claims most notably of Caligula, who not only introduced the hated practice of

prostration (προσκύνησις/προσκυνέω) before himself as a god, but also asserted his authority to bestow and remove kingdoms (G. Theissen, *The Gospels in Context: Social and Political History in the Synoptic Tradition* [Minneapolis: Fortress, 1991], pp. 206–21). For Theissen the temptation stories are modeled on this act of self-humiliation before the emperor, to which the Jews took particular exception inasmuch as it clashed with their monotheistic convictions (cf. Philo *De Legatione ad Gaium* 116–17, 352–53). Hence the underlying motivation of the narratives is to encourage Christians to follow the example of Jesus by not "falling down" before the imperial claimants to deity. Without following Theissen's whole reconstruction, his data support the thesis of this study in that the first Christians were to resist the worship of idols in any form, because Jesus is to be worshiped. He, not Caesar, is God.

30. Davies and Allison, *Critical and Exegetical Commentary,* 1:360; and Gundry, *Matthew,* p. 55. Cf. especially Matthew 17:7 and 28:18, where the transfigured and resurrected Jesus approached His disciples.

31. On Luke's portrayal of Jesus as the Lord God tested by Satan, see S. Brown, *Apostasy and Perseverance in the Theology of Luke* (Rome: Pontifical Biblical Institute, 1969), pp. 18–19, esp. n. 59.

32. See Best, *The Temptation and the Passion,* p. 7; Gundry, *Matthew,* p. 55; Davies and Allison, *Critical and Exegetical Commentary,* 1:355; and W. Wilkens, "Die Versuchung Jesu nach Matthäus," *New Testament Studies* 28 (1982): 481–82.

33. Thus, for example, J. A. Fitzmeyer, *The Gospel according to Luke,* 2 vols., Anchor Bible (Garden City, N.Y.: Doubleday, 1981), 1:507. On the temple-Jerusalem motif in Luke see J. B. Chance, *Jerusalem, Temple, and the New Age in Luke-Acts* (Macon, Ga.: Mercer University Press, 1988); and P. F. Esler, *Community and Gospel in Luke-Acts: The Social and Political Motivations of Lucan Theology* (Cambridge: Cambridge University Press, 1987), pp. 131–63.

34. Donaldson, *Jesus on the Mountain,* pp. 89–90.

35. Gundry, *Matthew,* p. 56; Donaldson, *Jesus on the Mountain,* p. 89; and Stegner, "Wilderness and Testing," p. 27.

36. Gerhardsson, *The Testing of God's Son,* pp. 76–79; Gundry, *Matthew,* p. 56.

37. Davies and Allison, *Critical and Exegetical Commentary,* 1:352.

38. Donaldson, *Jesus on the Mountain,* pp. 101–4.

39. Ibid., p. 96.

40. The Jewish materials are surveyed by Mauser, *Christ in the Wilderness,* pp. 53–61; J. A. Kirk, "The Messianic Role of Jesus and the Temptation Narrative: A Contemporary Perspective," *Evangelical Quarterly* 44 (1972): 16–21; Joachim Jeremias, "Μωυσῆς," in *Theological Dictionary of the New Testament* 4 (1967): 848–73, 862; Hengel, *The Zealots: Investigations into the*

Jewish Freedom Movement in the Period from Herod I until 70 A.D. (Edinburgh: Clark, 1989), pp. 249–55.

41. See Stegner, "Wilderness and Testing," and Milik, *Ten Years of Discovery,* pp. 115–16. If the sect is at all in the background of the temptations, Thompson would be right that Jesus is represented as the truly obedient Israelite in contrast to the sect's peculiar claims ("Called-Proved-Obedient," p. 8).

42. Josephus, *The Jewish War* 6.351.

43. Ibid., 2.258–33; Josephus *The Antiquities of the Jews* 20.97, 169–72; cf. Hengel, *The Zealots,* p. 255.

44. See Donaldson, *Jesus on the Mountain,* pp. 62–70, 73–76.

45. A number of scholars, while acknowledging that Jesus stands in for Israel, are not convinced that Matthew consciously depicted Him in Moses-like terms (e.g., W. D. Davies, *The Setting of the Sermon on the Mount* [Cambridge: Cambridge University Press, 1966], pp. 45–48). However, all the Gospels draw on a broad conceptual framework in which Moses and Israel are virtually one and the same. Moses was the covenant mediator and therefore embodied in himself the people as well as the Torah, both of which were to become "pillars" of second-temple Judaism. In addition, the forty days of fasting finds a point of contact with Elijah, significant because the synoptic Transfiguration accounts are to the effect that Jesus replaces both Moses and Elijah, who represent the Law and the prophets.

46. Gundry, *Matthew,* p. 55. Cf. E. Earle Ellis, *The Gospel of Luke,* 2d ed. (London: Marshall, Morgan & Scott, 1974), p. 94.

47. D. A. Carson, "Matthew," in *The Expositor's Bible Commentary,* 8:113.

48. Davies and Allison, *Critical and Exegetical Commentary,* 1:362.

49. J. Nolland, *Luke 1–9:20,* Word Biblical Commentary (Dallas: Word, 1989), p. 181.

50. In Matthew the same point is made in 26:53. Moreover, at the Crucifixion the Jewish leaders mockingly called for Jesus to come down from the cross and save Himself, since He said, "I am the Son of God" (Matt. 27:39–43).

51. J. A. T. Robinson, "The Temptations," in *Twelve New Testament Studies* (London: SCM, 1962), p. 56.

52. Dunn, *The Partings of the Ways: Between Christianity and Judaism and Their Significance for the Character of Christianity* (London: SCM, 1991), p. 33; on the importance of the temple for first-century Judaism, see pp. 31–35; cf. pp. 37–74; Donaldson, *Jesus on the Mountain,* pp. 51–83; Chance, *Jerusalem, Temple, and the New Age,* pp. 5–33; E. Schürer, *The History of the Jewish People in the Age of Jesus Christ,* rev. and ed. Geza Vermes et al., 4 vols. [Edinburgh: Clark, 1973–1987]); S. Safrai, "The Temple," in *The Jewish People in the First Century: Historical Geography, Political History, Social, Cultural and Religious Life and Institutions,* ed.

S. Safrai et al. (Philadelphia: Fortress, 1987), 2:865–907; and E.
P. Sanders, *Jesus and Judaism* (Philadelphia: Fortress, 1985), pp.
77–90; cf. pp. 61–76.

53. Davies and Allison point out that in 11QT 45–47 Jerusalem is but
an extension of the temple (*Critical and Exegetical Commentary,*
1:365). Dunn shows that the whole land of Palestine, another of
the "pillars" of second-temple Judaism, was focused in the temple
(*The Partings of the Ways,* pp. 31–35).

54. Josephus *Antiquities* 15.412. *Epistle of Aristeas,* pp. 83–84.

55. Davies and Allison relate a rabbinic tradition that the temple was
the highest point on earth (*Critical and Exegetical Commentary,*
1:365). Also see Donaldson, *Jesus on the Mountain,* pp. 59–61.

56. See Kirk, "Jesus and the Temptation Narrative," pp. 91–95.

57. A. A. Anderson, *The Book of Psalms,* New Century Bible, 2 vols.
(Grand Rapids: Eerdmans, 1972), 2:659.

58. See Donaldson, *Jesus on the Mountain,* pp. 100–103.

59. Carson, "Matthew," p. 113.

60. Numbers 14:22; Psalms 78:17–20, 40–42, 56–57; 95:8–11; 106:6–7;
Hebrews 3:7–11; *'Abot* 5.4. Also see Gerhardsson, *The Testing of
God's Son,* pp. 28–31.

61. See Dupont, "L'arriere-fond biblique du récit des temptations de
Jesus," pp. 296–98.

62. D. Daube, *Studies in Biblical Law* (New York: KTAV, 1969), pp.
24–39; Davies and Allison, *Critical and Exegetical Commentary,*
1:370–71. In Genesis 13:14–15, as taken up by 1QapHab 21, God
showed Abraham the land that would be his possession.

63. See Davies and Allison, *Critical and Exegetical Commentary,*
1:422–23; and G. Von Rad, *Genesis: A Commentary,* 2d ed.
(Philadelphia: Westminster, 1972), p. 79.

64. In Apocalypse of Abraham 20–32 (esp. 20–23), Abraham is cast
in the Adam role and is made to look on glories of the age to
come.

65. In the background is Deuteronomy 12:1–14, which warns Israel
against the idolatrous sacrifices of the Canaanites conducted on
the "high mountains." In Deuteronomy 32:17; Psalm 106:37–39;
and 1 Enoch 99:7 idolatry and demon worship are joined. Also
Abraham was tested on a mountain (Gen. 22; Apoc. Abram 12–13).

66. K. H. Rengstorf, "Old and New Testament Traces of a Formula of
the Judean Royal Ritual," *Novum Testamentum* 5 (1962): 241; P.
Doble, "The Temptations," *Expository Times* 72 (1960): 92;
Donaldson, *Jesus on the Mountain,* pp. 94–95; and Lövestam, *Son
and Savior,* p. 100.

67. Donaldson, *Jesus on the Mountain,* p. 95. He presents as evidence
the expectation that the eschatological Zion would be a lofty site
(Isa. 2:2; Mic. 4:1), a mountain high enough that the pilgrimage of
the Jewish exiles and the nations could be seen (Bar. 4:36–37;
5:1–9; Ps. Sol. 11:1–3). Also the phrase "high mountain," which

crops up in Jewish apocalyptic literature (e.g., 4 Ezra 13:6), is connected in the Old Testament with Zion as the cosmic/ eschatological mountain of the final consummation (see the Septuagint of Isa. 40:9; Ezek. 17:22; 20:40; 34:14; 40:2).

68. Davies and Allison, *Critical and Exegetical Commentary,* 1:372.

69. Donaldson, "Zealot," in *International Standard Bible Encyclopedia* 4 (1988): 1179.

70. The view taken here is defended by a number of scholars (e.g., Kirk, "Jesus and the Temptation Narrative"; Dupont, "L'arrier-fond biblique du récit des temptations de Jesus," pp. 303–4; Kelly, "The Devil in the Desert," p. 213; Pokorny, "The Temptation Stories," pp. 122–25; P. Hoffmann, "Die Versuchungsgeschichte in der Logienquelle: Zur Auseinandersetzung der Judenchristen mit dem politischen Messianismus," *Biblische Zeitschrift* 13 [1969]: 207–23).

71. Kirk, "Jesus and the Temptation Narrative," p. 24.

72. See in particular Hengel, *The Zealots,* pp. 149–228; and Don B. Garlington, "Burden Bearing and the Recovery of Offending Christians (Galatians 6:1–5)," *Trinity Journal* n.s. 12 (1991): 153–58.

73. See Jeremias, "Μωυσῆς," 4:860, 862; Barrett, *Gospel Tradition,* pp. 51–52; Strack and Billerbeck, *Kommentar zum Neuen Testament aus Talmud und Midrasch* 2:481; Lövestam, *Son and Savior,* p. 99; and T. F. Glasson, *Moses in the Fourth Gospel* (London: SCM, 1963), pp. 45–47.

74. See Raymond E. Brown, "Incidents That Are Units in the Synoptic Gospels but Dispersed in St. John," *Catholic Biblical Quarterly* 23 (1961): 152–55.

75. See Hengel, *The Zealots,* pp. 229–45; "The insistence on the 'sole rule of God' that was so closely associated with the revolt against Roman rule was for the Zealots the first step towards bringing about the kingdom of God, the coming of which was at least partly dependent on the personal participation of God's people" (p. 228); for them "the course of the eschatological events was determined not only by God, but also by the actions of Israel" (p. 123; cf. p. 127); at the same time it is also true that the Zealots were prepared to "carry the cross" and die a martyr's death, if God so chose (pp. 256–71); in all probability, the expression "carry the cross" was a Zealot motto (p. 260), played on by Jesus (Matt. 10:38 = Luke 14:27; and Matt. 16:24 = Mark 8:34; Luke 9:23).

76. France, *Jesus and the Old Testament,* p. 149.

77. Davies and Allison, *Critical and Exegetical Commentary,* 1:367, n. 32.

78. Again in Josephus a would-be deliverer, the Egyptian prophet, sought to follow this path to victory, in imitation of the exodus from Egypt (*Antiquities* 20.169–72). See Hengel, *The Zealots*, pp. 229–36, who also discusses the idea of the temple as the final battleground (pp. 221–24).

79. Kelly, "The Devil in the Desert," p. 213.
80. Hengel contends that apart from the temptations, Matthew 5:5 (= Ps. 37:11) possibly contains an authentically anti-Zealot tendency: "These words of Jesus were in very sharp contrast to the Zealot teaching and must have struck the Zealots, who called for retributory violence as a response to all injustice, as a form of enthusiasm" (*The Zealots*, p. 309).
81. Ibid., pp. 225, 303; Hengel cites as applicable to the Zealots, *mutatis mutandis*, *Num. Rab.* 21.3 (on Num. 25:13): "Everyone who sheds the blood of godless men is like one who offers a sacrifice" (p. 85). Cf. Kirk, "Jesus and the Temptation Narrative," 96–97. Matthew 26:51–56 mirrors Jesus' repudiation of zealot tactics when Peter played the part of the "zealot" by attacking the servant of the high priest with a sword: "all those who take up the sword shall perish by the sword," a prophecy fulfilled in A.D. 70. Therefore it was wholly inappropriate for the mob to come out against Him with swords and clubs, as though He were a "robber" (vv. 47, 55), Josephus's favorite term for the Zealots.
82. Robinson, "The Temptations," p. 57.
83. Cf. Kirk, "Jesus and the Temptation Narrative," pp. 96–100.
84. N. T. Wright, "Adam in Pauline Christology," in *Society of Biblical Literature Seminar Papers 1983*, pp. 360–65; and Wright, *The Climax of the Covenant: Christ and the Law in Pauline Theology* (Minneapolis: Fortress, 1991), pp. 21–26.
85. See Garlington, "Burden Bearing," p. 156. Especially striking is 11QT 64, which equates crucifixion with Yahweh's curse, a curse that falls on traitors to Israel. See Y. Yadin, *The Temple Scroll: The Hidden Law of the Dead Sea Sect* (London: Weidenfeld and Nicolson, 1985), pp. 204–8.
86. A recent example is Dunn, *The Partings of the Ways*, esp. pp. 163–229, 244–47.
87. For example S. Sandmel, *The Genius of Paul* (Philadelphia: Fortress, 1979), p. 21; N. A. Dahl, "The One God of Jews and Gentiles (Romans 3.29–30)," in *Studies in Paul* (Minneapolis: Augsburg, 1977), p. 191; F. Watson, *Paul, Judaism and the Gentiles: A Sociological Approach* (Cambridge: Cambridge University Press, 1986), p. 21; Sanders, *Paul, the Law, and the Jewish People* (Philadelphia: Fortress, 1983), p. 160; H. Räisänen, *Paul and the Law* (Tübingen: Mohr, 1983), pp. 171–72; Räisänen, "Galatians 2.16 and Paul's Break with Judaism," *New Testament Studies* 31 (1985): 550; and Räisänen, "Paul's Conversion and the Development of His View of the Law," *New Testament Studies* 33 (1987): 412.

Chapter 8

1. W. M. Clow, *The Secret of the Lord* (New York: Hodder & Stoughton, 1910), p. 166.

2. Ibid., pp. 166–67.
3. The altitude of Mount Hermon, 9,300 feet, fully meets the demands of the adjective ὑψηλόν (high). The early church traditionally placed the event on Mount Tabor and eventually erected monasteries and churches there—three of the latter to correspond to the three tabernacles Jesus refused to allow Peter to construct (cf. Richard Chenevix Trench, *Studies in the Gospels,* 6th ed. [London: Kegan Paul, Trench, Trübner, 1896], pp. 199–200).
4. C. E. B. Cranfield, *The Gospel according to Saint Mark* (Cambridge: University Press, 1959), p. 294.
5. The subjunctive of emphatic negation found here (οὐ μὴ γεύσωνται) is strong. While it is true that it is not so strong a construction in the New Testament as is it in classical Greek, it still must be admitted that it is the strongest form of prohibition in the New Testament. It is confined largely to Old Testament citations, the sayings of the Lord, and the Apocalypse. The expression here lays great stress on the fact that physical death shall not intervene between the present moment and the vision of the Son in His kingdom (Cf. James Hope Moulton, *A Grammar of New Testament Greek,* vol. 3: *Syntax,* by Nigel Turner [Edinburgh: Clark, 1963], pp. 95–96).
6. His reasoning includes the following questionable points: (1) The verb ἴδωσιν (see) refers to intellectual perception instead of physical sight. However, this verb is explained by the words ἔμπροσθεν αὐτῶν (v. 2), ὤφθη (v. 3), and εἶδον (v. 8). (2) In Mark 9:1 ἐληλυθυῖαν (has come) is to be taken as referring to an action that is past, or complete, before the time of their perception. That is all well and good, for the perfect tense would indicate that its action does precede the perception. But Dodd then made the fatal blunder of claiming that the action must have been complete at the time Jesus was speaking. But the Greek tense does not say this at all, for the perfect merely means that when some see the kingdom, they will see it as a kingdom that has come (C. H. Dodd, *The Parables of the Kingdom,* rev. ed. [New York: Scribner, 1961], pp. 53–54.)
7. Alan Hugh McNeile, *The Gospel according to St. Matthew* (London: Macmillan, 1915), p. 248.
8. Vincent Taylor, *Jesus and His Sacrifice* (London: Macmillan, 1951), pp. 8–9.
9. Cf. A. C. Craig, *Preaching in a Scientific Age* (New York: Scribner's Sons, 1954), pp. 40–41.
10. The question of whether the event was only a vision or something actually seen in a physical sense is another matter. The use of the word ὅραμα (vision) in 17:9 is not decisive for it may refer to something seen in an ordinary way (cf. Cranfield, *Mark,* p. 294).
11. Alfred Plummer, *A Critical and Exegetical Commentary on the Gospel according to S. Luke,* International Critical Commentary, 5th ed. (Edinburgh: Clark, 1922), pp. 249–50,

12. Peter's words in 1 Peter 5:1 have been misunderstood by many. The word χοιυωνός (partaker) refers to those at the time of his writing, not to the future. The glory will be revealed, but Peter was already a partaker of it—by reason of his experience on the mount. Selwyn has correctly rendered the clause, "who have also had experience of the glory that is to be revealed" (Edward Gordon Selwyn, *The First Epistle of St. Peter,* 2d ed. [London: Macmillan, 1947], p. 228).

Chapter 9

1. Ethelbert Stauffer, *Christ and the Caesars,* trans. K. and R. Gregor Smith (Philadelphia: Westminster, 1955), p. 101.
2. Arthur John Gossip, "The Gospel according to St. John," in *Interpreter's Bible,* ed. George A. Buttrick, 12 vols. (New York: Abingdon, 1952–1957), 8:657.
3. He pictured Christ as a forlorn and weary Jew, who, doubting what lay before Him, moved forward in despair to death as His last attempt to win the favor of the nation failed. In the light of history it is not Christ who is the forlorn and beaten One; it is Nietzsche, the philosopher whose god was dead—really
4. James S. Stewart, *The Life and Teaching of Jesus Christ* (London: Student Christian Movement, 1933), p. 158. McNeile comments, "The synoptists clearly convey the impression that Jesus deliberately rode into the city as the Messiah, and that He was acclaimed as such by the crowds that accompanied Him" (Alan Hugh McNeile, *The Gospel according to St. Matthew* [London: Macmillan, 1915], p. 297).
5. A. M. Hunter, *The Work and Words of Jesus* (Philadelphia: Westminster, 1950), p. 113.
6. Alfred Edersheim, *The Life and Times of Jesus the Messiah,* 2 vols. (reprint, Grand Rapids: Eerdmans, 1962), 2:363.
7. The clause may have been suggested by the νέον of Zechariah 9:9 (LXX, πῶλον νέον).
8. F. Godet, *Commentary on the Gospel of John,* 3d ed., 3 vols. (Edinburgh: Clark, 1890), 2:286. Cf. Numbers 19:2; Deuteronomy 221:3; and Luke 23:53.
9. As is well known, Matthew mentioned two animals while the other gospels mentioned only one. McNeile feels that Matthew misunderstood the Hebrew synonymous parallelism of Zechariah 9:9 and spoke "mistakenly of two animals" (*Matthew,* p. 294). The passage, then, becomes a shining example of a prophecy which, erroneously interpreted, creates a new and erroneous tradition. But this is not a necessary view at all, though many eminent interpreters have suggested it. It is more in accord with the context to have Matthew introduce the second animal to emphasize the fact that the colt was unused, as the synoptics indicate. The mother animal

was necessary since the unbroken young donkey would not have submitted to being ridden amid the tumultuous crowds unless she were along (for a full discussion see Robert H. Gundry, "The Use of the Old Testament in St. Matthew's Gospel with Special Reference to the Messianic Hope" [Ph.D. thesis, University of Manchester], pp. 230–33).

10. Hunter, *Work and Words of Jesus,* p. 113.

11. The word used in Luke 19:41 (ἔκλαυσεν, "wept") may be contrasted with the different word for "wept" used in John 11:35 at Lazarus's tomb. The latter word (δακρύω) means "to shed tears," but Luke's word means "to weep audibly" (C. K. Barrett, *The Gospel according to St. John* [London: SPCK, 1955], pp. 331–34).

12. Edersheim, *Life and Times,* 2:366. Cf. 2 Kings 9:13.

13. McNeile calls attention to Matthew's careful use of the Greek tenses here: "Part of the crowd spread their cloaks once (ἔστρωσαν) when the ride began, and when the colt had passed over them they would pick them up and follow, and part continued to pluck (ἔχοπτον) branches and to spread them (ἐστρώννυον) as they moved in front" (*Matthew,* p. 295).

14. Edersheim, *Life and Times,* 2:367.

15. The word "Hosanna" transliterates נא הושׁע, meaning, "Save, we pray Thee." It had come to be used as a shout of praise to God, as the following dative shows.

16. Cf. Hermann L. Strack and Paul Billerbeck, *Kommentar zum Neuen Testament aus Talmud und Midrasch* (Munich: Beck, 1922–1956), 1:846–50.

17. Cf. W. Graham Scroggie, *The Psalms,* 4 vols. (London: Pickering & Inglis, 1948–1951), 3:152.

18. Edersheim, however, makes a strong case for the presence of no special reference in the shouts (*Life and Times,* 2:371–72).

19. Cranfield maintains that the messianic hiddenness of Jesus was still maintained in the entry and that Jesus manifested His messiahship only in a veiled way. But in the light of the preceding evidence, it is plain that He went out of His way to assert His office. It is true that the disciples did not understand this clearly, but His actions are obvious. True, they did not understand, but it was not because they did not have sufficient evidence (cf. C. E. B. Cranfield, *The Gospel according to Saint Mark* [Cambridge: University Press, 1959], pp. 352–54).

20. The article refers to the Lord as being well known; it is not meant to connect Him with the prophet of Deuteronomy 18:15–18, though He is that Prophet (McNeile, *Matthew,* p. 297).

21. The point at which Matthew inserted his comment regarding Zechariah 9:9 in the narrative is in harmony with this view. Plummer remarks, "It is worth noting that Mt. inserts the prophecy (which Jn. also quotes) immediately after Christ's prediction of what the two disciples will find, not (as we might have expected)

after the procession had taken place. He intimates that Christ was consciously fulfilling the prophecy" (Alfred Plummer, *An Exegetical Commentary on the Gospel according to S. Matthew,* trans. Richard and Clara Winston [New York: Knopf, 1959], p. 285).

22. The perfect tense seems to say that the entire action stands there before the reader as proof of the fulfillment.

23. Cf. Stauffer, *Jesus and His Story,* trans. Richard and Clara Winston (New York: Knopf, 1960), p. 110.

24. James Stalker, *The Life of Jesus Christ* (New York: Revell, 1909), p. 112.

25. Ibid., p. 111.

26. A passage in the Babylonian Talmud illustrates this. Rabbi Joshua ben Levi asks, "It is written in one place, 'Behold, one like unto the Son of man came with the clouds of heaven,' but in another place it is written, 'lowly and riding upon an ass.' How is this to be understood? The answer is, If they be righteous (or deserving) He shall come with the clouds of heaven; if they be not righteous, then He shall come lowly, and riding upon an ass." Cf. E. B. Pusey, *The Minor Prophets with a Commentary,* 8 vols. (London: Nisbet, 1906–1907), 8:220–29; Strack and Billerbeck, *Kommentar zum Neuen Testament aus Talmud und Midrasch* 1:842–44.

Chapter 10

1. See, for example, Johnston M. Cheney, *The Life of Christ in Stereo* (Portland, OR: Western Baptist Seminary Press, 1969); Alfred Edersheim, *The Life and Times of Jesus the Messiah,* vol. 2 (Grand Rapids: Eerdmans, 1974); John H. Kerr, *A Harmony of the Gospels* (Old Tappan, NJ: Revell, 1924); A. T. Robertson, *A Harmony of the Gospels* (New York: Harper & Row, 1950); William M. Reese, "The Interwoven Gospels," in *The System Bible Study* (Chicago: John Rudin & Co., 1967); and J. Macartney Wilson, "Pilate, Pontius," in *International Standard Bible Encyclopedia* 4 (1939): 2396–98.

2. J. M. Wilson, "Pilate, Pontius," p. 2396.

3. Jérôme Carcopino, *Daily Life in Ancient Rome,* ed. H. T. Rowell, trans. E. O. Lorimer (New Haven, CT: Yale University Press, 1975), pp. 56–61.

4. J. M. Wilson, "Pilate, Pontius," p. 2396. See also "Pilate," in *Unger's Bible Dictionary* (Chicago: Moody Press, 1960), p. 865.

5. Josephus, *The Jewish Antiquities* 18. 3. 1; 2. 19. 2–3.

6. Ibid. 18. 3. 29; and Josephus *The Jewish Wars* 2. 9. 4.

7. Philonis Alexandrini, *Legatto ad Gaium,* xxxviii, ed. and trans. E. Mary Smallwood (Leiden: Brill, 1961), pp. 128–30. That this event is dated at A.D. 32 has been adequately presented by Harold W. Hoehner, "The Year of Christ's Crucifixion," *Bibliotheca Sacra* 131 (October–December 1974): 344–45.

8. References to both criminal law and *ius privatum* are included in the discussion in order to illustrate the full concept of Roman law at the time of Christ.

9. Wolfgang Kunkel, *An Introduction to Roman Legal and Constitutional History,* trans. J. M. Kelly, 2d ed. (London: Oxford University Press, 1975), p. 40.

10. Francis Lyall, "Roman Law in the Writings of Paul—Aliens and Citizens," *Evangelical Quarterly* 48 (January–March 1976): 12.

11. John James Maclaren, "Jesus Christ, Arrest and Trial of," in *International Standard Bible Encyclopedia* 3 (1939): 1671.

12. Lyall, "Roman Law in the Writings of Paul," p. 12.

13. Peter Garnsey, *Social Status and Legal Privilege in the Roman Empire* (London: Oxford University Press, 1970), p. 139.

14. Ibid., pp. 74–75.

15. Ibid., p. 262.

16. Lord Mackenzie, *Studies in Roman Law,* 6th ed. (Edinburgh: Blackwood & Sons, 1886), p. 84.

17. A. H. J. Greenidge, *The Legal Procedure of Cicero's Time* (London: Oxford University Press, 1901), p. 410.

18. A. H. M. Jones, *Studies in Roman Government and Law* (Oxford: Blackwell, 1960), p. 124.

19. Kunkel, *Constitutional History,* p. 85.

20. Ibid., pp. 41–42.

21. H. F. Jolowicz, *Historical Introduction to the Study of Roman Law* (Cambridge: University Press, 1954), p. 412.

22. Garnsey, *Social Status and Legal Privilege,* p. 121.

23. Greenidge, *Legal Procedure of Cicero's Time,* p. 413.

24. Jolowicz, *Study of Roman Law,* p. 413.

25. William Riley Wilson, *The Execution of Jesus* (New York: Charles Scribner's Sons, 1970), p. 130. This type of procedure was established by Augustus and is known as *cognitio extra ordinem;* it is described in some detail by Kunkel (*Constitutional History,* pp. 69–74).

26. Paul Winter, *On the Trial of Jesus* (Berlin: de Gruyter, 1961), p. 65.

27. Garnsey, *Social Status and Legal Privilege,* p. 127.

28. Mackenzie, *Studies in Roman Law,* p. 395.

29. W. R. Wilson, *The Execution of Jesus,* p. 130.

30. Ibid., p. 18.

31. Allen Clark, "The Court Trials of Jesus: Illegal," *Faith for the Family,* March/April 1976, p. 15.

32. Greenidge, *Legal Procedure of Cicero's Time,* p. 410.

33. J. M. Wilson, "Pilate, Pontius," p. 2398.

34. Edersheim, *Life and Times,* 2:580.

35. Hoehner, "The Year of Christ's Crucifixion," pp. 332–48. Not all will agree with Hoehner on this date, but his arguments are cogent and persuasive and seem to account best for all the available evidence.

36. Frederick Louis Godet, *Commentary on the Gospel of Luke,* 2 vols. (Grand Rapids: Zondervan, n.d.,), 2:326.
37. Josephus, *Antiquities* 18. 4. 1–2. Also see M. P. Charlesworth, "Tiberius," in *The Cambridge Ancient History,* vol. 10, ed. S. A. Cook, F. E. Adcock, and M. P. Charlesworth (Cambridge: University Press, 1934), pp. 649–50.
38. Eusebius, *Ecclesiastical History* 2.7.

Chapter 11

1. Sherman E. Johnson, *A Commentary on the Gospel according to St. Mark* (New York: Harper, 1960), p. 177.
2. James Stalker, *The Life of Jesus Christ* (New York: Revell, 1909), p. 118.
3. G. C. Berkouwer, *The Work of Christ,* trans. Cornelius Lambregtse (Grand Rapids: Eerdmans, 1965), p. 145 (italics his).
4. Stalker, *Life of Jesus Christ,* p. 116.
5. Joseph Klausner, *Jesus of Nazareth,* trans. Herbert Danby (New York: Macmillan, 1946), p. 332.
6. The proper noun is derived from the Aramaic גַּת שֶׁמֶן, "press of oils." Olives were trodden in an oil press (Mic. 6:15). Cf. Gustaf Dalman, *Sacred Sites and Ways* (New York: Macmillan, 1935), pp. 321–27.
7. Alfred Edersheim, *The Life and Times of Jesus the Messiah,* 2 vols. (reprint: Grand Rapids: Eerdmans, 1962), 2:534.
8. Traill, cited by David Brown, "Matthew—John," in *A Commentary, Critical, Experimental, and Practical, on the Old and New Testaments,* by Robert Jamieson, A. R. Fausset, and David Brown (1878; reprint, Grand Rapids: Eerdmans, 1945), 5:332.
9. For a full treatment of Klaas Schilder's view one should consult his fine work on the passion (*Christ in His Suffering,* trans. Henry Sylstra [Grand Rapids: Eerdmans, 1938]). He makes a lot of Luke 22:44, "And being in agony He was praying very fervently; falling down upon the ground."
10. Donald Grey Barnhouse, "Let This Cup Pass from Me," *Eternity,* September 1952, pp. 5–6, 39–42.
11. John Calvin, cited by C. E. B. Cranfield, *The Gospel according to Saint Mark* (Cambridge: University Press, 1959), p. 434.
12. Berkouwer, *The Person of Christ,* trans. John Vriend (Grand Rapids: Eerdmans, 1954), p. 256.
13. When Jesus said, "the spirit is willing, but the flesh is weak," He used "spirit" in reference to the human spirit but in its renewed condition (cf. Mark 2:8; 8:12).
14. Berkouwer comments, "Schilder has correctly pointed out that in the first prayer the main petition is that the cup may pass away, while in the second the main petition is: Thy will be done" (*The*

Person of Christ, p. 257). In addition, the first petition contains a first-class condition, while the second also contains a third-class condition. The progression in the prayers reflects a progression in the Lord's experience.

15. Edersheim, *Life and Times,* 2:541. Possibly a brief period of time transpired between the events recorded in verses 45 and 46. In verse 45 Jesus had said to the three, καθεύδετε λοιπόν, "Sleep on now," (KJV). As an adverb, λοιπόν usually means "henceforth," and McNeile suggests that this is a rare instance of irony in Jesus' words. McNeile paraphrases the two Greek words, "Sleep on, uninterrupted by further calls to prayer!" (Alan Hough McNeile, *The Gospel according to St. Matthew* [London: Macmillan, 1915], p. 392).
16. Stalker, *Life of Jesus Christ,* p. 119.
17. Edersheim, *Life and Times,* 2:538–39.
18. This is the common derivation of the word, but Lightfoot's disagreement is enough to make one somewhat doubtful and also to curb dogmatism (J. B. Lightfoot, *Saint Paul's Epistle to the Philippians* [1868; reprint, Grand Rapids: Zondervan, 1956], p. 123). Also note the use of the verb ἀδημονέω in Philippians 2:26.

Chapter 12

1. Louis Berkhof, *Systematic Theology,* rev. ed. (Grand Rapids: Eerdmans, 1953), p. 379.
2. Ibid., pp. 380–81.
3. Charles Hodge, *Systematic Theology,* 3 vols. (London: Clarke, 1960), 2:613.
4. John Murray, *Redemption, Accomplished and Applied* (London: Banner of Truth, 1961), p. 28.
5. George Smeaton, *The Doctrine of the Atonement* (Grand Rapids: Zondervan, 1957), p. 110.
6. Loraine Boettner, *The Atonement* (Grand Rapids: Eerdmans, 1941), p. 59.
7. Berkhof, *Systematic Theology,* p. 381.

Chapter 13

1. Helmut Thielecke, *The Silence of God,* trans. G. W. Bromiley (Grand Rapids: Eerdmans, 1962), pp. 67–69.
2. The perfect participle ἐσταυρωμένον (crucified), an extensive perfect, lays great stress on the cross. It suggests that Paul in his preaching painted the picture so vividly before them that it remained indelibly imprinted on their minds (1 Cor. 1:23; Gal. 3:1). Moule remarks that the perfect tense looks at the event as "an abiding force" (C. F. D. Moule, *An Idiom Book of New Testament Greek,*

2d ed. [Cambridge: University Press, 1959], pp. 14, 202). The anarthrous construction supports this emphasis. Phillips has caught its force beautifully: "You may as well know now that it was my secret determination to concentrate entirely on Jesus Christ Himself *and the fact of His death upon the Cross"* (J. B. Phillips, *Letters to Young Churches* [New York: Macmillan, 1947], p. 40 [italics added]). Way renders the words this way: "I determined to make no display of knowledge before you, except of the Messiah—and of Him only as a crucified Messiah" (Arthur S. Way, *The Letters of St. Paul,* 7th ed. [London: Macmillan, 1935], p. 25).

3. The term *Calvary* is derived from the Latin Vulgate. In Latin *calvaria* means a skull. The hymns that have made the term *Calvary* so meaningful to evangelical Christians as the place where redemption was accomplished is thus indebted to the Latin Vulgate. "Golgotha" comes from the Aramaic *gulgolta'.* An ancient legend has it that Adam was buried there, which suggests tantalizing correspondences. The identification, of course, cannot be proved.

4. The Greek texts of Matthew and Mark differ slightly in the opening words of the cry. Matthew reported the two words of address in their Hebrew form *("Eli, Eli")* while Mark reported them in Aramaic *("Eloi, Eloi,"* 15:34). Though it was difficult to be sure of the exact words of the cry, the doctrine of verbal inspiration is not affected by the question. It was the prerogative of the writers to report Jesus' words in either language. He undoubtedly spoke often in Aramaic, and yet His words are almost always reported in Greek by the evangelists.

The words are evidently a citation of Psalm 22:1, with Mark's rendering in its entirety being independent of the Septuagint (cf. T. W. Manson, "The Old Testament in the Teaching of Jesus," *Bulletin of the John Rylands Library* 34 [1951–1952]: 327–28).

The Matthaean version with Hebrew in its opening address and Aramaic in its interrogation is perhaps original. "Eli" would be more easily confused with Elijah's name (v. 47). Further the Targum Onkelos has this same *'eli, 'eli* in its rendering of the psalm, so the rendering would be familiar to every Aramaic-speaking Jew (Gustaf Dalman, *The Words of Jesus* [Edinburgh: Clark, 1909], pp. 53–54), although this was less likely in this Aramaic context. This is also the judgment of Joachim Jeremias ("El(e)ias," in *Theological Dictionary of the New Testament,* 2 [1964]: 937).

One thing is certain: The words are not invented. They formed a constant source of embarrassment to some early believers, as is perhaps evidenced by their omission in Luke and John and by the variations in the textual tradition (C. E. B. Cranfield, *The Gospel according to St. Mark* [Cambridge: University Press, 1959], p. 455).

5. Jeremias, *The Central Message of the New Testament* (London: SCM, 1965), pp. 14–17.

6. Arthur W. Pink, *The Seven Sayings of the Saviour on the Cross* (Swengel, Penn.: Bible Truth, 1919), pp. 75.
7. Charles Haddon Spurgeon, *The Treasury of the New Testament,* 4 vols. (Grand Rapids: Zondervan, 1951), 3:744.
8. Thielecke, *The Silence of God,* p. 74.
9. Gustaf Aulén, *Christus Victor,* trans. A. G. Hebert (New York: Macmillan, 1969), p. 4. This theory should not be confused with the ransom-to-Satan view.
10. Cranfield, *Mark,* pp. 458–59.
11. George A. Buttrick, "The Cry of Dereliction," in *Great Themes of the Christian Faith,* comp. Charles W. Ferguson (New York: Smith, 1930), p. 18.
12. James S. Stewart, cited by James W. Reapsome and Herschel O. Engebretson, "Princeton—Then and Now," *Sunday School Times,* June 16, 1962, p. 104.

Chapter 14

1. The name Κλεόπας is probably contracted from Κλεόπατρος, like Ἀντίπας for Ἀντίπατρος. This Cleopas is therefore a different person from Clopas (Κλῶπας, John 19:25), elsewhere called Alpheus (Ἀλφαῖος, Mark 3:18).
2. Second Maccabees 3:34 has ἀφανεῖς ἐγένοντο of angels.

Chapter 15

1. A. T. Robertson, *Paul: The Interpreter of Christ* (New York: Doran, 1921), p. 40.
2. A. C. Headlam, *St. Paul and Christianity* (London: Murray, 1913), p. 79.
3. D. Somerville, *St. Paul's Conception of Christ* (Edinburgh: Clark, 1897), p. 16.
4. Lewis Sperry Chafer, *Grace* (1922; reprint, Grand Rapids: Kregel, 1995), p. 22.
5. W. J. Sparrow-Simpson, *The Resurrection and Modern Thought* (New York: Longmans, Green, 1911), p. 288.
6. Headlam, *St. Paul and Christianity,* p. 137.
7. Sparrow-Simpson, *The Resurrection and Modern Thought,* p. 303.
8. William Milligan, *The Resurrection of Our Lord* (New York: Macmillan, 1881), p. 140.
9. Sparrow-Simpson, *The Resurrection and Modern Thought,* p. 296.
10. John Kennedy, *The Resurrection of Jesus Christ,* rev. ed. (London: Religious Tract, 1895), p. 115.

Chapter 16

1. Isbon T. Beckwith, *The Apocalypse of John* (New York: Macmillan, 1919), p. 258.

2. Ibid., p. 249.
3. Illustrations of varying interpretations could be multiplied. The girdle about the breast has been taken variously to mean majesty, princely rank, priestly office, and kingly office. Commentators have understood the eyes as a flame of fire to speak of energy, power of command, judgment, dynamic force, and zeal. And so the list grows, seemingly ad infinitum.
4. The Greek term is ποδήρη, and though it cannot be seen in an English translation of the Hebrew text, it is found in Exodus 28:4 and Zechariah 3:4, as well as in other passages dealing with the high priest.
5. The Greek replaces the Hebrew לְדֻשׁ בַּדִּים "clothed in linen," in Ezekiel. See also Daniel 10:5, ἐνδεδυμένος βυδδιν, which represents the same Hebrew expression. In the light of John's obvious dependence on the Septuagint here and elsewhere, it is surprising to find Charles saying, "John translated directly from the O.T. text. He did not quote from any Greek version though he was often influenced in his rendering by the LXX and another later Greek Version" (R. H. Charles, *A Critical and Exegetical Commentary on the Revelation of St. John*, 2 vols. [Edinburgh: Clark, 1920], 1:lxvi). The approach of Swete to this question seems more probable: "The Apocalyptist generally availed himself of the Alexandrian version of the Old Testament. . . . On the other hand many of the references depart widely from the LXX, in particular words, where the writer has either rendered [the Hebrew] independently, or has used another version" (Henry Barclay Swete, *The Apocalypse of St John*, 3d ed. [London: Macmillan, 1909], p. clv).
6. Charles's attempt to find other instances of a priestly ministry is futile, the nearest corresponding designation being "the Lamb," found thirty-eight times in Revelation (Charles, *The Revelation of St. John*, 1:cxiii). It is more proper to limit the significance of the symbol to the aspect dealing with judgment (Beckwith, *The Apocalypse of John*, p. 438).
7. James Moffatt, "The Revelation of St. John the Divine," in *The Expositor's Greek Testament*, ed. W. Robertson Nicoll, 5 vols. (reprint, Grand Rapids: Eerdmans, n.d.), 5:344; and Charles, *The Revelation of St. John*, 1:28. Josephus wrote that the high priest wore the high girding and that it was not adaptable to laborious service (*The Antiquities of the Jews* 3.7.2). Thus to be girded about the breast was a mark of dignity, while girding about the loins signified service or activity.
8. Beckwith, *The Apocalypse of John*, p. 438.
9. Swete, *Apocalypse of St. John*, p. 16.
10. Arthur E. Bloomfield, *All Things New* (Minneapolis: Bethany Fellowship, 1959), p. 45.
11. Swete, *Apocalypse of St. John*, p. 16.

12. Ibid., p. 17. In Daniel 10:6 the Greek wording differs, but the picture is generally the same.
13. The author at this point depended on the Hebrew text of Ezekiel, for the Septuagint does not contain this simile. It should also be observed that John deviated slightly from the corresponding simile in Daniel 10:6, "like the voice of a multitude," which would be a more confused roar (ibid., p. 18).
14. Of the ten descriptions of Christ this seems to be the only one that does not draw on the Old Testament in any way.
15. Beckwith, *The Apocalypse of John,* p. 440.
16. Richard Chenevix Trench, *Commentary on the Epistles to the Seven Churches in Asia,* 3d ed. (London: Macmillan, 1867), p. 41.
17. One need not try to form a pictorial representation of what John saw. As is often the case in this book, the figures envisioned defy any attempt at graphic reproduction. They are merely intended to portray various moral characteristics of who or what was being described.
18. E. W. Bullinger, *The Apocalypse, or The Day of the Lord,* 2d ed. (London: Eyre & Spottiswoode, 1909), p. 56.

Chapter 17

1. William F. Arndt and F. Wilbur Gingrich, *A Greek Lexicon of the New Testament and Other Early Christian Literature* (Chicago: University of Chicago Press, 1957), p. 278.
2. Ibid., p. 208.
3. Joseph Henry Thayer, *Greek-English Lexicon of the New Testament* (reprint, Grand Rapids: Zondervan, 1962), p. 159.